CW01509430

Books written previously by the same author:

'Our Birth on Earth'

'When Scorpio Ruled the World'

'Heaven's Message – How to Read it Nowadays'

'Character Portraits of England's Plantagenet Kings'

'Concise Character Portraits of England's Tudor, Stuart and Protectorate Rulers'

'Character Portraits of England's Germanic Monarchs'

'**Simply Now** – Our Simple A.D. 2020 Situation'

SIMPLY NOW 2

PERSONALITY AND LOVE

CHRIS STUBBS

Order this book online at www.trafford.com
or email orders@trafford.com

Most Trafford titles are also available at major online book retailers.

Print information available on the last page.

ISBN: 978-1-4907-9058-9 (sc)
ISBN: 978-1-4907-9059-6 (hc)
ISBN: 978-1-4907-9060-2 (e)

Library of Congress Control Number: 2018956438

Trafford rev. 08/31/2018

 www.trafford.com

North America & international
toll-free: 1 888 232 4444 (USA & Canada)
fax: 812 355 4082

To the memory of Ronald C. Davison (1914 – 1985),
Past President of 'The Astrological
Association' and the
Author of 'Synastry'

CONTENTS

ACKNOWLEDGEMENTS

The Staff of Wirral Libraries, Eastham Branch, kindly obtained books for me; my wife Angela, once again, has made time for me to write this book and Cara Selgas, of Trafford Publishing, has shown admirable patience on dealing with me, over matters concerning the book.

FOREWORD

Previously, we have tried to establish the best method of producing a complete and impartial horoscope for a single person. We recommended a slightly modified Morinus House System as the one simple and elegant method of choice. We found that we could apply this Morinus system to the theory of 'The Pre-Natal Epoch' and determined an Epoch time from a given time of Birth. From this, we determined its corresponding Ideal Time of Birth. Impartial interpretations of Epoch and Ideal Time of Birth charts were taken from books by notable astrologers and combined in an organised way to produce an understandable whole as that person's Character Portrait/Person Summary/Personality. Character Portraits of England's royalty were compared satisfactorily with their independent biographies. The question then arises, "Can we extend the method to produce a relationship horoscope between any two people by the process of 'Synastry'?"

Probably, the difficulty of the man – woman relationship is the most important concern in the lives of most people. There are no simple rules, and the only way appears to consist of assessing the horoscopes of the two people concerned, starting with general comparisons and then moving on to the more specific considerations of 'synastry'. Two pairs of horoscopes, with everything found to be harmonious, will never be found, but likely sources of disharmony may be identified, guarded against and so minimised. On the other hand, sources of harmony should be built on.

The results of two control 'synastry' exercises, closely familiar to the author, seemed to accord well with experience, so that two more such exercises for World famous couples could also prove to be reasonably correct. Chapter 6 presents some final results for all four of them.

CHAPTER 1

Love and Personality

<u>Love:</u> Apparently, conjugation (sexual dualism) has evolved mainly as a means of accelerating and intensifying the double effect (multiplication and diversification) obtained beforehand by asexual reproduction. Biologically, we can say that for every individual there have been several steps that led up to, and included, conception. Between central steps, i.e. between egg development in the mother and the egg's fertilisation by an acceptable sperm, there has been the mutual selection of the father and the mother. The conscious result of the mother's DNA (her personality) attracts the conscious result of the father's DNA (his personality), and *vice-versa*, in the process called 'love', or the selection of an appropriate mate. Ideally, love has occurred when each can say to the other:

"It is not so much the way you look, or what you are, although these are important, but rather the way that I feel, or how you make me feel, when I am with you."

Love is important for the rearing of children because not only do you love those parts of the child that derived from yourself, but also those parts that derived from your loved one.

1

The question now arises: "How do we sense love?" "Is it just simply by a combination of our five senses, namely those of sight, hearing, touch, smell and taste, or is something else involved as well, such as intuition?" But we won't try to answer these questions now, but a way forward may come from the application of Astrology, particularly that part of it called "Synastry". The word comes from the Greek: 'syn' standing for 'mutual bringing together' and 'astron' meaning 'star'. To return to basics just once more, we can say that:

The fundamental biochemical processes that underpin all animal senses predate the emergence of multicellular life. In the search for the origin of the senses, we don't need to go very far because the single, eukaryotic-celled creature, a paramecium, developed the sense of touch. It has no brain, but as soon as it bumps into an obstacle, it changes direction. The biochemical mechanism underlying this touch response is an 'action-potential'. It is ancient, as well as electrical. An 'action-potential' is a short-lasting, electrical pulse that produces a simple response from within the nervous system. The ability of an organism to sense its environment is based on the transformation of an external stimulus – be it a chemical, light, sound, or touch, into a change in a cell membrane potential, which is an 'action-potential'. The advantages are the speed of transmission, and the controlled nature of the electrical pulse. 'Action-potentials' can travel at over 100 metres per second (through ion channels) and the shape plus intensity of the pulse does not alter over long distances. Every sensation we have, is relayed to our brains by 'action-potentials'. This is 'Simply Now'.

Although the mechanism by which information is transmitted to the brain from the various senses, is the same for all of them, different parts of the brain deal specifically with the information from each sense. For example, the visual cortex (at the back of the brain!) deals with the reception and interpretation of vision. Similarly, the auditory cortex (part of the temporal lobes) deals with sound data; the olfactory cortex (situated at the front of the cerebrum) deals with signals from the nostrils, and the sensations of touch have to do with the somatosensory cortex (located in the parietal lobes). These regions of the senses are called *primary* because they are concerned with the input to, and the output from, the brain. Near to these *primary* regions lie the *secondary* ones, which deal with more abstract levels. The data from the various senses is processed at these associated *secondary* levels. The remaining regions of the cerebral cortex are called *tertiary*, and the most abstract and sophisticated activity of the brain is carried out here. The information from the different senses is analysed and combined; memories are laid down, pictures of the outside World are constructed, general plans are conceived, evaluated and speech is understood, or formulated. The *hippocampus* participates strongly in laying down long-term (permanent) memories. The *hypothalamus* is the seat of emotion – pleasure, rage, fear, despair and hunger, for example. The *thalamus* itself, is a processing centre and relay station, whereas the *reticular formation* is responsible for the general state of alertness, or **awareness**, involved in the brain, as a whole. However, the *reticular formation* is an ancient part of the brain, but the more complicated activities of the *cerebral cortex* would give that region the strongest claim for being capable of harbouring **consciousness.**

With the foregoing in 'mind', let us return to the phenomenon of 'love'. Earlier, we said that the conscious result of the mother's DNA (i.e. her overall personality) attracted the conscious result of the father's DNA (i.e. his overall personality), and *vice-versa*, in the process called 'love'. Clearly, we have here two people **sensing** each other. The data from this is transferred to each of their brains, in time-honoured fashion by action-potentials, where it becomes analysed finally in the *tertiary* regions of the *cerebral cortex*. At first thought, it would seem that no additional, specific area is required to handle this sort of information. Yet sensing each other's personality, initially, can take place very quickly, followed by a slower confirmation of the initial, favourable impression, and so on. Earlier, we used the word 'personality', but we could just about have used the word 'horoscope' instead. Could we possibly take a step further and suggest that the sensing of 'personality'/'horoscope' is essentially the same as sensing the state of each other's planets at their moments of epoch and birth? After all, all of us are members of the solar system, even though we are, naturally, Earthlings first. And we can test the validity of this proposal to see whether there is agreement between the proposed results of love, and the actual ones, between sets of two specific people, i.e. from their 'synastry' exercises.

Usually, the greatest value of 'synastry' consists of its ability to assess the compatibility of partners in marriage. Couples might want to know, before marriage, whether they are suited to each other. Many young people are anxious to have confirmation of their feelings before taking an irrevocable step. Marriage partners may need advice with problems within their relationship, hoping that these may be solved by an assessment of their strengths and weaknesses, followed by making appropriate allowances. The difficulty of the man-woman relationship is probably the most important concern in the lives of most people. There is no single rule and the only way consists of assessing the horoscopes of the two people involved, starting with general comparisons, and then moving on to more specific considerations. In no pairs of horoscopes will everything be found to be harmonious, but likely causes of disharmony may be identified, guarded against and so minimised. Probably, it is better if two people can realise that they do not combine well in certain ways, then, if they can admit this openly, their relationship should improve. On the other hand, sources of harmony should be built on*. Astrologically, there should be strong points of similarity in the horoscopes of marriage partners, but, at the same time, points of contrast, in order that each may learn from the other, and absorb some of his/her different habits of thought and body.

All that has been said, allowing for different circumstances, applies to partnerships other than marriage, such as those of parent and child, as well as those of business/professional partnerships. Interestingly, comparison of the horoscope of someone who has a strong liking for the work of a particular composer, for example, with that composer's horoscope, will show unmistakeable indications of rapport between the two, even though the composer in question is now dead.

The 7th House represents all that is complementary to our personal selves (shown by the 1st House) and contains all that we lack, and seek in others, to supplement our deficiencies. It is the House of all yearnings and seeking after the unattainable, or the far distant; the House of the Ideal, as opposed to the actual (again, shown by the 1st House). Thus, the general circumstances of marriage are shown by the 7th House.

Personality: In our previous seven books, we have pursued the task of trying to establish the truth of natal astrology, and the best way of carrying it out, as applied to individual persons. We recommended the Morinus House system as the one simple and elegant method of choice. But we have modified it slightly by taking the original House boundaries and converting them into the House centres. Using this modified system we showed that the theory of 'The Pre-Natal Epoch' seemed more readily applicable than it had been before. Instead of just one chart of birth, we determined an Epoch from it, as well as its corresponding Ideal time of Birth. Interpretations of Epoch and Ideal-Birth-Time charts' factors were taken from books published by notable astrologers, who had had no connection with the person whose horoscope was being prepared. The combination and organisation of the charts' impersonal interpretations so obtained, led to an essentially complete and understandable horoscope for the person, or that person's character portrait/person summary. The method was used to produce character portraits of England's kings, queens and rulers from Henry II to Elizabeth II, which could be compared with independent biographies of the self-same monarchs and rulers, bearing in mind the possibly unreliable birth data, the inherent inaccuracy of astrological interpretations and the biases sometimes found in royal biographies.

Nevertheless, we were encouraged by the results, which we are now proposing to extend to the interactions between two people, whose birth data are reasonably well-known. Firstly, we have produced the character portraits, or personalities, of the seven people making up our study, and have presented them in the Appendix for introductory reference purposes. Three of them have been used as controls, disguised by request, namely Jack Sprat, Jill Hillside and Gillian Gray. These people were well-known by the author for significant periods of his life, and their horoscopes, in the opinion of the author, appeared to fit them rather well. Similarly, the results obtained for their 'synastry' exercises seemed to accord well with experience, thereby increasing the author's confidence that what he was producing was reasonably correct. Then the method was applied to two World famous couples, namely the Duke and Duchess of Windsor, and the actor Richard Burton with the actress Elizabeth Taylor, in the hope that the results from them would prove reasonably correct, too. The final chapter of the book presents and discusses the results obtained from all four 'synastry' exercises.

- -

*Often charts should be compared to see whether planets for one, are coming, or have come, to planets in the other by progression, but perhaps this is a bit too far ahead of our presentation of 'synastry' in this book, where we are concerned with establishing a basic 'synastry' method.

- -

CHAPTER 2

A 'Synastry' Exercise for the Duke and Duchess of Windsor.

'Synastry' can identify areas in a partnership where the chances of compatibility are greatest, and where they are least, so that partners can build on the strengths of a relationship and eventually overcome weaknesses.

Having described the Duke and Duchess individually from their charts in some detail, (see the Appendix) including their attitude to love and lovers, we can gain a general idea of their likely interaction, and so form an impression of how suitable they would have been as a couple, simply by considering the make-up of their individual charts. We can then move on more specifically to the two-way interaction of close, major cross-aspects between each of their two charts.

General considerations from the Duke's natal charts.

Firstly, we recall that the Duke is mainly subjective, i.e. the majority of his planets lie below the Earth in the lower hemisphere. We see that his destiny lies both in his own hands (all his planets lie to the East in his Epoch chart) and also depends on others and circumstances (most of his planets lie to the West in his Birth chart). Jupiter leads the

'Bowl' shape of his Epoch chart indicating that he 'captures experiences' and 'takes them in'. The Moon (his female principle) leads the locomotive shaping of his Birth chart suggesting that he would be affected by factors in his public and social environment. We notice that 11 planets (out of 22) lie in the 'external Air' triplicity (intellectual and communicative) and that the majority (17) of his planets find themselves in the Cardinal (outgoing) and Mutable (adaptable) quadruplicities. Notice also that he has 9 quintile aspects and 2 decile aspects altogether, indicating high intelligence.

Concerning partnership, we see that the Duke in his 7th House (of his partner) has no planets residing there, but Pisces is on the 7th House centre at Epoch, and Leo on the 7th House centre at Birth. Respectively, these indicate that fickleness is a threat to relationships (Pisces), which should be guarded against, and that marriage and partnerships will play a major role in his life, and may well bring a rise in status (Leo). Similarly, Libra is the sign of the Partner and we see that the Duke has Mars, the Sun, Mercury and Saturn in this sign. Generally, the Sun shows that the establishment of harmony will be a major aim in his life. He would have identified this aim with a sense of pride, self-esteem and a need for achievement. There was a good chance of his building smooth relationships but some difficulty would have arisen through wounded pride, and a belief that he had been unfairly treated. Mars in Libra shows that his energy was committed to the establishment of a satisfactory state of equilibrium in life, and that his passions required fulfilment through a spiritual response from his partner. Mercury in Libra shows that harmony is largely a mental concept for him and that mental compatibility was desired in partnership. Saturn in Libra shows that his drive for security helps his partnerships to be as sociable and as practicable as possible. There would have been a sense of duty and a strong feeling of obligation towards his partner. Great trouble would have been taken to find a mate able to demonstrate integrity. The likelihood was that he would have married at a later age – a desire for perfection may have made him too demanding, but here, on balance, despite difficulties in his relationships with women and with his mother, an enduring relationship was indicated.

General considerations from the Duchess's natal charts.

Firstly, we see that Wallis was both objective and subjective, i.e. that, on balance, her planets are distributed equally between the upper and lower hemispheres (i.e. above and below the Earth) of her natal charts. However, most of these planets (14) lie in the Eastern hemisphere (rather than in that of the Western one), showing that her destiny lay mainly in her own hands. Wallis's charts consist of a 'Bowl' shape at Epoch, led by the Moon, (suggesting a public life) mainly of the 'captures experiences' and 'takes them in' type. The shape of her Birth chart is a 'Bucket' one (indicating a particular and rather uncompromising direction to her life effort) with Mars in Aries (its own sign) in the 11th House, as the conservatively placed 'handle' planet, which is also a singleton that provides extra emphasis to her energy expended on friendships and objectives. 'Bowl' to 'Bucket' types tend to combine rather well. 13 planets (out of 22) in 'Air' make it Wallis's triplicity, and, as with the Duke, her quadruplicities are Cardinal and Mutable. Notice that Wallis's charts contain five quintile family aspects and six decile family aspects indicating very good intelligence.

Concerning partnership, there are no planets in Wallis's 7th House. Aries and Sagittarius lie at the centre of the 7th Houses. Respectively, these suggest that there would have been a tendency for Wallis to marry early in life to a strong, even dominating person, and that marriage and partnerships were likely to have brought great material benefits. Wallis has the Moon, Mercury, Venus and Chiron (twice) in Libra. Like the Duke, Mercury shows that, for Wallis, harmony is largely a mental concept so that mental compatibility would be desirable in partnership. Venus indicates a need for her to express her affection in the most harmonious way she can, whereas the Moon shows that her feelings were concerned with creating an harmonious atmosphere. An ability to sense instinctively how best to adjust to others would have greatly assisted putting them at their ease. Social acceptance would have been important and partnership would have been seen as something that can confer mutual benefits. When her feelings were hurt, then she would have "put a brave face on it".

The union of 'Air' to 'Air' people is rightly described as a meeting of minds. Both of them would have worked best together on an intellectual basis. There would have been easy communication between them, and an exchange of ideas on a variety of subjects, but with more debate rather than action. The danger was that they would have become too involved in abstract issues and theoretical problems, and so may have failed to devote sufficient time and energy to practical, near-at-hand issues. Both would have liked lots of social life, so that home life may have been neglected. Probably, this partnership needed more ballast.

A union of 'Cardinal' – 'Cardinal' quadruplicities may work well on an all-action basis provided both can agree on aims and ambitions to be realised jointly. Clearly defined spheres of action for each is needed to avoid clashing of competitive natures. Cardinal types need elbow room and do not like to be opposed. However, there can be a great deal of mutual admiration; each appreciates the achievements of the other.

The union of 'Mutable' – 'Mutable' types is likely to flourish best on the mental level. Both partners can be highly adaptable but someone needs to supply the continuity they lack. The tendency is for them to fail to act with sufficient thoroughness under circumstances that call for total commitment, but when the Earth element is lacking (perhaps as in this case) the partners may show a distaste for coping with practical issues, and those requiring caution.

The union of 'Cardinal' – 'Mutable' quadruplicities works best when both partners have a majority of planets in the same element ('Air' in this case, i.e. Libra and Gemini). Because mutable persons are willing to adapt to their more active partners, the result may be a very active partnership but that, unfortunately, lacks any kind of anchor. Some 'Fixed' quadruplicity is needed to supply a 'resistance to change'.

Between them Wallis and the Duke have their planets distributed fairly equally between the categories of Angular (outgoing), Succedent (resultant status) and Cadent (dispersion of ideas and energies) Houses.

Specific considerations from all four charts (see the charts at the end of the chapter).

Let us begin to be more specific concerning the relationship of the Duke and Duchess by listing the planets by their sign positions beginning from the first point of Aries. The following Table should help us to list all the cross-aspects from her two charts with his two, and *vice-versa;* the purpose of the latter is to enable us to specify the 'relocation' House of the planets making the cross-aspect from one chart to the other. Because there are many such aspects between them, i.e. from Epoch to Epoch, from Epoch to Birth and *vice-versa,* and from Birth to Birth, only the very strong cross-aspects (with an orb of 1^0 on each side of exactness for major ones, of 45' for sextiles and 30' for minor ones) have been considered. We shall see that these are indeed enough to give a very good idea of what their married relationship, and suitability for it, would have been like. We shall only consider aspects associated with the 1st, 2nd, 3rd, 4th, 6th and 12th harmonics, namely the conjunction, opposition, trine, square, sextile, semi-sextile and quincunx aspects that all divide easily into the 360^0 of the aspect circle. Less satisfactorily, we shall not be concerned with aspects of the 5th, 7th, 8th, 9th, 10th and 11th harmonics. Nevertheless, we shall find plenty that does seem quite relevant.

Table 1: The planets of the Epoch and Birth charts of the Duke and Duchess of Windsor listed by sign starting from the first point of Aries.

Duchess Epoch	Duke Epoch	Duke Birth	Duchess Birth
Mo 10⁰Ge15'	Ju 01⁰Ge01' Rx	Ma 00⁰Ar22'	Ma 21⁰Ar11'
Pl 12⁰Ge45'	Pl 10⁰Ge 40' Rx	Ve 23⁰Ta16'	Pl 12⁰Ge37'
Np 18⁰Ge02'	Np 13⁰Ge27' Rx	Pl 10⁰Ge47'	Me 16⁰Ge13' Rx

Ju 01°Le16'	Mo 28°Le01'	Np 13°Ge59'	Np 18°Ge10'
Su 18°Vr30'	Ch 14°Vr07'	Ju 18°Ge20'	Ve 23°Ge00'
Ma 28°Vr15'	Ma 02°Li24'	Su 02°Ca19'	Su 28°Ge33'
Ve 00°Li30' Rx	Su 13°Li05'	Me 27°Ca25'	Ju 08°Le45'
Me 07°Li56'	Sa 15°Li27'	Ch 16°Vr15'	Mo 10°Li54'
Ch 11°Li12'	Me 24°Li26'	Sa 18°Li25'	Ch 20°Li35'
Sa 04°Sc09'	Ur 09°Sc20'	Ur 11°Sc32' Rx	Sa 12°Sc59' Rx
Ur 16°Sc50'	Ve 22°Sc48'	Mo 03°Pi43'	Ur 21°Sc04' Rx

In the Table Rx stands for retrograde motion.

Following our allowances specified for cross-aspects, we find that the cross-aspects between the Duke's and the Duchess's charts' planets, both at Epoch (see columns 1 and 2) are: [Her]Mo[E] conjoint(S-M) [His]Pl[E]; [Her]Pl[E] conjoint(M-W) [His] Np[E]; [Her]Pl[E] trine(S) [His]Su[E]; [Her]Ju[E] sextile(S) [His]Ju[E]; [Her]Ch[E] trine(M-W) [His]Pl[E].

The cross-aspects between the Duchess's Epoch and the Duke's Birth charts' planets (see columns 1 and 3) comprise: [Her]Mo[E] conjoint(M) [His]Pl[B]; [Her]Np[E] conjoint(S) [His]Ju[B]; [Her]Ju[E] trine(VW) [His]Ma[B]; [Her]Su[E] semi-sextile(E-S) [His]Sa[B]; [Her]Su[E] square(E-S) [His]Ju[B]; [Her]Ma[E] sextile(W) [His]Me[B]; [Her]Ve[E] opposite(E-S) [His]Ma[B]; [Her]Ch[E] sextile(M) [His]Pl[B]; [Her]Ch[E] semi-sextile(M-W) [His]Ur[B]; [Her]Sa[E] trine(M) [His]Mo[B]; [Her]Ur[E] sextile(M-W) [His]Ch[B]; [Her]Np[E] trine(M) [His]Sa[B].

The cross-aspects between the Duchess's Birth and the Duke's Epoch charts' planets (see columns 4 and 2) consist of: [Her]Pl[B] conjoint(E) [His]Pl[E]; [Her]Pl[B] trine(M) [His]Su[E]; [Her]Me[B] trine(M-W) [His]Sa[E]; [Her]Su[B] sextile(M) [His]Mo[E]; [Her]Ju[B] square(M-W) [His]Ur[E]; [Her]Mo[B] trine(S) [His]Pl[E]; conjoint(VW) [His]Np[E]; [Her]Sa[B] quincunx(VW) [His]Np[E].

The cross-aspects between the Duchess's and the Duke's Birth charts' planets (see columns 4 and 3) are: $^{Her}Me^B$ square(E) $^{His}Ch^B$; $^{Her}Np^B$ conjoint(E) $^{His}Ju^B$; $^{Her}Np^B$ trine(S) $^{His}Sa^B$; $^{Her}Ve^B$ semi-sextile(M) $^{His}Ve^B$; $^{Her}Mo^B$ trine(E-S) $^{His}Pl^B$.

In the short-form identification of the individual, cross-aspects found, the superscripts His and Her stand for each of the partner's charts (see the ends of the relevant chapters). The capital (upper case letter) followed by the ordinary (lower case) letter, are the first two letters of the planets comprising the aspect. Similarly, the abbreviations for the type of aspect are straightforward. The strength of each aspect is given in brackets following the type of the aspect. Thus, E stands for exact; S for strong; M for medium, W for weak and V for very. Please note that the superscripts, E and B, that follow the abbreviations for the planets involved in the cross-aspect, signify Epoch chart and Birth chart, respectively.

The interpretations for all these cross-aspects are found in Davison's book: "Synastry". Taking a major one from each of the above four groups as illustrations, we find for:

$^{Her}Ma^E$ semi-sextile(S) $^{His}Mo^E$: His concept of the ideal woman would have been stimulated, i.e. she could have supplied a useful stimulus to his powers of imagination.

$^{Her}Sa^E$ trine(S) $^{His}Mo^B$: She may have hesitated to break any legal bond between them out of a sense of duty, whereas he may have become so accustomed to having her around that he may have developed a "better the devil I know" type of attitude about their relationship. She needed him as a means of showing her constancy, whereas he may have clung to her as a 'mother' figure, and have got into the habit of becoming dependent on her.

$^{Her}Su^B$ sextile (M) $^{His}Mo^E$: She stands for his ideal man and he stands for her feminine ideal, which is the opposite of normal expectation. Thus, she was likely to have played the leading rôle in their relationship, but she would also have adapted to his wishes.

$^{Her}Ve^B$ semi-sextile(M) $^{His}Ve^B$: A congenial, classic link is formed. This encouraged the development of a happy companionship, along with an affectionate consideration for each other's needs. Likes and dislikes of the partners should have clashed rarely.

If we take all the interpretations of the cross-aspects and organise them into a readily understandable whole, we obtain:-

The primary indicator of compatibility at the physical level was present (Venus in aspect with Mars), which suggests that there was a ready response to each other's animal magnetism. He took the initiative and she invited it but, in this case, it may not have been that easy for the partners to adjust each other on the physical and/or emotional level. His concept of the ideal woman would have been stimulated, i.e. she could have supplied a useful stimulus to his powers of imagination. Yet there was also a tendency that he was able to spark her enthusiasm. He tended to make her an object of adoration, with a desire to place her on a pedestal. He may also have been able to bring out all her latent ability to play her most attractive feminine rôle. This could have been most felicitous (it is frequently found between marriage partners) in which each may vie in lavishing gifts on the other. The partners could have agreed helpfully on matters of philosophy, ethics and general moral standards. There would have been a mutual tolerance and a broad-minded acceptance of the partner's way-of-life. She reinforced his belief in himself, whereas he provided an effective outlet for her subconscious drives. Altogether, this indicates a relationship brought about by destiny. As a result, a great deal of physical attraction would have been present. She stood for his ideal man, and he stood for her feminine ideal, the opposite of normal expectation. Thus, she was likely to have to have played the leading rôle in their relationship, but she would also have adapted to his wishes. Her mind was steadied by him, deepening her thinking by providing solid, practical advice. In response, she would have provided him with extra points to consider. Hence, a congenial, 'classic' link was formed, which encouraged the development of a happy companionship, along with an affectionate consideration for each other's needs. Likes and dislikes of the partners should have clashed rarely. Although they had a strong partnership, he may have flattered her, yet she still would have shown favouritism to him, thereby improving his situation. She showed a deep level of understanding of him, in general, so that there developed sympathy towards his outlook.

She may have hesitated to break any legal bond between them out of a sense of duty, whereas he may have become so accustomed to having her around that he may have developed a "better the devil I know" type of attitude about their relationship. She needed him as a means of showing her constancy, whereas he may have clung to her as a 'mother' figure, and have got into the habit of becoming dependent on her. She would have wanted him to be aware of his responsibilities as her partner, and he would have wanted her to be just the same as his partner. Both she and he would have been teachers in their both learning co-operation. Both of them would have exerted some kind of control over each other's more flamboyant extravagances. He may have taken advantage of her easy-going generosity. His ideas were challenged, but care was needed because too much 'constructive' criticism may have led him to resort defensively to verbal gymnastics. He may have resorted also to erratic action to break-up her irritating air of complacency that had provoked him into behaving unwisely.

A hypersensitive type of awareness was present. She could have introduced him to a less prosaic, and more idealistic, way of looking at things. She may have played on his phobias and fantasies, increasing any neurotic, or escapist, tendencies present. However, at best, she could have shown him how to give his ideals, inspirations and dreams, practical expression, and how to contain, and to put to effective use, his flights of fancy. As she sought his transformation, so he would have become more elusive and mysterious. Similarly, at best, he could have done exactly the same for her. But if he had known how to influence her moods, then he could have become a very unwelcome enemy. But as both partners were engaged in welfare, and/or in artistic affairs, then they were capable of acting with mature integrity, resulting in a successful collaboration.

She had difficulty in believing that his charitable inclinations were well-directed. Her own, balanced, wise and successful philanthropic ideas would easily have found an intense and creative reaction from him. This should have helped him in his career because he was connected with it through her, as well as helping him in his more unusual, independent, career interests. He could have fostered, and encouraged, her inspiration and ideals, whereas her compassionate nature could have helped him to find suitable, charitable outlets for his own philanthropic impulses. All this could have added a subtle, new dimension to his philosophical understanding.

- -

Planet 'Relocation' Interpretations

An additional result of examining cross-aspects concerns the effect of the planet making the cross-aspect on the House of the planet receiving the cross-aspect. There are interpretations for this effect and, once more, we find them by consulting R. C. Davison's book, "Synastry". We have said that aspects work in two, or both, directions, so that if a planet in the 2nd House of an Epoch chart makes a cross-aspect with another person's planet in, let's say, the 6th House of their Epoch, or Birth, chart, then not only do we have the two-way working interpretations of the cross-aspect itself but we also have the interpretations of the two planets making-up the aspect forming 'relocations' to the House of the other planet in the cross-aspect. Thus, the planet in the 2nd House can be considered to have an influence on the 6th House of the other person's chart, and *vice-versa*, i.e. the receiving planet in the 6th House of the other person's chart being 'relocated' to the 2nd House of the first person's chart. Unless the planets of the cross-aspect are the same, and in the same House, then the effects, and so the interpretations, of the 'relocations', will be different. Overall then, and in this way, the effects of one person upon the other, will be noticeably different. Let us consider, for example, the 1st House in the Duke's Birth chart. There we find the Moon that has the Duchess's Saturn at Epoch in cross-aspect to it. Thus, her

Saturn influences his 1st House, i.e. it becomes 'relocated' into it, and there is an interpretation for this, as follows: *Something in his personality may have convinced her that she could have depended on him. He may have valued her as a stabilising influence and so he may have developed his own sense of responsibility more effectively. Possibly, his conduct may have made demands on her patient understanding and so have tested her powers of endurance, but this could also have been an indicator of a lasting relationship.*

If we take the all the 'relocation' interpretations of the Duchess's planets to the Houses of the Duke's charts, and combine and organise them into a readily understandable whole, then for mainly her effect on him, we obtain:-

He may have felt an instinctive liking for her, and have felt very much at home with her. She may have assisted him to beautify his home, or to have put him in touch with opportunities for improving his environment, or to have helped him to acquire property. She may have felt tempted to adopt a maternal attitude towards him. He, out of admiration, may have tended to emulate her habits and instinctive reactions. He would have found that she would have been easy to talk to, so that she may have monopolised a good deal of his time in conversation. But she may also have been inclined to boast, exaggerate, or even bluff, when he was unsure of his facts. She may not have been able to recognise when his sense of proportion was being distorted, leading to trouble. Also, she may have been telling him what she thought he may have liked to hear, with similar results.

She will have been attracted to him by the way in which he deployed his talents, and by his general attitude to the whole area of creative and pleasurable activities. She would have proved an appreciative audience, encouraging him to display his talents, and enjoying his sense of humour. She may have been able to appeal to his sense of the dramatic and have assisted him in the process of self-dramatization. Usually, under favourable conditions, these attractions would have contributed to a happy association. She may have succeeded in taking advantage of his generosity by playing on his sympathies, or by his "showing off". Alternatively, she may have been able to increase his artistic vision as well as his leisure time activities. She may have brought a new sense of idealism into those activities nearest to his heart. There would have been dreams of romance, or of shared romantic fantasies, challenging him to live up to the highest romantic ideals. These he would have cherished, and have reminded him that true love may have caused him to develop a greater intuitive recognition of the fact that she was the object of his affection, which needed elevation. On the other hand, she may have subtly drained away his vitality, or have encouraged him to dissipate it in fruitless enterprises. However, at best, she may have provided him with the inspiration to reach the height of his creative endeavours. In fact, there was a stimulus from her towards more creative activities, either by inspiring him to emulate her example, or by giving enthusiastic support to his projects, enterprises and hobbies. Usually, she was able to evoke a warm, emotional response from him, so that he felt uplifted by her presence. As a result, he may have become particularly indulgent about any of her shortcomings. All this was good for friendship and she would have had the capacity to bring joy into his life. Also, she would have taken pleasure in his affectionate responses.

Something in his personality may have convinced her that she could have depended on him. She may have valued him as a stabilising influence and so she may have developed her own sense of responsibility more effectively. Possibly, her conduct may have made demands on his patient understanding, and so have tested his powers of endurance, but this could have resulted in confirming a lasting relationship. And yet, she would have been able to exert a stabilising and vivifying effect upon him as a person. His psychological orientation would have encouraged her to be her own essential self more effectively. He would have appreciated her worth as an individual to the extent that he would have seen his own external characteristics and outward method of approach shown in mature fashion by her, as if they had belonged to the very essence of her being. Much mutual attraction would have resulted.

She may have had a particularly beneficial effect on him, not only in material affairs, but also in spiritual and emotional ones. Her sense of values would have made her aware of his good qualities, giving him a feeling of well-being. Often, she was likely to have gone out-of-her-way to assist him. Hence, there was likely to have been a good understanding between them. She could have had a special talent for detecting any shortcomings in the way in which he handled his financial arrangements, and she may have been able to provide helpful suggestions for augmenting them. She may have been able to give good advice on how to increase his material resources and she may have been instrumental in helping him to cultivate a more realistic sense of values, but, possibly, her advice could have been ill-founded. Yet also, she may have been able to provide him with a greater sense of security and have helped him to develop a more prudent and responsible attitude towards financial affairs, advising him as to the best way to insure against risk, and how to avoid doubtful investments. He may have owed her some debt, which could have been most suitably repaid on a material basis. Here, any debt should always have been punctiliously discharged. Altogether, his experiences with her may have caused him to become aware of his most deep-seated motives that regulated his attitude to money and possessions. The way she acted may have caused him to ask himself on what his standard of values was really based, and to examine his whole attitude towards the question of security. She may have been the means of bringing him much financial gain.

She understood his subconscious motivations better than most, and could have hinted at how he might best attain some self-transformation. If she appreciated his sense of inner values, then this could have proved most rewarding. However, she may have used her knowledge of his inner motivations for her own advantage. It just may have been unwise for him to enter into any financial transactions with her.

Wallis would have kept him on his toes, challenging him to put forward his best efforts, and to summon-up his courage when faced with an emergency. She would have been a courageous advocate for his cause, but she would have expected him to display some degree of independence and self-sufficiency. For his part, he may well have responded with his own complementary thoughts, thereby leading to an effective collaboration. She may have challenged him to show his efficiency and technical know-how, while, at the same time, being ready to apply her own skills and knowledge, if they had been needed. She could have given him useful assistance when jobs needed doing. He would have found that she had no trouble in keeping him busy, and she may even have been inclined to dwell on the virtue of work for its own sake, as well as of making efforts for the welfare of others.

His experiences with her may have led him to undertake radical self-appraisal, and so have effected an important transformation in his being. She may have been the means of interesting him in a study of economics. There could have developed a contest between them about who should exercise control over the family budget. He may have been able to kindle her interest, and she may have stimulated his interest, in occultism, and so enabled him to view the phenomenon of death in a new light. A considerable, and mutual, physical attraction may have been experienced.

She would have provided him with warmth and reassurance. She could have inspired him in his search for a vital and transcendent life philosophy. She may have acted as a 'guru' for him. Indeed, she may have had a very uplifting and spiritualising effect upon his whole outlook on life. Through her vision, he may have been encouraged to widen his frontiers and to have cultivated a more receptive attitude towards ideas. She would have been happy to publicise his achievements, and in making them known to a wider audience. But misunderstandings may have resulted unless they had made a special effort to ensure that messages had been properly received. For example, she may have attempted to give his ideas a communistic, etc. slant.

Wallis may have been able to offer him considerable help in his career and provide him with valuable encouragement while he sought to realise his aims, because she appreciated the value of what he was trying to achieve. He would always have been able to retain her good opinion of his worth, and he would have found that any show of loyalty to her on his part, usually would have been repaid amply. She may have been instrumental in making possible improvements in his status, perhaps through putting him in touch with influential people, or through wise advice based on her own personal experience. She may have given him a taste for success, or, by her good opinion of him, given him an extra incentive to succeed so that he did not let her down. She may have taken pleasure in playing the rôle of 'father' to him, because she appreciated the aims he had in mind. Her objective would have been to strengthen his belief in himself and to encourage him to achieve his ambitions through applying his efforts wisely. Possibly, he may have aimed higher than of what he was capable, thereby weakening his resolve, perhaps by having had his path made too easy, and perhaps by having had his progress hampered through his receiving bad advice. She may have played some definitive rôle in his career. She would have encouraged him to develop a realistic approach to his responsibilities and to have assisted him to obtain a higher level of achievement and self-development. She may even have been guilty of envying him, his position.

Instinctively, she would have understood what he was aiming at in life, would have shared his interests, and would have wanted him to succeed in them. Because of this manifest belief in his abilities, she may have been inspired to pull out that little bit extra that would have made all the difference between success and failure. She would have known how to nurture his ambitions, and would have been able to make suggestions that would have helped to draw out some of his latent talents. She may even have felt it incumbent upon herself to adopt a somewhat parental attitude towards him, gently pushing him towards a certain goal and being particularly concerned to shield his reputation from attack from any source. All of this can be found between a husband and wife. He could have become more sensitive to the fact that one's reputation depends, to a large extent, on the goodwill and support of others, and that any blemish on his own reputation may have reflected poorly upon the reputations of those around him. Thus, she may have exercised some degree of control, or influence upon his career, or have been the means of him entertaining certain ambitions. As a result, he may have adopted a more definitive attitude to positions of power and authority. He may have found that, in the process, he became aware, for the first time, of some hidden motivations, that had, hitherto, governed the direction of his ambitions, and of his whole attitude towards making his way in the World. This would have helped him to transform his aims, and to have tested his integrity, when he had been called upon to occupy positions of authority.

- -

To complete our example of a 'relocation' exercise, i.e. the reverse half of the cross-aspect between her Saturn at Epoch with his Moon at Birth, we can write $^{His}Mo^B$ trine(S) $^{Her}Sa^E$. As the Duchess's Saturn occupies her 2nd House, then it is his Moon at Birth, which is 'relocated' there and the interpretation for this is: *He may have recognised in her a stabilising influence, and so have taken an interest in helping her to make the most of her resources. He may have made a practical show of his interest by giving her presents, thereby gaining pleasure himself. Importantly, she should have been grateful for his generosity. Possibly, he would have worried unduly about her financial problems, and so may have hindered and/or cramped her style.*

Similarly, we can gather together, organise and combine into a readily understandable whole, all the 'relocation' interpretations of the Duke's planets into the Houses of the Duchess's charts, which will give us mainly, his influence on her:-

He may have gone out-of-his-way to seek her friendship and have taken practical steps towards making her dreams come true. Her aspirations may have fired his enthusiasm, which gave her more hope of achieving them. He was likely to have become her friend in the best sense of the term, but she may have needed not to take too much advantage of his generosity of spirit, or to have taken him too much for granted. Possibly, too much indulgence, over-optimism, or self-esteem, would have spoilt the overall effect.

He may have expected her to be reliable and self-sufficient in those very areas where she was likely to have been the most vulnerable. He may have brought one of her weaknesses to light in a disconcerting way, arousing his doubts about her ability, and simultaneously arousing her resentment. On the one hand, she may have received an incentive to eradicate her weaknesses. Fortunately, she was able to summon-up fresh courage to tackle her problems after his bolstering of her self-assurance. Alternatively, he may have made testing demands on her sympathetic and charitable instincts. He was likely to have wanted to find out what made her tick, and she may have been encouraged to share confidences with him, despite his possible lack of stable discretion.

Her personality would have encouraged him to take a benevolent interest in her, resulting in the formation of a rewarding friendship. She would have been likely to receive favours from him, and his company would always have put her in a good mood, so that she tended to feel completely relaxed with him. Very often, they would have shared common aspirations and a respect for each other's qualities. She may have been doing him a favour by providing an outlet for his altruistic instincts. She will have been particularly aware of his charm, whereas her personality would have struck an harmonious chord in his psyche. She would have felt 'at home' with him and enjoyed his company, whereas he would have encouraged her to be her own, natural self. Something in her personality may have convinced him that he could have depended on her. She would have valued him as a stabilising influence, so that she may have developed her sense of responsibility more effectively. Her conduct may have made demands on his patient understanding and so tested his powers of endurance, but this could well have led to a lasting relationship. He may have been attracted to her by some potentialities she appeared to possess. Their relationship may have developed within her an urge to become more and more her essential self. He may have challenged her (perhaps unwittingly) to become conscious of some hidden motive for action, of which, previously, she had been unaware, perhaps having suppressed it psychologically. She may have been able to effect some kind of transformation in herself that had made her more complete and better integrated.

There was a similarity between his essential self, his inner being and the way she was seeking to project herself outwardly. She could have appreciated his worth as an individual, resulting in much mutual attraction that she then showed as admiration for him, which, in turn, made him happy. Thus, a sensitive link between the two was likely to have existed. Each felt that it was good to be in the other's company. His impulse to protect and cherish would have been projected in her direction. He may have been able to stimulate her imagination, so that there could have become a marked physical attraction between them. The way in which he thought may have appealed to her and he would have derived a mental stimulus by exchanging ideas with her. This would have proved helpful as they shared common interests and intellectual pursuits. He would have been able to keep her on her toes, challenging her to produce her best efforts, and to summon-up her courage, independence and self-sufficiency in the face of an emergency.

There was a tendency that his most effective channel of communication was through her emotions and charitable impulses. She may have begun to feel more deeply about the under-privileged. He may have been able to interpret her dreams and explain her fantasies, but she needed to have been careful that her illusions were not being fostered at the same time. His effect may have been relaxing and soothing and so she may have become able to dramatize herself more effectively. She may have had to guard herself against identifying too much with his emotions, and against allowing him to sway her sympathies unduly. She understood his unconscious motivations better than most, and could have hinted at how he might have attained some sort of transformation regarding his charitable inclinations.

Whereas he may have recognised in her a naturally stabilising influence and have taken an interest in helping her to make the most of her resources, even to the extent of making a practical show of his interest by giving her presents (that also gained him pleasure for himself) importantly, for her part, she should have been grateful for his generosity. Although his careful charity connected well with her finances and possessions, and have helped to mitigate changes occurring in her resources and feelings, any advice he gave her may have proved ill-founded. Possibly, he would have worried unduly about her financial problems, and so may have hindered, or cramped, her style. Financial transactions with him probably would not have worked out well for her.

On the other hand, he may have given her an entirely new slant on life, through new information, which gave her the opportunity to develop a quite different mental perspective, leading to a higher degree of mental rapport. More basically, for example, he may have suggested valuable, time-saving cuts in her method of travel.

He may have been responsible for making her aware of her latent, creative talents, which he may have enabled her to develop with dramatic effect. Many contemporaries may have affected her and she may have become compelled eventually to transform her whole attitude and approach to affairs of the heart. He may have been in a position to offer her some kind of service. She could have relied on his aid, although he may have put on her to return the compliment, especially as he was likely to have valued her services. There was unlikely to have been any emotional involvement as a result of this from her, but any reticence about emotional involvement was unlikely to have originated from him. She could have felt (perhaps wrongly) that she would have been better off without his help and advice. In any event, he would still have sympathised with her, and have had a soothing effect upon her.

Whereas she could have introduced him to a less prosaic and more idealistic way of looking at things, he may have been instrumental in focusing her thoughts upon religious, or philosophical, issues, leading her to adopt a more serious attitude to the important facts of life. He may have been a source of inspiration to her in her search for a more vital and transcendent philosophy of life. He would have had a great effect upon her religious and philosophical views. His ideas may have challenged her to examine her own ideas in a depth not previously contemplated. In the process, she may have uncovered some unconscious motivation that seemed to compel her to adopt a certain kind of outlook. In fact, he could have had a very uplifting and spiritualising effect upon her. In many ways, he may have broadened her horizons spiritually, mentally and physically. He may have had the happy knack of being able to stimulate her ideas on a variety of subjects, helping her to widen her horizons, which would have led to mutual trust and happiness. Through the ways in which he was guided by his beliefs, he became a 'guru' of their relationship.

Once again, the contact between them may have arisen through travel. They may have met first while travelling by sea, or air. He may have stimulated in her a restless desire for travel, based on his own accounts. He may have been the means of putting her in touch with foreign countries, and so have brought her responsibilities connected with them.

- -

Figure 1: Duke of Windsor-Epoch.

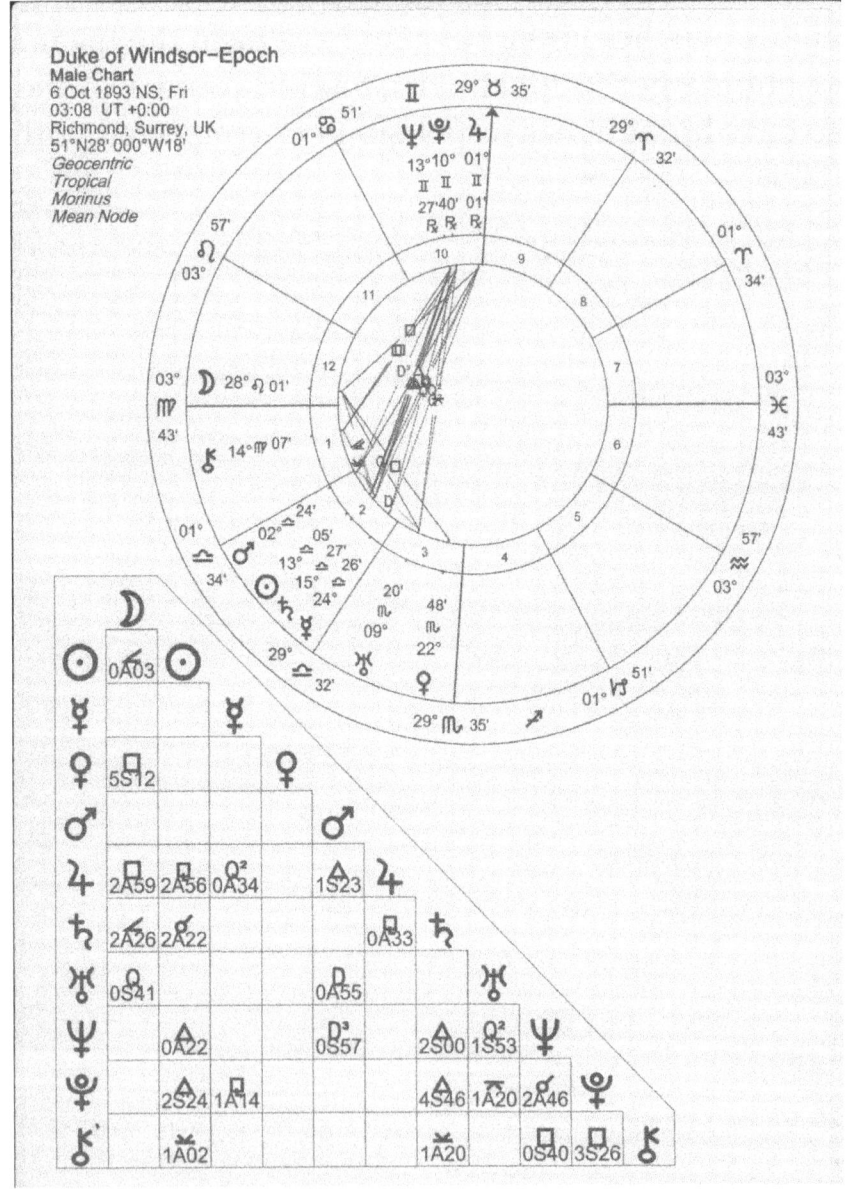

Figure 2: Duke of Windsor-Birth.

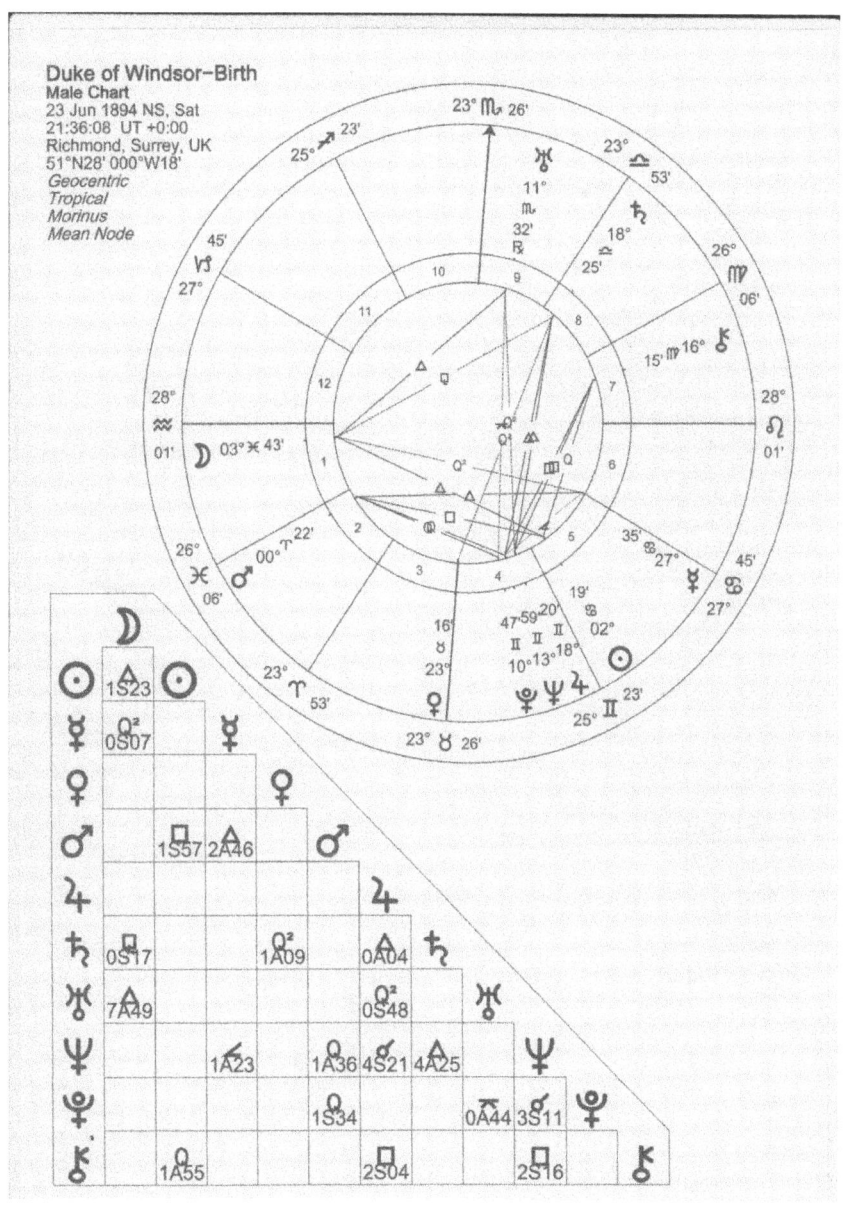

Figure 3: Wallis, Duchess of Windsor-Epoch.

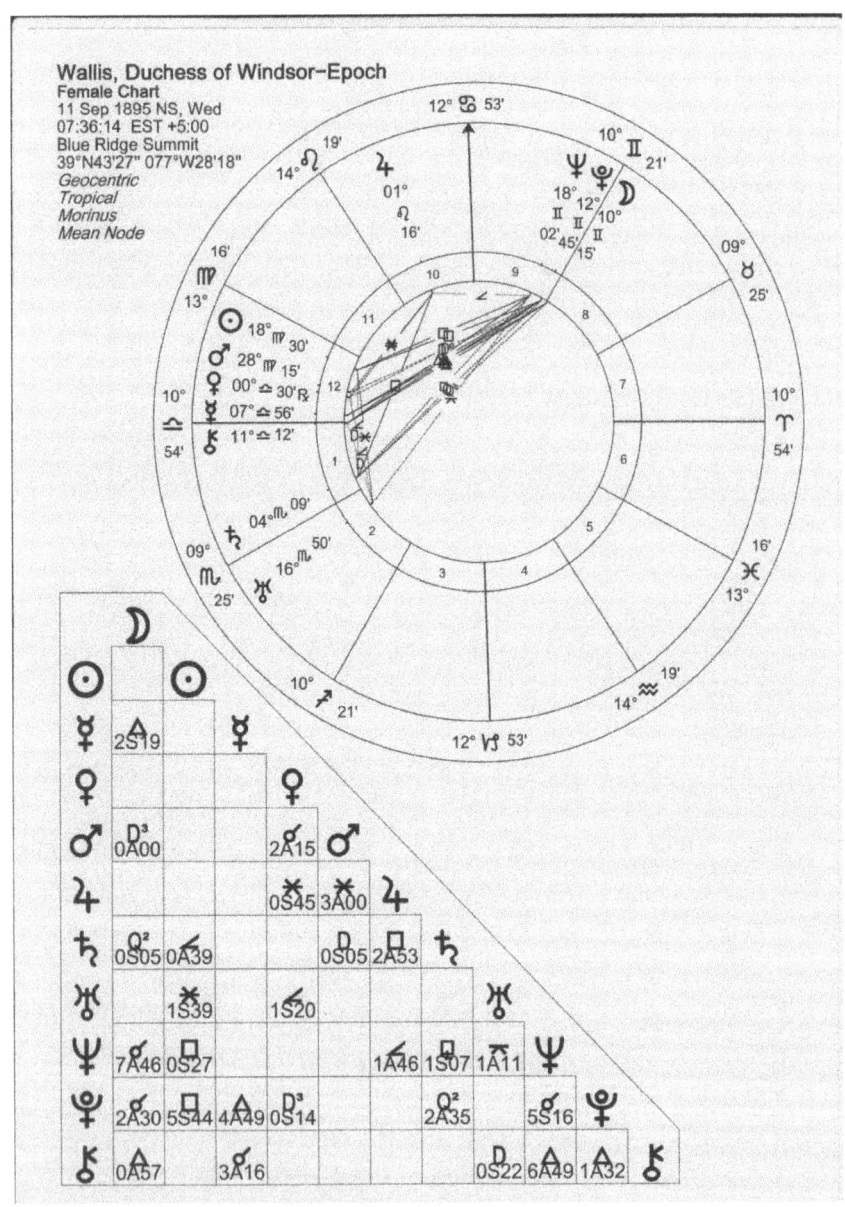

Figure 4: Wallis, Duchess of Windsor-Birth.

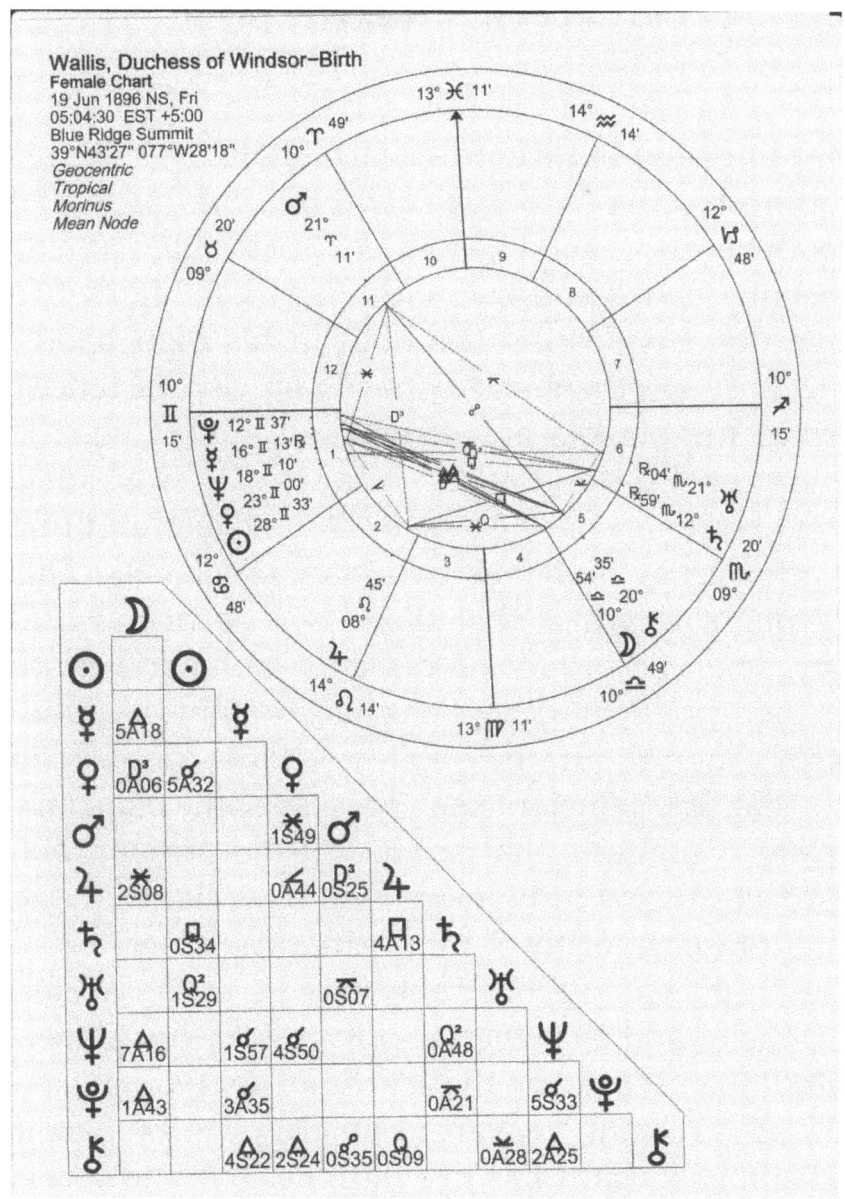

CHAPTER 3

A 'Synastry' exercise for Richard Burton and Elizabeth Taylor.

Examination of Richard's charts shows that he was both objective and subjective, i.e. the planets of both charts, taken together, are distributed almost equally above and below the Earth. Similarly, we see that his destiny lies both in his own hands, in those of others and depends on circumstances, since his planets are distributed almost equally between East and West. Additionally, we notice that both his charts have 'bucket' shapes and that each bucket chart has two 'handle' planets. This strongly indicates that there is a particular and rather uncompromising direction to his life effort. Moreover, Richard's Epoch chart contains a Grand-trine kite about the Jupiter – Pluto opposition as the kite's major axis. This specific planetary pattern suggests that strain will be present, but, in fact, there will be more ease than strain due to the presence of the Grand-trine. We observe that seven planets out of twenty two lie in the 'Water' triplicity and that the majority (17) of his planets find themselves in the Cardinal (outgoing) and Fixed (resistant to change) quadruplicities. Notice also that Richard has five quintile, and one decile, aspects in total, suggesting good intelligence.

Considering partnership, we see that Richard only has Mercury in Sagittarius present in his 7th House (of his partner). This implies that he sought a partner who could have assisted him at the intellectual level, although the mild square aspect of Mercury to the Moon indicates attraction to a highly-strung type. Hence, he may have had to learn to control his argumentativeness. Virgo lies at the centre of his 7th House at Epoch, and similarly, Sagittarius lies there at Birth. Respectively, these indicate that marriage may occur to a younger person, and that marriage could bring great material benefits. Analogously, Libra is the sign of the partner, and we see that whereas his chart at Epoch contains no planets in Libra, that he does have Mars in Libra at Birth. This suggests that his energy is committed to the establishment of a satisfactory state of equilibrium in his life, and that his passions required fulfilment through a spirited response from his partner. He may have wished to lead in all co-operative enterprises, and may have become quarrelsome (medium semi-square of Mars to the Moon) when feeling that he was losing the initiative – resentment may have been felt as a result.

Examination of Elizabeth's charts shows that she was somewhat more objective (12 planets above the Earth) than subjective (10 Planets below it). We see that her destiny depended mostly on others and on circumstances (16 planets to the West) rather than lying in her own hands (only

6 planets to the East). Also, we see that both her charts are of the 'bucket' type. Saturn is her anti-clockwise (conservative) 'handle' planet at Epoch, and the Moon is her vertical (emphasised) 'handle' planet at Birth. As for Richard, this strongly suggests that there was a particular and rather uncompromising direction to Elizabeth's life effort, involving both control (Saturn) and the public (the Moon). Notice that in Elizabeth's case, there are only two planets in the 'Air' triplicity, suggesting a lack of intellectual and/or communicative skills. However, although her planets are well-distributed among the quadruplicities, ten of her planets lie in 'Cadent' Houses, indicating a dispersal of ideas and energies. Notice also that Elizabeth has 10 quintile and 4 decile aspects altogether, suggesting high intelligence (to make-up for her lack of intellect?).

Concerning partnership, we see that Elizabeth has four planets in her 7th Houses, namely Mercury, Venus and Chiron at Epoch, and Uranus at Birth. Like Richard, she sought a partner who could have assisted her at the intellectual level, although her Mercury's square to Mars suggests that she, too, should have had to learn to control her argumentativeness. Her Venus here, shows appreciation of the value of a relationship, but there could have been an inordinate craving for affection, which could have placed a relationship on a rather fragile basis. Her 7th House Chiron indicates that a partner interested in philanthropy, would have provided a strong attraction for her.

Uranus in her 7th House at Birth, suggests the presence of unusual elements in a partnership, and possibly the need for both partners for greater 'elbow-room'. However, if one partner's capacity for self-development expands faster than the other partner's, then spouses can change, and so divorce may become likely. The exact semi-square of Uranus to Mars here, has to have been a source of explosiveness, despite its strong conjunction with Venus, its trine to Jupiter but not its square to Pluto. Taurus lies at her 7th House centre at Epoch and so the remarks made for Venus may have applied to a lesser degree in Elizabeth's case. Generally however, this indicates that marriage, or other romantic partnership, would have tended to play an important part in her life. Aries lies at her 7th House centre at Birth, and the interpretation here is that Elizabeth would have tended to marry early in life, the partner being a person of strong, and/or even dominating, character.

Concerning partnership generally, and the triplicities, the obvious feature in Richard and Elizabeth's relationship, concerns the combined, relative lack of 'Air' between them (6 planets out of 44). Hence, there may have been a lack of shared mental interest as well as an inability to communicate effectively. Others may have been at a loss to understand them. They can fail to plan ahead, act without due foresight and needlessly dissipate their energies in abortive, unwise and impulsive actions. Progress tends to be made only through trial and error. However, this may only have been a tendency. There is a small preponderance (14 out of 44 planets) of the 'Water' triplicity making for an emotional partnership. Both partners were likely to have been intuitive, but sympathies could have been misplaced. For optimum results, each should have made allowance for the other's moods, or mutual resentment would have resulted. However, positive reassurance may have been required to lift either Elizabeth, or Richard, out of the doldrums.

Concerning the quadruplicities, there is a small lack of the mutable (flexible) type (11 planets out of 44), and so a small excess of both the Cardinal (outgoing) [16 planets] type and of the Fixed (resistant to change) [17 planets] type. Compromise may have been difficult. Concerning the Houses, the outstanding observation is that both Richard and Elizabeth have an excess of planets [20 out of 44] in 'Cadent' (dispersal of ideas and energies) Houses. Thus, there could have been difficulty for both of them in finding an effective way of self-expression. Partners can compensate for this through dedication to a life of service, i.e. acting as agents, or go-betweens, and adapting to a variety of different people and circumstances, could have proved satisfying.

There would have been a tendency for both of them to live too much in their heads, so that they both may have tended to withdraw into an abstract World. As a result, mental compatibility would have been important to them, and they needed partners who could have drawn them out, and so helped them to realise their latent potential. They themselves, may have tended to concentrate on planning and perfecting a theoretical approach.

- -

Specific Inferences from all four of their Charts

Earlier, for the Duke and Duchess of Windsor, we mentioned and specified limitations for cross-aspects. For Richard and Elizabeth the following Table lists the planets of their Epoch and Birth charts by sign, starting from the first point of Aries

Table 2:

Elizabeth Epoch	Richard Epoch	Richard Birth	Elizabeth Birth
Mo 03⁰Ar27′	Ch 21⁰Ar07′	Ch 25⁰Ar03′ Rx	Ur 17⁰Ar05′
Ur 18⁰Ar32′	Ma 07⁰Ta37′	Pl 14⁰Ca36′ Rx	Ve 18⁰Ar01′
Ch 20⁰Ta43′	Pl 11⁰Ca19′ Rx	Np 24⁰Le42′	Ch 19⁰Ta07′
Ve 23⁰Ta27′	Np 21⁰Le01 Rx	Mo 11⁰Vr51′	Pl 20⁰Ca11′ Rx
Me 27⁰Ta22′	Sa 14⁰Sc17′	Ma 28⁰Li09′	Ju 15⁰Le05′ Rx
Su 17⁰Ge52′	Mo 09⁰Sg47′	Sa 17⁰Sc07′	Np 06⁰Vr34′ Rx
Pl 19⁰Ca33′	Ju 13⁰Cp32′	Su 17⁰Sc54′	Mo 26⁰Sc00′
Ju 21⁰Ca55′	Ve 11⁰Aq38′	Me 07⁰Sg06′	Sa 00⁰Aq23′
Ma 29⁰Le30′	Me 15⁰Aq38′	Ve 04⁰Cp16′	Ma 02⁰Pi08′
Np 03⁰Vr10′	Su 28⁰Aq07′	Ju 18⁰Cp23′	Su 08⁰Pi01′
Sa 22⁰Cp13′ Rx	Ur 20⁰Pi09′	Ur 21⁰Pi43′	Me 08⁰Pi49′

In the Table Rx stands for retrograde motion.

Because cross-aspects are just aspects, they are two-way. Following the allowances for cross-aspects listed earlier, we find that the cross-aspects between Richard's and Elizabeth's Epoch charts' planets (see columns 1 and 2) are: $^{Her}Ch^E$ square(S-M) $^{His}Np^E$; $^{Her}Ch^E$ sextile(M-W) $^{His}Ur^E$; $^{Her}Me^E$ square(W) $^{His}Su^E$; $^{Her}Pl^E$ trine(M-W) $^{His}Ur^E$ and $^{Her}Ju^E$ square(M-W) $^{His}Ch^E$.

Similarly, the cross-aspects between Elizabeth's Epoch chart's planets and those of Richard's Birth Chart, (see columns 1 and 3) comprise: $^{Her}Mo^E$ square(W) $^{His}Ve^B$; $^{Her}Ur^E$ square(E-S) $^{His}Ju^B$; $^{Her}Su^E$ quincunx(E) $^{His}Su^B$; $^{Her}Su^E$ quincunx(W) $^{His}Ju^B$; $^{Her}Pl^E$ opposition(W) $^{His}Ju^B$; $^{Her}Ju^E$ trine(E-S) $^{His}Ur^B$; $^{Her}Np^E$ trine(VW) $^{His}Ve^B$ and $^{Her}Sa^E$ sextile(M-W) $^{His}Ur^B$.

Again, the cross-aspects between Elizabeth's Birth chart's planets and those of Richard's Epoch chart (see columns 4 and 2) consist of: $^{Her}Ch^B$ sextile(VW) $^{His}Ur^E$; $^{Her}Pl^B$ trine(E) $^{His}Ur^E$; $^{Her}Ju^B$ square(W) $^{His}Sa^E$; $^{Her}Ju^B$ opposition(M) $^{His}Me^E$; $^{Her}Np^B$ trine(W) $^{His}Ma^E$; $^{Her}Su^B$ sextile(M) $^{His}Ma^E$; $^{Her}Pl^B$ square(W) $^{His}Ch^E$ and $^{Her}Me^B$ square(W) $^{His}Mo^E$.

Finally, the cross-aspects between Elizabeth's and Jack's Birth charts' planets (see columns 4 and 3) comprise: $^{Her}Ur^B$ quincunx(E) $^{His}Sa^B$; $^{Her}Ch^B$ trine(W) $^{His}Ju^B$; $^{Her}Np^B$ square(M) $^{His}Me^B$; $^{Her}Su^B$ square(W) $^{His}Me^B$; $^{Her}Ve^B$ quincunx(E) $^{His}Su^B$; $^{Her}Ve^B$ square(S-M) $^{His}Ju^B$ and $^{Her}Ju^B$ semi-sextile(W) $^{His}Pl^B$.

<u>Shared and combined cross-aspects – organised.</u>

Although a highly educational start may have begun their relationship, one partner may have had to nurse the other, or to have shouldered some of the other's burdens. There was a tendency that there was a purity of affection. Elizabeth showed glamour to Richard, which was illusory rather than real. Nevertheless, the tendency was that she was able to increase his feelings, sensitivity and desire for her. She may have helped him to appreciate the values of gentleness and compassion, whereas he may have provided her with more direction and drive. All round, he was able to identify his self with his own concept of manliness, thereby further stimulating his desire nature. Possibly, significant achievements developed through good teamwork, in which he supplied the drive for her grand strategy. Good fellowship promoted generosity of spirit and mutual respect. Each would have taken pleasure in the other. His individuality and originality were expressed more dramatically and effectively by her mobilisation of support to help him to achieve his goals and to spur him on to greater efforts. Simultaneously, he could have shown her new ways of reaching her goals. These collaborations could have produced exciting results. She would have tolerated his related, independent behaviour and have given him sympathetic support for any of his metaphysical interests. His warmth could have drawn a great deal of affection from her because she recognised his worth, which made him feel flattered. She could also have teased him, when he became too dictatorial. His originality could have stimulated her charitable leanings by indicating new ways. Possibly, he could have made her aware of her generous and charitable impulses, and to have helped her to realise deeper levels underlying her understanding of philosophical concepts. She tended to increase his optimism and understanding, so that he could have achieved his ambitions more smoothly. By return, he may have been able to help her financially. Conversely, her generosity may have been encouraged, but also possibly exploited by him.

The tendency became that he may have indulged her too much, or have created disharmony by his too casual approach to matters of affection. He may have turned on the charm to take advantage of a temporary relationship, or she may have responded, for the sake of flirtation, to gain a short-term benefit, but these, perhaps, were only of a minor nature. Nevertheless, she could have favoured him to his advantage. All of a sudden, he may have become the recipient of her bounty.

The tendency was that Richard could have provided an imaginative focus of interest for her intellectual activity. Yet he may have appeared to be too aloof and unable to comprehend her feelings. She may have objected to his plans because they would not have been conducive to their mutual happiness. Each tended to be at cross-purposes with the other. He tended to find her ideas to be frivolous, or unworthy of serious attention, whereas she may have felt that he was incapable of appreciating the spirit in which her ideas were conceived and communicated. At the same time, he may also have felt that she was unable to appreciate the spirit in which his ideas were conceived and communicated. He may have felt that she was less than frank and that she tended to take allegorical illustrations as literal truth. Thus, they may have misunderstood each other because his logical thinking tended not to blend with her sensitivity and imagination. Her flights of fancy, poetic imagination and impracticality would have failed to find his sympathy.

Elizabeth's lack of directness, combined with Richard's everlastingly brash approach, would have led to problems following an initial, glamorous fascination. Perhaps he would never have felt completely secure, or satisfied. However, he may have known how to enhance her self-esteem, even, possibly, to his own advantage. In this case, flattery to deceive her, may have led her astray as a result of his over-confidence, leading to an eventual lack of good faith. Thus, there was a tendency, on the material level, that she may have suffered financially. Also, her buoyancy may have become somewhat deflated.

They may have had difficulty agreeing on a common goal, and have failed to appreciate each other sufficiently. Give-and-take could have helped them here, as well as a good pattern of interplay between them. They may well have had different approaches to charitable problems and they may have been too critical of each other's dealings here, even though they both were inclined to support charitable causes. Psychological tension developed between them as there was difficulty for them to feel truly at ease in each other's company. There could have been a notable lack of sympathy between them. He may have regarded her extravagant behaviour with distaste and disapproval. This could have provoked her into even more extravagant behaviour, thereby 'helping' him to adopt a more modern, original lifestyle.

Elizabeth may have resorted to erratic action to break-up his irritating air of complacency, provoking Richard into reacting unwisely. She may have exploited his ideas and abilities, and have become out to capitalise, as much as possible, on their relationship. There was also a tendency that she may have refused obstinately to accept his philosophy of life and moral standards, whereas he would have found her to be too single-mindedly set on her own course of action, and completely unwilling to make any concessions.

- -

Interpretations for Elizabeth's planets 'relocated' through cross-aspects to Richard's Houses in his Charts – Organised.

Their relationship may well have been significant. It could have developed within him an urge to become more and more his essential self. His experiences with her may have made him undertake some radical reappraisal, or that he would have been able to transform some important aspect of his being. She may have challenged him (perhaps unwittingly) to become conscious of a certain, hidden motive for action, of which, previously, he had been unaware, perhaps having suppressed it psychologically. He may have been able to effect a certain kind of transformation within himself that made him feel more complete and better integrated. Greater self-knowledge would have been obtained. His feelings for her would have become deeply rooted, yet he may not always have been sure of the true reasons for her emotional reactions; whether they were sympathetic, or the opposite. Still, he may well have felt that she was the ideal partner for him, which she may have been able to recognise without difficulty. She may have found herself attracted to him by certain potentialities that he appeared to possess. Some rivalry between them may have been present. She might have been tempted to exploit her knowledge of his vulnerable areas, and thus have thrown him completely off-balance. At best, she could have proved a desirable partner for him, but, at worst, a formidable opponent.

Yet she could have been the person to whom he turned in times of trouble. She would have been interested in finding out what made him tick. Unfortunately, she may not always have been discreet in keeping his confidences to herself. As a result, they may have had to guard against scandal.

Thus, there was a tendency for the relationship to have been an all-or-nothing one, with her feelings being strongly involved. It was never likely to have been lukewarm, and his feelings for her would have been keen, but kept under control. He would have come to realise the hidden depths of feelings in others, and so have had to add an extra measure of self-control, when his own feelings were stirred by them. Although there would have been considerable physical attraction, experimental attitudes could have led to unwanted complications.

Elizabeth may have seemed to be possessed by some mysterious allure, much of which may have been based on physical attraction, from which there was no great guarantee of a permanent association. Richard may have found that he had allowed himself to be deluded by a mirage of unattainable bliss, and the wonderful union that he had envisaged, may never have been realised. Nevertheless, some fascinating glamour may have remained to suggest the eternal promise of some sort of mystic union. More realistically, a compassionate understanding of temperamental differences between these two people, would have helped to dissolve the barriers between them. As a result, he may have gained much self-enlightenment.

Richard became aware of some subtle discontent engendered by their relationship. Perhaps this was due to an unconscious recognition of the need for some sort of transformation in his being. This might have proved a good link, if they had shared an interest in the metaphysical, in the psychic, or in the occult. However, he may have become uncomfortably aware of some defect in his character, which would have required a change of attitude from himself. Also, there may have been some sort of the most deep-seated and subconscious motivations that governed his desire/ behaviour. Any attempt to surrender power to Elizabeth would have been unwise, even though physical attraction may have become enhanced. If he could have become tolerant of criticism, then he might have been able to take himself in hand, and have been able to stand more on his own.

The way in which Elizabeth thought may have appealed to him and although he may not have been mentally stimulated by her, he would have appreciated the mental stimulus she was trying to give him. Usually, she would have listened to him, and have encouraged him, to develop his ideas on a broad basis, thereby resulting in a lively, mental, but mainly platonic companionship. Yet still there may have been a fundamental lack of understanding between them, despite frequent communication. Possibly, her input upon his mental processes was to help him to develop his powers of imagination, and poetic appreciation, by adding intuitive awareness to his common-sense reasoning. Yet, she may have appeared to him to have become consistently wrong-headed, which may have led him astray, or to have made him become muddle-headed.

Elizabeth was likely to have taken much pleasure in rendering him various services, e.g. by showing him how to perform his chores more easily, and by introducing him to labour saving devices that would have helped to make his work easier. He could have remained assured that he could have relied on her aid. Her whole-hearted support may have encouraged him to make sure that he was functioning as efficiently as he could, otherwise he may have found that she would have been ready to suggest ways that would have improved his system, making it more reliable. Occasionally, in return, she may have called upon him to return the compliment by performing some unusual service on her behalf, especially as she was likely to have valued his services. However, something about her presence may have proved unsettling to him, e.g. through implied criticism. At some point, he may have had cause for concern regarding her health, and so have needed his care and support.

Elizabeth may have been instrumental in making possible improvements to his status, perhaps through wise advice. She may have given Richard a taste for success, or a feeling that he hadn't to let her down. She may have been able to make suggestions, which helped him to further his career, by pointing his ambitions towards a certain direction, and by understanding what it was that he was trying to do. Unfortunately, she may have caused him to aim higher than that of which he was capable. Idle gossip, reflecting badly on his reputation, may have occurred here. She may have been in a position to offer him material help, or to have given him advice, which enabled him to increase his material resources. She would have rewarded him strictly according to his desserts. She may even have gone out-of-her-way to thwart him, to test his ambition, and he may have found that, in the long run, such action had strengthened his will to succeed. She may have been inclined to adopt a parental attitude towards him, and would have encouraged him to adopt a more realistic approach to his responsibilities. Her concern was that he should have been able to do justice to himself. She may have been able to provide him with valuable advice about the best way to handle his philanthropy. She may have been able to advise him about the best way to get philanthropic jobs done. She could have hinted at how he might have attained some sort of change of attitude concerning his charitable/philanthropic inclinations. Possibly, this advice may have proved unsettling, and improvements recommended, may have resulted in snags arising. In charitable cases, she may have encouraged him to spend unwisely, so that her advice here, may have been ill-founded.

His psychological orientation would have encouraged her to project her essential self into that sector of his life connected with the way in which he related to his environment, and with how he gathered information of a practical nature. She may have been able to introduce him to a wide range of philosophical teachings, and in the process, have given him a greater insight into some of the more abstract problems that she had been unable to solve satisfactorily. He may well have been able to help here. A happy relationship, based on mutual trust, could have developed. However, feelings of unfilled desire, may have arisen here also.

- -

Interpretations for Richard's planets 'relocated' through cross-aspects to Elizabeth's Houses of her Charts – organised.

Elizabeth and Richard may have met first while travelling for charitable causes. They both may have made the same journey at frequent intervals and having spoken superficially at first, they then started to exchange philanthropic ideas. He may have developed a very strong impulse to seek her out as a friend, and she may have shared this impulse. Just possibly, and initially, she may have felt somewhat uncomfortable in his presence. On the other hand, his independence may have made him appear to be rather casual, and if she was to engage in a close relationship with him, she may have had to be prepared to meet him more than half-way. In times of emergency, he may have reacted surprisingly and offered her his help, when she had least expected it. He would have had her best interests at heart. Considerable physical attraction was present, as well as an appreciation of each other's good qualities, which could have created a solid relationship. Each would have acted in good faith towards the other. She may first have been attracted to him because of his conventional abilities and the quality of his intellect. He may have been able to understand the ideals she held dear, and have been able to put her in touch with those similarly motivated.

She may have felt that he was the ideal partner for her but she may have found herself to be deluded by a mirage of unattainable bliss. The wonderful union she had envisaged may never have been realised, even though some fascinating glamour remained to suggest the eternal promise of some sort of mystic communion. This experience may have brought home to her the need to make sacrifices, if a truly harmonious partnership was to have been formed. Generally, understanding temperamental differences helps to dissolve barriers between people. He may have placed her in a situation, perhaps unwittingly, where she had to make some radical change in order to maintain their relationship on an even keel. Their relationship was likely to have remained delicately poised, being subject to abrupt changes of course, either through him, or through circumstances that arose with disconcerting suddenness, for example, being due to enforced separation during their careers. As a result, she may have decided to change her line of approach to other people.

They may have had a very critical relationship. If she had measured up to his standards, then she would have made a friend for life. However, his method of testing her could have proved irksome, which she would have resented. She may have needed to live by the precept, "do as you would be done by", but even this may not have guaranteed an effusive response from him. She may even have been challenged to show a reciprocal dependability to match his integrity. Possibly, as a result of their experiences together, she may have felt a need to examine, in some depth, the real reasons underlying her most cherished hopes and wishes, and to have redefined her attitude towards communal activities of all kinds. Her experiences with him may have determined, to some extent, her attitude to all her friends. Their relationship may have generated a good deal of intensity.

Elizabeth was made uncomfortably aware of a character defect that would only have been rectified satisfactorily by some kind of transformation in herself. Richard may have been the means of making her aware of some hitherto neglected facet of her being, either positive or negative, an asset or a liability. As a result, she could have concentrated on enhancing, or enriching, some special attribute, or on attempting to transform a defect, in such a way as either to eliminate it as a negative factor, or to have turned it into a positive source of benefit. She may have had to tap resources, of which, previously, she had been unaware. A great deal may have depended upon her self-esteem and on her powers of self-protection. If she could have been mature enough to tolerate criticism, then she may have been able to disarm her would-be critic, when appreciation of her would have grown in proportion to the extent to which she had been able to take herself in hand, and have stood on her own. With mutual respect, a lasting relationship could have been achieved. However, she may have turned against him through his conservative and ultra-cautious attitude. She may have had to call upon a great deal of tolerance, and willingness to make sacrifices on her part, for the relationship to prosper.

Richard may have been the means of providing her with an entirely new slant on life, providing her with the opportunity to develop different mental perspectives. He may have been instrumental in causing her to review her whole philosophy of life, which would have been different from his own. He may have brought to her notice, books that stimulated her to branch out into new directions, to think more originally and to have shown a greater interest in foreign countries. He would have drawn upon his own experience to help her to expand her understanding and to stimulate her ideas on a variety of subjects, thereby helping her to widen her horizons. She would have tended to value his good opinion of her, and he would have trusted her with confidences, leading to a happy, and mutually trusting, relationship. He may have been able to put forward alternative means of providing charity that complemented and rounded-out hers. He would have liked to compare her charitable interests with his own. His willingness to co-operate with her charitable interests could have improved the results for them both. A high degree of mental rapport became possible. He could have reminded her that issues were not always clear-cut, and that incomplete theories may have to be changed considerably in the light of new evidence.

Richard may have been in a position to render Elizabeth valuable services and have taken pleasure in so doing. He may have been instrumental in introducing her to societies and organisations dedicated to the furtherance of some of her cherished ideas, or have put her in touch with a variety of friends. He may have been able to provide her with a new understanding of the concept of brotherhood. His special 'know-how' may have complemented and augmented her own, so that new techniques would have helped her to perform her routines with greater ease. He may have challenged her to show her efficiency and technical knowledge, while being ready to apply his own skills and knowledge when needed. Possibly, he may not approved of her way of doing things, or have become impatient, if she had appeared to be taking too much time over a job. This would have proved irritating to her.

Richard was likely to have had an instinctive awareness of the areas in which Elizabeth needed support. But he may have been inclined to fuss and worry unduly, and so paving the way to be irritating to her, and even of lowering her morale. He would have been acting as a 'do-gooder', showing to himself that he was capable of sympathy towards others. Generally, however, he would have supported her welfare and well-being. He may have helped her with her diet and physical fitness, with changes in her environment and have suggested time-saving cuts in her methods of travel. He may have provided her with know-how to get her jobs done well, and when stressed, with effective advice, but his advice may have been unsettling. There may even have been a contest between them about who should have control over the family budget. Perhaps unwisely, he would have allowed her to assume the senior status, and so have tried to ensure that his own interests would have been looked after also.

Richard may have given her a greater insight into some of the more abstract problems that previously, Elizabeth had been unable to solve satisfactorily. He may have taken a special interest in the way in which she adjusted to life as a whole. He may have become aware of her vulnerable points, and have pointed out inconsistencies in her behaviour. He would have tended to make her aware of those areas of her psyche over which she normally had little control. If these had been weak, then he might have had reservations about accepting her friendship. He may have needed to have known her for a long time before he decided finally to consolidate their relationship. As a result, Elizabeth may have felt the need to make some kind of attitude transformation, so that their relationship would have operated more smoothly. Richard may have given her good advice, but she may have been inclined to resent it, or to have found it particularly difficult to put into practice. He would have brought home to her, her areas most in need of extra attention and transformation.

A very critical relationship may well have grown between them. He may have found her Achilles' heel. He may have known just how to play on her psychological weakness, in order to upset her. As a result, she may have made a more effective appraisal of herself, and have been challenged to be honest with herself, while cultivating a straight-forward approach to others. Any attempt to cover up her weaknesses may have made her seem insincere to him. However, he may have been able to help her to fortify her weak points, shielding her from attack on her weak points and championing her until he had encouraged her to develop enough self-sufficiency to stand on her own two feet.

Richard may also have been able to help Elizabeth to make a more realistic assessment of the best way to achieve her hopes and wishes. However, there was a tendency that he would have taken a more practical interest in helping her to achieve her ideals, if she had been prepared to work hard at them, and if he had believed that they were truly worthwhile, and within the bounds of possibility to achieve. A strong friendship would have resulted but she would have needed to convince him that she was a solid, dependable and genuine person. He may have made demands on her friendship inconveniently, so that she would have had to make sacrifices in order to have responded as he would have wished. But he would always have been willing to place his experience at her disposal. All told, this may well have led her to feel antipathy towards him, so that she may have preferred to avoid, rather than to cultivate, his company.

Figure 5: Richard Burton – Epoch Chart.

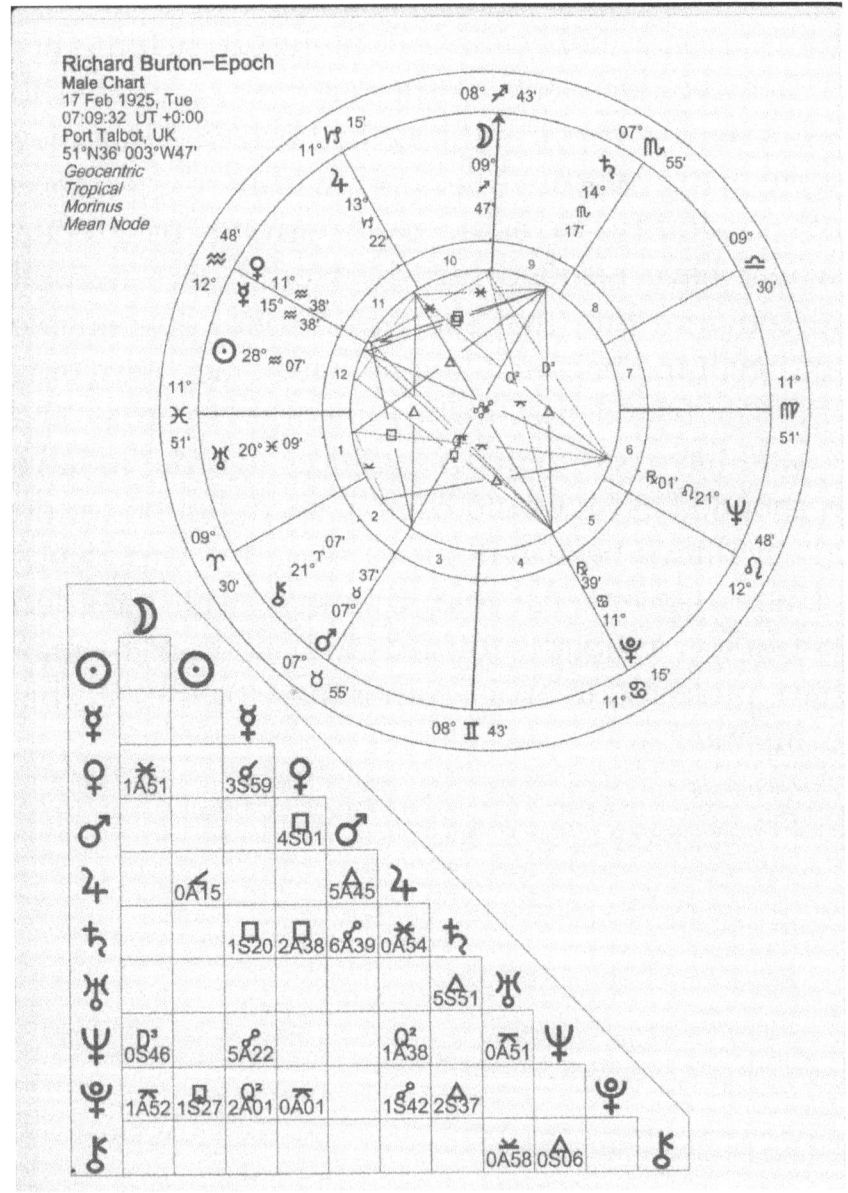

Figure 6: Richard Burton – Birth Chart.

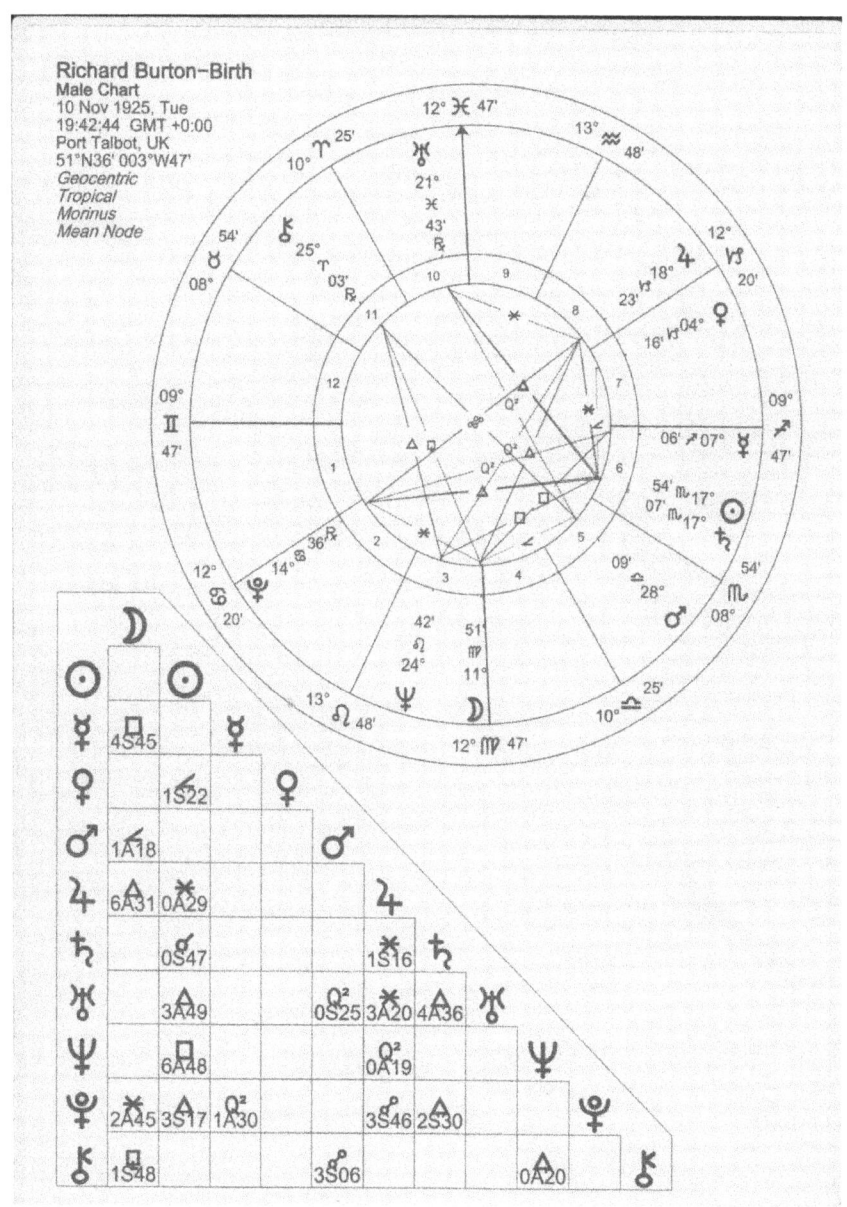

Figure 7: Elizabeth Taylor – Epoch Chart.

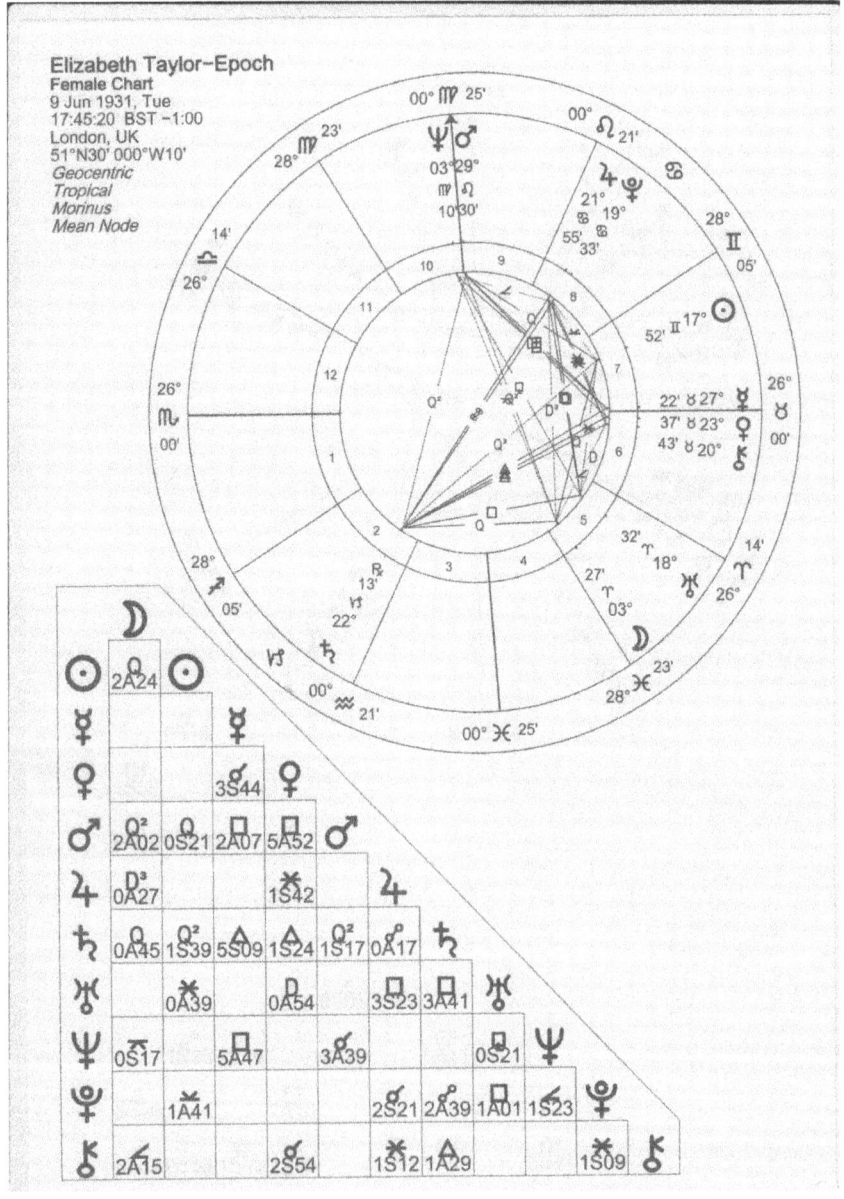

Figure 8: Elizabeth Taylor – Birth Chart.

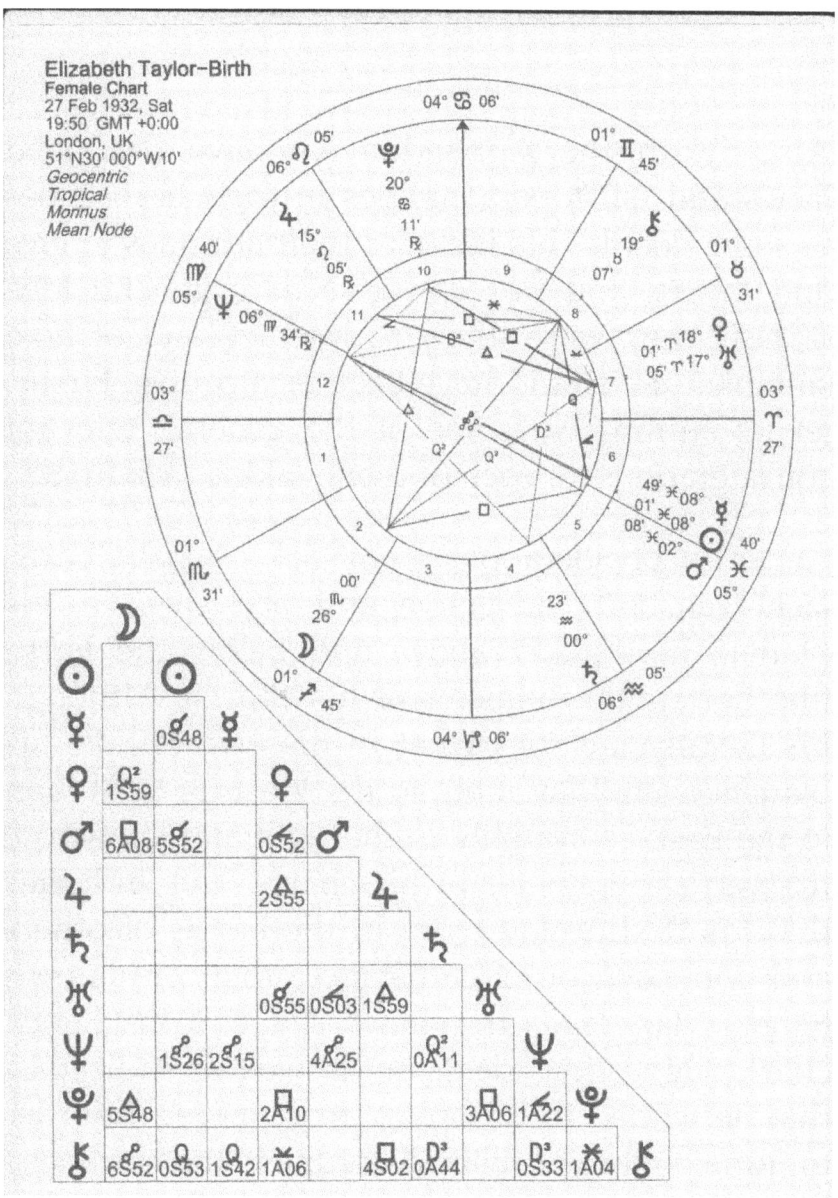

CHAPTER 4

A Control 'Synastry' Exercise for Jack Sprat and Gillian Grey – Adult Love

Already, in the Appendix, we have described Jack's and Gill's personalities in their horoscopes in some detail. This includes their attitudes to love and lovers, and this can give us a general idea of how they were likely to interact, and of how suitable they would have been as a couple. Firstly, let us summarise some of the general, relevant considerations for each of them, taking Jack first.

General Considerations from Jack's Natal Charts: Jack was both subjective and objective, i.e. his planets lie equally above and below the Earth (the horizontal diameter of his charts). Although his destiny lay somewhat in his own hands, his planets overall lay more to the West (14 to 8) than to the East, i.e. roughly to the right and left across the vertical diameter of his charts. This indicates that his destiny lay more in the hands of others and depended on circumstances than in his own hands. Mars leads the 'bowl' shape of his Epoch chart, suggesting idealism, as well as indicating that he tended to 'scoop-up' experiences, in order to initiate more of them. Neptune is the clockwise (impulsive) 'handle' of the 'bucket' shape of his Birth chart, suggesting a particular and rather uncompromising direction to his life-effort. Notice that the summation of his quadruplicities and triplicities of his planets leads to a preponderance of Fixed Earth (Taurus), with some Fixed Air (Aquarius) as well as with some Fixed Water (Scorpio). Notice also, that there are shortages of 'Cardinal' (initiatory) and of 'Fire' (keen, ardent) that equate to Aries (assertive energy). Taken together, his planets (10 out of 22) lie mainly in 'Cadent' (dispersion of ideas and energies) Houses. In addition, notice that he has six quintile and two decile aspects in his two charts, suggesting good intelligence.

Concerning Partnership: We see that Jack has his Mercury and Chiron at Epoch, and his Sun at Birth, in his 7th House (of his partner); that at Epoch, he has the sign of Cancer at its centre point, and that similarly at Birth, he has the sign of Aquarius there. Respectively, these two signs indicate that marriage and partnerships are both likely to be advantageous, but that a quality of inconstancy can, if not mastered, lead to difficulties. The Sun in the 7th House indicates that marriage and partnerships are likely to assume a paramount role in his life, and that he would have sought a partner who could have encouraged him to be his real self. Mercury in his 7th House suggests that he may have given much thought to partnership and marriage, and that he may have looked to marriage to provide mental satisfaction. Similarly, Chiron in his 7th House leads to charitable feelings/actions as a result of marriage and partnerships. Analogously, Libra is the sign of the partner, but none of Jack's planets resides there.

General Considerations from Gill's Natal Charts: Gill was mainly objective, i.e. her planets (16 out of 22) lay above the Earth. We see that her destiny lay somewhat more (13 to 9) in the hands of others and depended on circumstances, than in her own hands. Mars in Aries in her 7th House is the leading planet of the 'bowl' shape of her Epoch chart, and as it lies between the 10th and 4th House centres, it suggests that she was inclined to 'capture' things, or consummate various phases of life. The 'bowl' shape itself, indicates that she tended to be an idealist, or reformer. The 'splay' shape of her Birth chart suggests the presence of purposeful emphases in her life according to her very own special tastes. She would have been particular, and yet impersonal, in her interests with a 'splay-foot' certainty in every approach that she made to her life-problems. The summation of all her planets' quadruplicities and triplicities shows mainly Cardinal, but some Mutable, 'Air' (Libra and Gemini), 'Fire' (Aries and Sagittarius) and 'Water' (Cancer and Pisces), but a shortage of 'Fixed' (resistance to change) and 'Earth' that equates to Taurus (i.e. practical and cautious). Overall, Gill's planets (12 out of 22) lie in Angular (initiatory) Houses. Notice also, that Gill has six quintile aspects, and one decile aspect, in both her charts, suggesting good intelligence.

<u>Concerning Partnership</u>, we see that Gill has no planets in her 7th House (of her partner) at Birth, but the sign of Aries lies at her 7th House centre. This suggests that there was a tendency to marry early in life, and that the chosen person would likely have been one of strong, and even dominating, character. However, Gill has the Moon, Mercury, Venus and Mars occupying her 7th House at Epoch, with, once again, the sign Aries at her 7th House centre. When the Moon is in the 7th House, there may have been some indecisiveness in choosing a partner, especially as her feelings were apt to be influenced somewhat easily by those with whom she came into contact. Marriage may have been undertaken with the object of establishing a home. Hence the domestic qualifications, plus the family and social background of a prospective partner may have acquired a disproportionate priority in her reasons for choosing a partner. When Mercury lies in the 7th House, she may have been inclined to look to marriage principally to provide mental satisfaction. She should have learned to control her argumentativeness and desire to criticise. Analogously, when Venus occupies her 7th House, then much appreciation may have been given to the value of the relationship, but it may have been accompanied by an inordinate craving for affection, which may have made the partnership

fragile. With Mars in her 7th House, her energies were most naturally mobilised in seeking to adjust to others, and a good deal of stimulus would have been expected from social contacts, even sparring partners! She may have had an over-demanding attitude!

Libra is the sign of her partner, and at Epoch Neptune lies in Libra. Neptune also lies in Libra at Birth, along with the Moon, Chiron and Jupiter. Neptune in Libra signifies that she channels her sense of idealism in her search to establish a significant rapport with those around her. She needed to establish a partnership in which disharmony, or imperfection, are absent. Ideally, a mystical union would have been desired, such as a highly spiritual, or even platonic one. She may even have deceived herself concerning the true nature, deceptive, or otherwise, of her partner.

The Moon in Libra indicates that her feelings were very much involved in the creation of an harmonious atmosphere. An ability to sense instinctively how best to adjust to others, could have led to putting them at their ease. Social acceptance would have been important. Even when feelings are hurt, there would have been a tendency to "put a brave face on it", but this would have had its limits! Jupiter in Libra can lead to an expansive attitude to the establishment of harmony, and a well-developed sense of proportion could have resulted in a prosperous and fruitful union. An improvement of status through marriage often results in the choice of a professional partner, but care would have been needed to balance true love with improved social status. Finally, Chiron in Libra suggests that compatible attitudes towards philanthropy could have improved the quality of a marriage partnership.

General Comparisons between Jack's and Gill's Charts: We have seen that Jack's charts are lacking in the 'fire' triplicity, thereby tending to be deficient in ardour and keenness, but this could have been compensated for by Gill's charts that contain sufficient (6) planets in 'fire'. Conversely, we have also seen that Gill's charts are deficient in the 'Earth' triplicity, thereby tending to lack practicality, patience and caution, whereas Jack's charts can readily compensate for this, having sufficient planets (7) in 'Earth'. The combination of 'Fire' and 'Earth' in a marriage represents spirit working with matter. 'Fire' may find 'Earth' too slow and plodding, whereas 'Earth' criticises 'Fire' for leaping impulsively without looking. 'Fire' can be foolhardy, whereas 'Earth' needs vision, imagination and a touch of daring. Similarly, regarding the quadruplicities, we find that in Jack's charts there is a shortage (3) of 'Cardinal' planets that is strongly compensated by Gill's 'Cardinal' planets (12). Conversely again, we see that Gill's charts are deficient (3) in 'Fixed', whereas Jack's charts contain an excess of 'Fixed' planets (11). The combination of a 'Cardinal' (initiatory) person with a 'Fixed' (resistance to change) person can seem like the irresistible force coming into contact with the immovable object. A great deal will depend upon the way the 'Mutable' (adaptable) quadruplicity plays its part, since this will be needed by both partners. 'Fixed' is apt to find that 'Cardinal' is too rash and careless, whereas 'Cardinal' finds that 'Fixed' is too lazy and unenterprising, and too concerned with maintaining his position, and holding-on to his resources. On the other hand, 'Fixed' establishes the position gained by its enterprising 'Cardinal' ally.

Analogously, for the Houses, we see that Jack's planets (10 out of 22) lie in 'Cadent' (dispersion of ideas and energies) Houses, whereas Gill's planets (12 out of 22) lie in 'Angular' (outgoing) ones. 'Angular' people want to feel themselves at the centre of everything, and may desire to take the lead in a relationship. On the other hand, 'Cadent' people tend to hide their personalities, and often have difficulty in finding effective, self-expression. Mental compatibility is more important to them, but they need a partner who can draw them out to realise their latent potentialities. Usually, however, there is less chance of an harmonious relationship of the 'Angular' with the 'Cadent' type.

Concerning the comparison of chart shapes, we find that Gill's 'splay' type is likely to have become the most self-sufficient, independent and least likely to adapt to a partner type, although they may be satisfied if the partnership were run on their terms. Yet Gill's 'bowl' shape, being idealistic, provides her with a concern for people and causes. Jack also has an idealistic 'bowl' shape, which has advantages, and his single-minded 'bucket' may find good support from her 'bowl' shape. The occupied hemispheres of Jack's 'bucket' and Gill's 'bowl' roughly coincide, so that there could have been a greater attraction than otherwise, cross-aspects permitting. But for all the foregoing, general considerations gathered here, the advantages and disadvantages are not that clear-cut. A final judgement may well depend on whether the cross-aspects between their charts are favourable, or not, which now becomes the subject of the following, more specific, section.

Specific Considerations concerning all Four of their Natal Charts (see the end of the chapter):

Let us try to be more specific concerning Jack's and Gill's relationship by listing their planets by their sign positions, from the first point of Aries, in their four separate charts, as given in Table 3. Then we can list all the cross-aspects from Gill's two charts with Jack's two.

Table 3: The Planets of the Epoch and Birth charts of Jack Sprat and Gillian Gray, listed by sign, starting from the First Point of Aries.

Gill Epoch	Jack Epoch	Jack Birth	Gill Birth
Ma 05⁰Ar14'	Sa 21⁰Ta02'	Sa 22⁰Ta43'	Ur 13⁰Ge24' S
Ve 17⁰Ar20'	Ur 27⁰Ta04'	Ma 24⁰Ta58'	Ma 14⁰Ca07' Rx
Mo 17⁰Ar51'	Ju 01⁰Ge29'	Ur 26⁰Ta35'	Sa 18⁰Ca40' Rx
Me 22⁰Ar41'	Su 10⁰Ge55'	Ju 12⁰Ge08'	Pl 10⁰Le11' Rx

Su 18°Ta38'	Ve 22°Ge28'	Mo 16°Ca47'	Np 08°Li10' Rx
Ur 11°Ge45'	Me 04°Ca04'	Pl 03°Le56' Rx	Mo 14°Li31'
Sa 07°Ca23'	Ch 28°Ca31'	Ch 09°Le36' Rx	Ch 21°Li05' Rx
Pl 07°Le59'	Pl 02°Le30'	Np 29°Vr04' Rx	Ju 27°Li15' Rx
Ju 17°Vr33' Rx	Mo 27°Le44'	Ve 05°Aq45'	Su 00°Pi38'
Ch 27°Vr11' Rx	Np 24°Vr54' Rx	Me 12°Aq32'	Ve 05°Pi04'
Np 03°Li59' Rx	Ma 11°Pi05'	Su 07°Pi29'	Me 07°Pi51'

In the Table, Rx stands for retrograde motion and S stands for stationary.

Following the allowances for cross-aspects listed previously, we find that the cross-aspects between Jack's and Gill's Epoch Charts' planets (see columns 1 and 2) are: $^{Her}Me^E$ sextile(S) $^{His}Ve^E$; $^{Her}Ur^E$ conjoint(W) $^{His}Su^E$; $^{Her}Ur^E$ square(W) $^{His}Ma^E$; $^{Her}Ch^E$ semi-sextile(W) $^{His}Mo^E$ and $^{Her}Np^E$ square(E-S) $^{His}Me^E$.

Similarly, the cross-aspects between Gill's Epoch Chart's planets and Jack's Birth Chart's planets (see columns 1 and 3) comprise: $^{Her}Ma^E$ sextile(M-W) $^{His}Ve^B$; $^{Her}Ve^E$ square(M) $^{His}Mo^B$; $^{Her}Mo^E$ square(VW) $^{His}Mo^B$; $^{Her}Me^E$ semi-sextile(E) $^{His}Sa^B$; $^{Her}Ur^E$ conjoint(S-M) $^{His}Ju^B$; $^{Her}Ur^E$ trine(W) $^{His}Me^B$; $^{Her}Sa^E$ trine(E) $^{His}Su^B$; $^{Her}Pl^E$ quincunx(W) $^{His}Su^B$; $^{Her}Ju^E$ sextile(W) $^{His}Mo^B$; $^{Her}Ch^E$ trine(M) $^{His}Ur^B$ and $^{Her}Np^E$ sextile(E) $^{His}Pl^B$.

Again, the cross-aspects between Gill's Birth Chart's planets and Jack's Epoch Chart's planets (see columns 4 and 2) consist of: $^{Her}Pl^B$ sextile(W) $^{His}Su^E$; $^{Her}Ch^B$ quincunx(E) $^{His}Sa^E$; $^{Her}Ju^B$ quincunx(E-S) $^{His}Ur^E$; $^{Her}Ju^B$ sextile(M-W) $^{His}Mo^E$; $^{Her}Su^B$ square(W) $^{His}Ju^E$ and $^{Her}Ve^B$ trine(W) $^{His}Me^E$.

Finally, the cross-aspects between Gill's and Jack's Birth Charts' planets (see columns 4 and 3) comprise: $^{Her}Ur^B$ trine(W) $^{His}Me^B$; $^{Her}Pl^B$ conjoint(M) $^{His}Ch^B$; $^{Her}Np^B$ quincunx(VW) $^{His}Su^B$; $^{Her}Ju^B$ quincunx(VW) $^{His}Ur^B$; $^{Her}Ve^B$ semi-sextile(VW) $^{His}Ve^B$ and $^{Her}Me^B$ conjoint(S-M) $^{His}Su^B$.

Now, we need to gather together all the interpretations of these cross-aspects by finding them in R. C. Davison's book: "Synastry", bearing in mind the strengths of the aspects (in brackets above) and the particular state of each of all of the planets, i.e. whether they are in Epoch, or Birth, charts, and how they interact with the other planets in their respective charts, i.e. the nature of the aspects that they receive there. Then we organise them into a readable and understandable whole, according to the individual nature of the planets, or by the subject matter contained in the interpretations. For example, we find that:

The Organised, Combined Interpretations for the Cross-Aspects between Jack's and Gill's Natal Charts are:

There was a tendency towards good fellowship, generosity of spirit, mutual respect, appreciation and encouragement in their marriage. This helped to sustain their partnership in the face of difficult cross-aspects between them. Toleration was evident, but Gill should have guarded against the effects of Jack's flattery. Yet Jack was a willing listener, encouraging Gill to communicate and to put over ideas. Jack may have provided Gill with opportunities for literary endeavour, or have suggested areas of study that may have proved fruitful. As a result, Gill would have felt that she had a partner who understood her. Gill was likely to have found a helpful collaborator in Jack, provided that she listened to his responses with attention and due deference. Conversely, Gill could have proved to be an efficient interpreter of, and a helpful agent for, Jack's ideas. Just possibly, a common bond of idealism could have encouraged a subtle feeling of camaraderie, while Gill's capacity for capturing inspirations may have intrigued Jack, who could have encouraged Gill to try further along these lines, thereby perhaps leading to some self-transcendence on her part. Additionally, there was a tendency that excitement and stimulus took the place of possible boredom and frustration. Gill would have been inclined to keep Jack on his toes, but both Jack and Gill should have allowed each other freedom, by respecting each other's right to some independent existence. There was a further tendency only, that Gill could have reinforced Jack's belief in himself, whereas he could have provided Gill with an effective outlet for her subconscious drives, and so have encouraged him in his support for their partnership. Destiny could have been involved here, with enhanced physical attraction as a result. On the other hand, there was an indication only, that there could have been a mutual sense of some deep-seated and basic lack of compatibility that prevented the development of a rewarding association. Rivalry and a struggle for supremacy, could have resulted in Gill blocking Jack's plans and remaining aloof, while Jack tested Gill's capability to stand alone. Gill would have made Jack aware of his responsibilities to her. She would have been the teacher, providing lessons of seriousness, initiation and co-operation, with opportunities for learning them, thereby providing Jack with valuable experience. Also, Gill could have provided some control over Jack's more flamboyant extravagances. Conversely, Jack could have provided the warmth and reassurance that Gill needed. Integrity, combined with duty and determination to fulfil responsibilities could have guaranteed the continuity and durability of their marriage.

Fortunately, an easy-going relationship helped to smooth-over any temperamental differences. Gill's aspiration, moral standards and good will appealed to Jack, who was likely to have held her in high esteem. He would have made special efforts to accommodate Gill, who respected conventional proprieties, and whose expansiveness made her feel comfortable at home. Perhaps there was some tendency that conflicting habit patterns and a failure to appreciate that each other's instinctive reactions to problem situations, could have resulted from a dislike of some of the other partner's personality traits. Gill may have indulged Jack too much, or disharmony could have resulted from a too casual approach regarding affections, particularly in the case of stressful situations.

Gill's ideas would have been received well by Jack, and *vice-versa*, but somewhat less so. He could have encouraged her and given her extra confidence to communicate her ideas further, and again, *vice-versa*, but less so. Gill would have had a tendency to stimulate Jack, so that he directed his ideas into new channels, or have taken-up new studies. Jack may have become intrigued by Gill's novel way of looking at things, which she could have brought to their relationship. Also, Gill may have tried to cause Jack to change some of his hitherto strongly held opinions, but this was less likely to succeed as his ideals tended to be rather 'Fixed'.

Gill's excitability should not have made Jack gamble needlessly, or act independently. Nevertheless, Gill may have resorted to erratic action to break-up Jack's irritating air of complacency, thereby provoking him into behaving unwisely. Jack acted to steady Gill's thinking by drawing attention to the more serious side of life, and by providing practical advice. He may even have dampened Gill's spontaneity, or his own fears may have caused him to object to Gill's plans, but there again, she may have found him to be a bit slow on the uptake. Jack's logical thinking probably would not have blended easily with Gill's sensitivity and imagination, so that misunderstandings could have arisen. Jack's practicality may have suggested to him that Gill had been less than frank, whereas Gill's nuances of meaning may have escaped Jack.

Nevertheless, a congenial link just may have been formed between Jack and Gill, which encouraged the development of happy companionship and affectionate consideration for each other. Their likes and dislikes would have clashed rarely. However, although Gill's harmony was strong, Jack's was cool, and so would have mitigated their congeniality. There was compatibility, but although this was important, other indications of compatibility needed to be present as well, to cement their marriage. None of this implied a lack of masculine qualities in Jack, nor a lack of feminine ones in Gill. But there was a tendency for disruption. Dynamism and energy, which helped physical attraction, may have caused irritation from too much contact and could have forced the need for an occasional break from each other.

Just possibly, Jack's occult interests, would have received Gill's support, who may have appreciated his unorthodox approach. If Jack and Gill had been engaged in welfare work, or in activities of an artistic nature, and both had been capable of acting with mature integrity, then a useful collaboration could have resulted.

There was a tendency only that Gill's philanthropy could have provided a focus of interest for Jack, who would have responded instinctively. But also, Jack could have stimulated Gill's charitable inclinations by directing her to take-up new directions/studies. Gill may have become intrigued by Jack's novel way of looking at philanthropy, thereby modifying some of her strongly held views. Jack acted to steady Gill's thinking about her philanthropy, checking her charity from his own experiences, and generally giving solid, practical advice. However, Gill may have found it hard work convincing Jack, who, as already indicated, may have been a bit slow on the uptake.

Planet 'Relocation' Interpretations

An additional result of examining cross-aspects concerns the effect of the planet making the cross-aspect on the House of the planet receiving the cross-aspect. There are interpretations for this effect and, once more, we find them by consulting R. C. Davison's book, "Synastry". Bringing them altogether, we achieve:-

The Organised, Planet 'Relocation' Interpretations to the Houses of Jack's Natal Charts, i.e. mainly Gill's effect on Jack.

Gill and Jack may have first met through both of them having an interest in the same hobby (tennis). [On the other hand, and just possibly, Jack's connection with Gill may have arisen through the treatment of some illness, or psychological trouble, that he was suffering from. In certain respects, her behaviour may have accentuated his health problems.] There could have been a very felicitous omen for their partnership. She would have wished to make it easier for him to use his creative faculties in the best possible way, and have helped him to discover his most effective means of self-expression. She would have enjoyed giving him pleasure, perhaps by providing him with opportunities he might have been denied otherwise. At the same time, she would have valued his support and his good opinion of her. He may have gained real pleasure through her companionship, particularly at social functions and entertainments. Although romantic friendship and mental affection were indicated, there may have been times when he had to have dealt with her tactlessness and bluntness.

Gill may have been the means of giving Jack an entirely new slant on life, putting him in touch with the opportunity to develop different mental perspectives. Their physical attraction would have been transferred to the mental realm, so that mental rapport became possible. She would have had the capability to keep Jack alert mentally. Gill may have been able to provide Jack with ideas that complemented and rounded-out his own. She may have been able to put forward a view opposite to his, providing him with the opportunity for comparison, and so of assessing their relative merits. She may have been instrumental in widening his circle of contacts so that others could have acted as a sounding board for his ideas. Gill's mental co-operation with Jack could have brought about profitable results. Also, Gill may have been the means of making Jack aware of some hitherto neglected facet of his being, which may have operated either as an asset, or as a liability, to him. She would have concentrated on enhancing, or enriching, some special attribute, or on attempts to transform a defect in such a way as to eliminate it as a negative factor and turn it into a positive source of benefit. Usually, Gill would have had his best interests at heart. Gill would have been able to appreciate why his ambitions led Jack in a certain direction and to have understood what he was trying to achieve. She may have been able to make suggestions, which helped him to further his career, perhaps drawing attention to details that he may have overlooked. She would have been happy to communicate his achievements to others, and perhaps have put him in touch with those who could have given him assistance. She may have been able to make improvements in Jack's status, and have even given him a taste for success, or by her good opinion of him, have given him an extra incentive to succeed, so that he did not let her down. She may have taken pleasure in playing the role of 'father' to him, thereby helping him to reach his goals. Her object would have been to strengthen his belief in himself, and have encouraged him to achieve his ambitions through applying his efforts wisely.

Gill could have appreciated why Jack's charitable inclinations led him in the way that they did, and have understood what he was trying to achieve. She may have adopted a too critical attitude to his charitable inclinations and have damned him with faint praise. Perhaps, she may have put him in touch with those who could have given him assistance with his charitable leanings. But Gill herself, may have been in a better position than most to appreciate his unconscious motivations, and so have provided him with valuable hints to further his charitable instincts.

Gill may have had a special talent for helping Jack to adjust to difficult situations, and have been able to suggest solutions to him when he had been faced with complicated problems. She may have had a special interest in easing his path as much as possible, and may not always have said what was in her mind for fear of upsetting him. She could have become a sympathetic companion to him, and have comforted him when he was distressed, and may have put him in touch with those who would have ministered to his bodily well-being, and spiritual needs. She may even have been instrumental in introducing him to a study of occult, or mystical, objects.

In times of emergency, Gill may have reacted surprisingly, and have offered Jack help when he had expected it least. Indeed, she may have been instrumental in introducing him to societies and organisations dedicated to the furtherance of some ideal that he cherished, or to have put him in touch with a wide variety of friends. She may have had to be prepared to meet him more than half-way. Generally speaking, she may have been able to give him a new understanding of the concept of 'brotherhood'.

Gill may have been in a position to offer Jack some kind of service. Jack could have rested assured that he could have relied on Gill's aid, although occasionally, she may have called upon him to return the compliment, as she was likely to have valued his services. He needed to function as efficiently as he could, otherwise Gill would have been ready to suggest improvements, but no emotional content would have been involved. Gill may have made demands on Jack's services. He may have found that his association with her became a continual challenge to him to overhaul (and to improve) his methods. Gill may have challenged him to show his efficiency and his technical know-how. At the same time, she would have been ready to supply her own skills and knowledge if needed. She may not always have approved of his ways of doing things, and have become impatient when he seemed to take too much time over a job. Such an attitude on her part could have proved a source of mutual irritation. She may have tended to set his nerves on edge, but simultaneously, he may have become concerned about her health. Something about her presence could have proved unsettling to him.

On the other hand, Gill would have been likely to take pleasure in rendering Jack various services, and in showing him how to perform his chores more easily. She would have been concerned to see that working conditions were congenial. She may have been able to provide Jack with valuable know-how about the best way to get his jobs done. Also, she may have been able to suggest new ways of doing things, and have introduced Jack to labour-saving devices that helped to make his work easier. All this, may have caused him to overhaul his methods to see what improvements could have been made.

Although some co-operation was possible between them, Gill's distaste for unpleasantness may not have helped. A very critical relationship was indicated, but one solid enough to stand the test of time. Alternatively, she may have become critical of his aims, and have even spread idle gossip, which reflected badly on his reputation. Jack may have resented her testing methods, and he may have needed to live by the precept: "do as you would be done by" but even this may not have guaranteed an effusive response from Gill. Although she may have been demanding, Gill would have displayed integrity, and her reliability would have provided Jack with a challenge to show a reciprocal dependability.

Jack's relationship with Gill may have tested to the utmost, his capability for total co-operation. His experiences with her may have caused him to explore the real nature of his inner motivations relating to partnership, and to have asked himself what he really required of his partner. In addition, she may have had a definitive effect upon his political outlook. Jack may never really have come to terms with Gill, and she may have adopted an attitude of permanent hostility towards him, because a deep-seated disturbance in his mind formed a continuing obstacle to an harmonious relationship between them.

Jack's experiences with Gill may have made him uncomfortably aware of those elements in his character that were apt to have played him false when he was under pressure. More disturbingly, may have been his realisation of subconscious compulsions towards certain types of action, or weaknesses, which he had not known about before their relationship began. Jack may have felt that Gill was in a position to exploit his Achilles' heel and perhaps have insidiously undermined his position. For her part, Gill may not consciously have acted in this way at all, but any feeling of insecurity on Jack's part may have transmitted itself to her in such a way that she came to believe him to be unreliable, or a bad risk. And so their relationship could easily have led Jack to seek some form of escapism, which could have resulted in him becoming more deeply involved with his difficulties, and have left him further than ever from a final solution. The main purpose of their association may have been his instinctive recognition of those really in need of his sympathy and support, and to have been on guard against foolishly confiding his secrets, and of exposing his weak points, to others. It may have challenged him to sacrifice all those aspects of his personality that worked against his best interests, and have hampered his spiritual progress.

Instinctively, Gill may have been able to recognise Jack's problems and have been able to sense his weak points. She would have been likely to adopt a particularly charitable attitude towards him, and she would have been anxious to protect him, if she had felt that he was in a situation where one of his vulnerable points would have been likely to be exposed to attack. She could have been the person to whom he most likely turned, in times of trouble. She may have been able to show him how to cope with any deficiencies in his character, or temperament, which may have involved him in disconcerting situations, and she would often have been able to bolster his self-assurance. Hence, he would have become able to summon-up fresh courage to tackle his problems. Sometimes, her concern could have proved embarrassing, and she would have been inclined to worry unduly about his problems, or state of health. Yet she was likely to have been well-disposed towards him. Perhaps it would have been better not to have concerned herself overmuch with his welfare, and to have left well alone. For his part, Jack would have become more aware of whom he could have best entrusted with his welfare.

Jack's experience with Gill may have involved some claim on her part, upon his sympathies and charitable impulses, and she may have been instrumental in changing his views about the sick, the suffering and the underprivileged. Jack may have felt that she was the ideal partner for him. However, he may have found that he had allowed himself to be deluded about a mirage of unattainable bliss, and about a wonderful union envisaged that may never have been realised. Possibly, it would have been better if he hadn't had cut and dried ideas about partnership with Gill because the whole object of his experience with her, may have been to accustom himself to the idea of allowing complete freedom of thought and action to others, and relying only on those links brought into being through compassionate understanding and through a feeling of spiritual identity. However, Gill's influence may have had a seductive effect upon Jack, causing him consciously, or unconsciously, to lose sight of his objectives, by exploiting his susceptibilities, and by playing on his sympathies, for her own ends. She would have been interested in finding out what made Jack tick, and possibly could have been able to awaken his interests in subjects that brought about a greater understanding of life's undercurrents.

Organised, Planet, 'Relocation' Interpretations to the Houses of Gill's Natal Charts, i.e. mainly Jack's effect on Gill.

Jack and Gill may have met first through both being interested in the same hobby (tennis), or through activities connected with children, or education. Some unusual facets of Jack's personality may have captured Gill's attention. There could have been a dynamic attraction. Initially, their friendship may have had both positive and negative factors. He may have regarded it as a privilege, and as a friend, to have offered advice on the way she conducted her affairs, but, as a friend, he would normally have been prepared to accept her for exactly as she was. But also, Jack may have been at particular pains to evaluate Gill's capability for establishing a happy relationship before he committed himself finally. But once he had become satisfied that she could have done so, then a particularly harmonious relationship was promised. However, caution might have been required regarding trouble and unpleasantness from confusion, deception, disclosure, upheavals and new starts. Thus, Jack may have known instinctively how to complement, and to balance, the most important facets of Gill's personality. He may have been the means of enlarging the circle of her friends, and generally, of making her reputation known more widely. Jack would have been inclined to regard Gill as an equal. They may have shared a number of interests, and when delicate negotiations of a personal nature were required, then Jack may have been able to operate as a sensitive go-between. Gill should have become more aware of her need to adapt, and to adjust, to others, becoming careful to respect their feelings and to realise that co-operation entails going at least half-way to meet the other person. Theirs would have been a critical, yet permanent relationship; one strong enough to have withstood the test of time. Nevertheless, the relationship may have been a particularly challenging one, as he may have caused her to bring forth all her latent powers of sympathy and understanding, in an effort to find the best way to deal with him. He may have had the knack of making her feel ill-at-ease and inadequate in some ways, whereas she may have had the feeling that he was hatching some secret plot to take advantage of her weakest points. She may have imagined that he was strongest where she was weakest, although if she had tried to copy his methods, then she may only have made matters worse. But Jack may have been able to recognise Gill's problems instinctively, and have sensed her weak points. He would have been likely to adopt a particularly charitable attitude towards her, and he would have been anxious to protect her if one of her weak points had become exposed to attack, but he could have overdone this when it would have been better to have left well alone. Gill should have become more aware of whom she could have trusted with her welfare best. However,

Jack may have adopted a too critical an attitude towards Gill's creative efforts, or that his ideas may have hindered rather than helped, the effective realisation of her creative projects. Yet their relationship was favoured by Jack wishing to make it easier for Gill to use her creative faculties in the best possible way, and to help her to discover her most effective means of self-expression. Jack would have enjoyed giving Gill pleasure, by providing her with opportunities that otherwise, she may have been denied. Indeed, Jack may have been a great source of pleasure to Gill, and she may always have enjoyed being in his company. Jack should have been appreciative of all her creative efforts, and would have encouraged Gill to present them in the most attractive and dramatic form. Their relationship should have flourished and endured. A high degree of mutual co-operation should have been possible.

Jack may have put Gill in touch with a new circle of friends, and have brought her into contact with a completely new environment. Jack may have found himself attracted to Gill by some potential she appeared to possess, or by some facet of her being, which was not immediately apparent to others. Something in Gill's personality may have convinced Jack that he could have depended on her. Jack would have valued Gill as a stabilising influence and, as a result, she may have developed her sense of responsibility more effectively. Jack's conduct may have made demands on

Gill's patient understanding and sometimes he would have tested her powers of endurance. But this, nevertheless, was an indication of a lasting relationship. Jack would have been the one to suffer more in this kind of situation.

However, a supportive, sensitive link was likely to have existed between them. Jack would have felt at home with Gill's familiar type of behaviour, instinctively recognising her everyday approach to life and those facets of her character that corresponded to his own patterns of temperament. Gill may have been willing to make any adjustment to render the relationship even more congenial. His impulse to protect and cherish was likely to have been projected in her direction. Jack needed to be alert to adapt his approach according to Gill's particular orientation. There was a similarity between Jack's inner being, and the way that Gill was seeking to project herself outwardly. At the same time, Gill's psychological orientation would have encouraged Jack to be his own essential self, more effectively. She would have appreciated his worth as an individual, and have gained a high regard for him. However, Jack's authority may not have been accepted passively and a struggle for supremacy could have developed. Possibly, a degree of antipathy would have arisen.

The way in which Jack thought, may have appealed to Gill and he could have derived a mental stimulus by exchanging ideas with her, but a lack of fundamental understanding between them may have been possible, even though communication was frequent. Jack may have tended to make Gill more restless than usual. However, ultimately, they had a helpful link through a common interest in intellectual pursuits. Jack may have brought to Gill's notice, areas that hitherto she had left unexplored. A deeper level of communication may have been possible resulting in a beneficial exchange of ideas and discussions on the more philosophical aspects of life. Jack may have been a source of inspiration to her in her search for a vital and transcendent philosophy of life. Through the ways he allowed his life to be guided by his beliefs, he may have caused Gill to become interested in the philosophical teachings to which he subscribed. In this case, Jack may have been acting as a 'guru', or mentor. Jack may have introduced Gill to a wider-range philosophy, and in the process have given her a greater insight into some of the more abstract problems. He may have had the happy knack of being able to stimulate her ideas on a variety of subjects. Also, Jack may have been able to provide Gill with the kind of inspiration to lead her to formulate her ideals more clearly, and so have helped her to realise them. Jack would have been able to supply a stimulus to Gill's thinking and have challenged her way of looking at life. He may have expected her to have had clearly defined views on a variety of subjects, and have attempted to use her as an encyclopaedia, but true communication may still have eluded them. Yet generally, Gill would have valued Jack's good opinion of her, and could have trusted him with her confidences. A happy relationship was indicated based on mutual trust.

Jack may have been in a position to offer Gill some kind of service. Gill could have rested assured that she could have relied on his aid, although, occasionally, he may have called upon her to return the compliment, especially as he was likely to have valued her services. His whole-hearted support may have encouraged her to make sure that she was functioning as efficiently as she possibly could, otherwise Gill may have found that Jack would have been ready to suggest ways that would have improved her system to make it more reliable. Often, there would have been no emotional content involved here, though any reticence over this would have been unlikely to have come from Jack.

Also, Jack may have been able to enhance her reputation and have put her in touch with influential contacts, who could have assisted her progress. In a way, he felt the need to accept some kind of responsibility for her behaviour. There may have been a shortcoming on her part that acted as a barrier to future progress. He might have been able to give her practical advice as to how it could have been guarded against. On the other hand, Jack may have felt that he needed Gill's support, or her acknowledgement of his abilities, in order to increase his self-esteem.

Moreover, Jack may have been able to understand the charitable ideals that Gill held dear. He may have been able to help her to make a realistic assessment of the best way to achieve these. Alternatively, his suggestions may have proved to be a hindrance, and he may have misrepresented Gill's ideas to others, placing her relationships in some difficulty, as a result.

The real reason for their relationship may have been to develop within Gill an urge to become more and more her essential self. Jack may have been more concerned about the qualities that Gill did not display immediately to the World, and he may have challenged her, unwittingly, to become conscious of some hidden motive for action, of which she had not been aware, having perhaps suppressed it for some psychological reason. Accordingly, Gill may have found that Jack had been the means of effecting some kind of transformation within herself that had made her a more complete and integrated person.

Jack may have challenged Gill, again unwittingly, by his being and lifestyle, to make changes in herself and, as the process of making such dramatic changes in one's way of living and thinking is rarely a congenial one, she may have found that such a challenge placed her in a very uncomfortable position. He may have wanted to dictate to her what she should do under certain circumstances, and his manner may have been such as to make her tense and nervous. Jack may even have been the source of her breaking-up with old associates, and finally, he may have disappeared from her life, as suddenly as he had entered into it.

Figure 9: Jack Sprat – Epoch Chart.

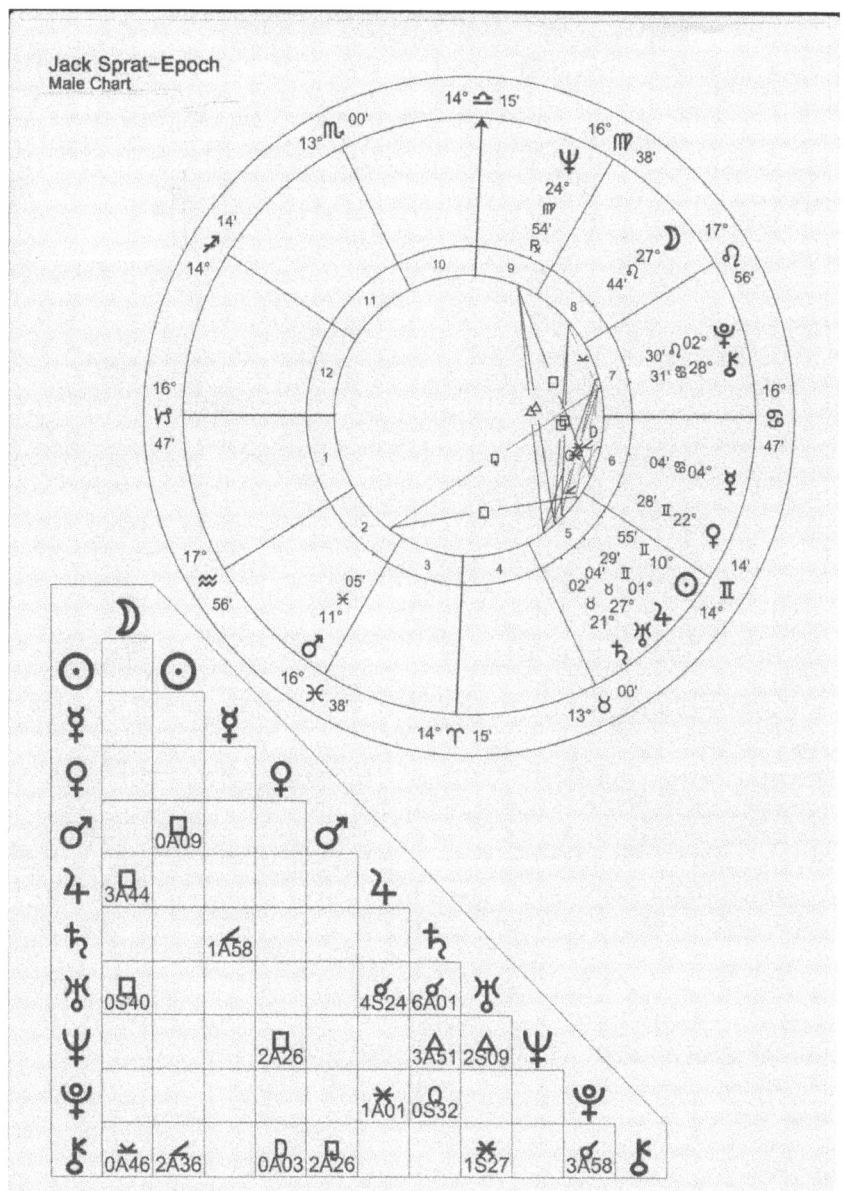

Figure 10: Jack Sprat – Birth Chart.

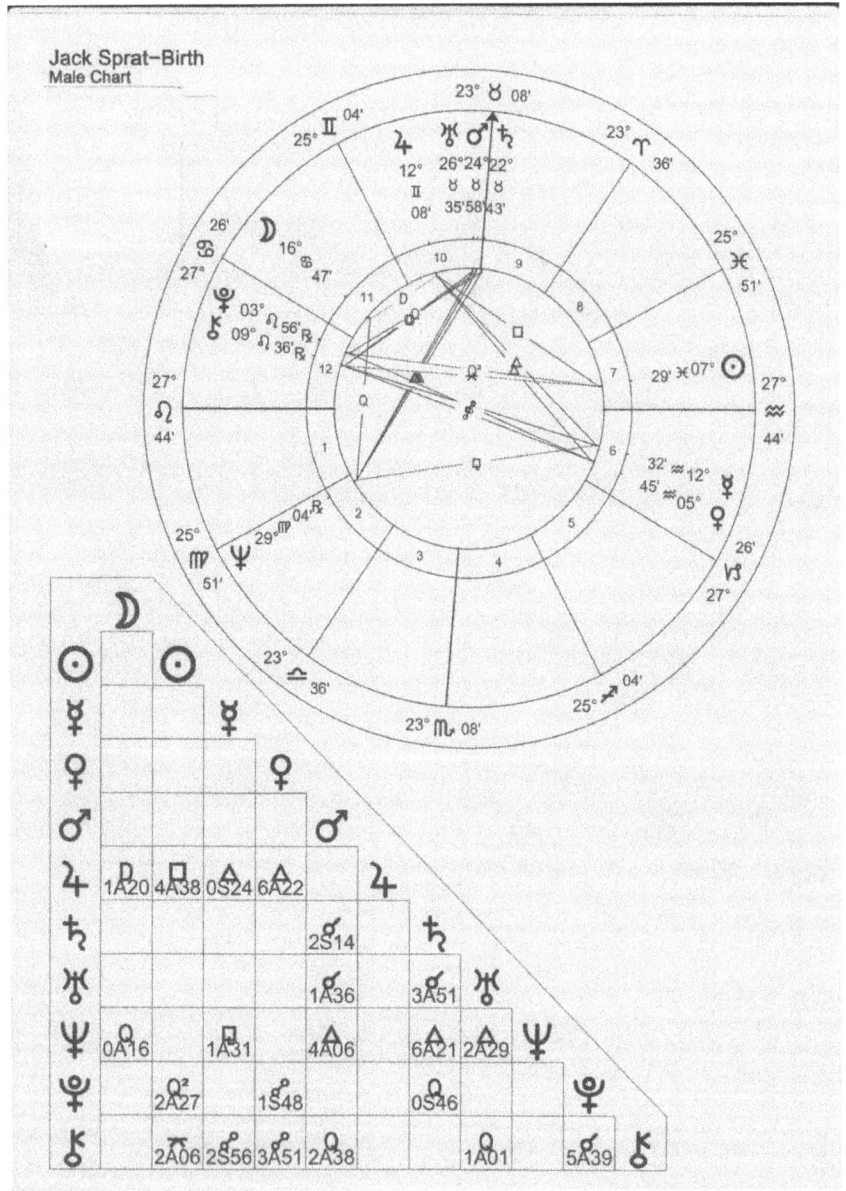

Figure 11: Gillian Gray – Epoch Chart.

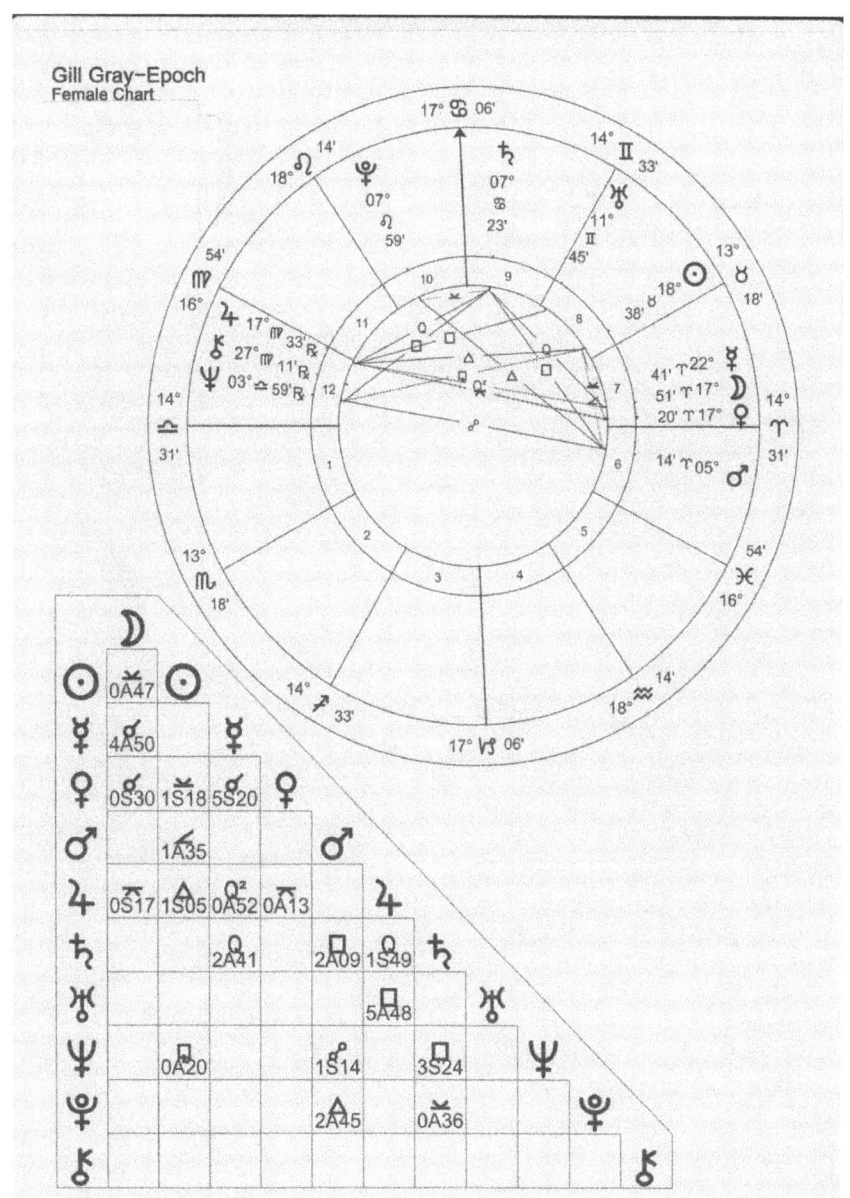

Figure 12: Gillian Gray – Birth Chart.

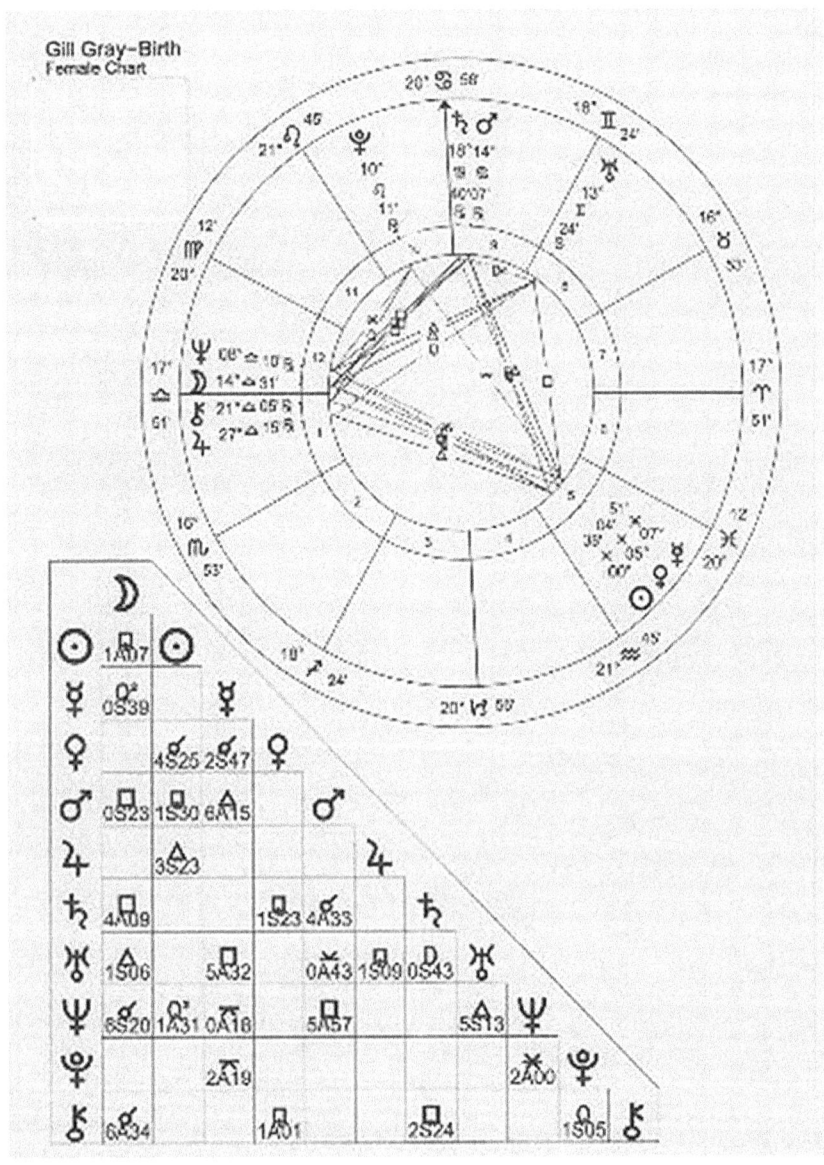

CHAPTER 5

A Control 'Synastry' Exercise for Jack Sprat and Jill Hillside – Young Love

<u>Speculative Only</u>

Having described Jack and Jill in their horoscopes (in the Appendix) in some detail, including their attitude to love and to lovers, we can gain a general feeling for their likely interaction, and obtain some sort of idea of how suitable they would have been as a couple, simply by considering the make-up of their personalities from their two natal charts. Let us summarise some of the general, relevant considerations for each of them.

<u>General considerations from Jack's Natal Charts</u>:-

Firstly, we recall that Jack was both subjective and objective, i.e. his planets lie about equally above and below the Earth. We have seen that his destiny lay in his own hands, in the hands of others and depended on circumstances, i.e. his planets overall lay more to the West (14 to 8) than to the East, of his charts. Mars leads the 'Bowl' shape of his Epoch chart, suggesting idealism, and indicating that he tends to 'scoop-up' experiences in order to initiate more of them. Neptune is the 'clockwise' (impulsive) 'handle' of the 'Bucket' shape of his Birth chart suggesting a particular, and rather uncompromising, direction to his life effort. We notice that the summation of the triplicities and quadruplicities of his planets leads to a preponderance of Fixed Earth (Taurus), some Mutable Earth (Virgo) and some Fixed Air (Aquarius) as well as some Fixed Water (Scorpio), whereas there is a shortage of Cardinal (initiatory) and Fire (keen, ardent), i.e. Aries (assertive energy). Altogether, his planets (10 out of 22) lie mainly in Cadent (dispersion of ideas and energies) Houses. Notice also, that he has six quintile aspects and one decile aspect in both his charts, suggesting good intelligence.

Concerning Partnership, we see that Jack has his Mercury and Chiron at Epoch, and his Sun at Birth, in his 7th House (of his partner), that, at Epoch, has the sign Cancer at its centre point, and similarly, at Birth, has the sign Aquarius there. Respectively, these two signs indicate that marriage and partnerships are both likely to prove advantageous, and that a quality of inconstancy can, if not mastered, lead to difficulties. His Sun in the 7th House indicates that marriage and partnerships are likely to assume a paramount role in his life, and that he would have sought a partner who could have encouraged him to be his real self. Mercury in his 7th House suggests that he may have given much thought to partnership and marriage, and that he may also have looked to marriage to provide mental satisfaction. Similarly, Chiron in his 7th House leads to charitable feelings/actions in marriage and partnerships. Analogously, Libra is the sign of the partner, but he has no planets residing there.

General Considerations from Jill's Natal Charts:-

Jill was mostly subjective, i.e. her planets (18 out of 22) lay below the Earth. We see that her destiny lay more in the hands of others and depended on circumstances (13 out of 22 planets lay to the West in her charts) than in her own hands. Uranus conjoint Mars leads the 'Locomotive' shape of her Epoch chart, suggesting that she felt a sense of need of a task to be achieved. Thus, she had a powerful, self-driving personality. All of her planets are confined into the 'Bundle' shape of her Birth chart, suggesting that her life would be held between narrow bands of opportunity. The summation of all her planets' triplicities and quadruplicities is mainly Mutable (adaptable) [10 out of 22] 'Air' and 'Earth', i.e. Gemini and Virgo, backed up by the Cardinal (outgoing) ones of Libra and Capricorn. Thus, there appears to be some deficiency of the 'Fixed' quadruplicity (resistant to change) and of the 'Fire' (energetic action) and 'Water' (emotional and sensitive) triplicities. Overall, Jill's planets lie mainly in 'Succedent' (resultant status) and 'Cadent' (dispersion of ideas and energies) Houses. Notice also, that she has five quintile family aspects and two decile ones in her two charts suggesting good intelligence.

Concerning partnership, we see that Jill has no planets in her 7th House (of her partner) but that Sagittarius lies at her 7th House centre at Epoch and that Scorpio lies there at Birth. The respective interpretations here are that marriage and partnership are likely to bring great material benefits, and that a certain quality of impetuousness may well lead to unusual domestic circumstances. Libra is the sign of her partner, and at Epoch her Neptune lies there, and at Birth Neptune also lies there as well as being occupied by Venus and by Mars. Neptune signifies that Jill channels her sense of idealism (and her desire to seek transcendental experiences) in her search to establish a significant rapport with those around her. Venus indicates that she seeks to express her affection in the most harmonious way that she can, and Mars implies that her energies are committed to establishing a satisfactory state of equilibrium in her life. Additionally, her passions require fulfilment through a spirited response from her partner.

General Comparisons between Jack's and Jill's Charts:- We have seen that both Jack's and Jill's charts are deficient in the fire triplicity, thereby tending to lack ardour and keenness, but the content of their triplicities is similar, making them alike, which has its virtues. Similarly, regarding the quadruplicities, we find that they both contain the mutable (adaptable) one, but Jill's summation is deficient in the fixed (resistance to change), unlike Jack, but she makes up for his deficiency in the cardinal one (initiatory), which she has. Thus, in certain respects, they could compensate for each other. However, the union of Jack's fixed with Jill's mutable could lead to unhappiness for Jill, unless she had been content to follow a mainly passive role. Jack will not have wished to follow Jill's eager appetite for variety and change, and he may also have failed to gain that degree of mental rapport that Jill would have been anxious to cultivate. Jill may have developed an admiration for Jack's 'strength of character' and Jack may have considered Jill to be too flighty and undependable, while she considered him to be too stolid, autocratic and unyielding. Yet, when signs of the same element predominate, 'Earth' in this case, then the partnership stands a better chance of success. Also, while both partners show 'cadent' (dispersion of ideas and energies) properties, Jill has more succedent (resultant status) content, whereas Jack has somewhat more of the angular (outgoing) sort.

Concerning the comparison of chart shapes, both the 'bowl' (Jack) and the 'locomotive' (Jill) are conscious of a sense of lack. The 'bucket' type (Jack) may have found in Jill's 'locomotive' type, the kind of drive he needs, as well as perhaps the decisive outlook of her 'bundle' type. But the advantages and disadvantages here are not clear cut. A final judgement may depend on whether the majority of cross-aspects between their charts are favourable, or not, but see the following section. The keyword here, and throughout a 'synastry' exercise, is 'understanding', leading to the making of allowances on both sides, if this is possible, and then moving on.

<u>Specific Considerations concerning all Four of their Natal Charts (see the end of the chapter)</u>:-

Let us begin to be more specific concerning Jack and Jill's relationship by listing their respective planets by their sign positions, from the first point of Aries, in their four separate charts, as in Table 4. We can then list all the cross-aspects from Jill's two charts with Jack's two:

<u>Table 4</u>: The Planets of the Epoch and Birth Charts of Jack Sprat and Jill Hillside, listed by sign, starting from the first Point of Aries.

Jill Epoch	Jack Epoch	Jack Birth	Jill Birth
Ur 05⁰Ge51' Rx	Sa 21⁰Ta02'	Sa 22⁰Ta43'	Mo 09⁰Ge01'
Ma 06⁰Ge55'Rx	Ur 27⁰Ta04'	Ma 24⁰Ta58'	Ur 13⁰Ge05'
Sa 22⁰Ge30'Rx	Ju 01⁰Ge29'	Ur 26⁰Ta35'	Sa 09⁰Ca02'
Pl 08⁰Le21' Rx	Su 10⁰Ge55'	Ju 12⁰Ge08'	Pl 09⁰Le35'
Ju 26⁰Le54' Rx	Ve 22⁰Ge28'	Mo 16⁰Ca47'	Ju 09⁰Vr35'
Ch 15⁰Vr45'	Me 04⁰Ca04'	Pl 03⁰Le56' Rx	Me 12⁰Vr17' Rx
Np 04⁰Li11'	Ch 28⁰Ca31'	Ch 09⁰Le36' Rx	Su 16⁰Vr06'
Mo 15⁰Sc53'	Pl 02⁰Le30'	Np 29⁰Vr04'Rx	Ch 20⁰Vr42'
Ve 17⁰Sc38'	Mo 27⁰Le44'	Ve 05⁰Aq45'	Np 03⁰Li18'
Su 00⁰Cp59'	Np24⁰Vr54' Rx	Me 12⁰Aq32'	Ve 06⁰Li12'
Me 20⁰Cp57'	Ma 11⁰Pi05'	Su 07⁰Pi29'	Ma 07⁰Li03'

In the Table Rx stands for retrograde Motion.

Following the allowances for cross-aspects listed previously, we find that the cross-aspects between Jack's and Jill's Epoch charts' planets (see columns 1 and 2) are: $^{\text{Her}}\text{Sa}^{\text{E}}$ conjoint(E) $^{\text{His}}\text{Ve}^{\text{E}}$; $^{\text{Her}}\text{Ju}^{\text{E}}$ square(E-S) $^{\text{His}}\text{Ur}^{\text{E}}$; $^{\text{Her}}\text{Ju}^{\text{E}}$ conjoint(W) $^{\text{His}}\text{Mo}^{\text{E}}$; $^{\text{Her}}\text{Np}^{\text{E}}$ square(E) $^{\text{His}}\text{Me}^{\text{E}}$; $^{\text{Her}}\text{Su}^{\text{E}}$ opposition(M) $^{\text{His}}\text{Ju}^{\text{E}}$ and $^{\text{Her}}\text{Me}^{\text{E}}$ trine(E) $^{\text{His}}\text{Sa}^{\text{E}}$.

Similarly, the cross-aspects between Jill's Epoch chart's planets and Jack's Birth chart's planets (see columns 1 and 3) comprise: $^{\text{Her}}\text{Ur}^{\text{E}}$ trine(E) $^{\text{His}}\text{Ve}^{\text{B}}$; $^{\text{Her}}\text{Ma}^{\text{E}}$ square(M) $^{\text{His}}\text{Su}^{\text{B}}$; $^{\text{Her}}\text{Sa}^{\text{E}}$ semi-sextile(M) $^{\text{His}}\text{Sa}^{\text{B}}$; $^{\text{Her}}\text{Ju}^{\text{E}}$ square(S-M) $^{\text{His}}\text{Ur}^{\text{B}}$; $^{\text{Her}}\text{Np}^{\text{E}}$ sextile(S-M) $^{\text{His}}\text{Pl}^{\text{B}}$ and $^{\text{Her}}\text{Mo}^{\text{E}}$ trine(W) $^{\text{His}}\text{Mo}^{\text{B}}$.

Again, the cross-aspects between Jill's Birth chart's planets and those of Jack's Epoch chart (see columns 4 and 2) consist of: $^{\text{Her}}\text{Ch}^{\text{B}}$ trine (S-M) $^{\text{His}}\text{Sa}^{\text{E}}$; $^{\text{Her}}\text{Np}^{\text{B}}$ square(W) $^{\text{His}}\text{Me}^{\text{E}}$ and $^{\text{Her}}\text{Np}^{\text{B}}$ sextile(W) $^{\text{His}}\text{Pl}^{\text{E}}$.

Finally, the cross-aspects between Jill's and Jack's Birth charts' planets (see columns 4 and 3) comprise: $^{\text{Her}}\text{Mo}^{\text{B}}$ sextile(M-W) $^{\text{His}}\text{Ch}^{\text{B}}$; $^{\text{Her}}\text{Ur}^{\text{B}}$ conjoint(W) $^{\text{His}}\text{Ju}^{\text{B}}$; $^{\text{Her}}\text{Ur}^{\text{B}}$ trine(M) $^{\text{His}}\text{Me}^{\text{B}}$; $^{\text{Her}}\text{Sa}^{\text{B}}$ semi-sextile(W) $^{\text{His}}\text{Ch}^{\text{B}}$; $^{\text{Her}}\text{Pl}^{\text{B}}$ conjoint(E-S) $^{\text{His}}\text{Ch}^{\text{B}}$; $^{\text{Her}}\text{Ju}^{\text{B}}$ semi-sextile(E) $^{\text{His}}\text{Ch}^{\text{B}}$; $^{\text{Her}}\text{Me}^{\text{B}}$ quincunx(M) $^{\text{His}}\text{Me}^{\text{B}}$; $^{\text{Her}}\text{Me}^{\text{B}}$ square(E-S) $^{\text{His}}\text{Ju}^{\text{B}}$; $^{\text{Her}}\text{Su}^{\text{B}}$ sextile(W) $^{\text{His}}\text{Mo}^{\text{B}}$; $^{\text{Her}}\text{Np}^{\text{B}}$ sextile(W) $^{\text{His}}\text{Pl}^{\text{B}}$; $^{\text{Her}}\text{Ve}^{\text{B}}$ trine(M) $^{\text{His}}\text{Ve}^{\text{B}}$ and $^{\text{Her}}\text{Ma}^{\text{B}}$ quincunx(W) $^{\text{His}}\text{Su}^{\text{B}}$.

The Combined Interpretations of all the Cross-Aspects between Jack's and Jill's Natal Charts.

A degree of good fellowship, generosity of spirit, mutual respect, appreciation, tolerance and encouragement existed between Jack and Jill.

There was a tendency that she represented his sub-conscious feminine ideal and that he stood for her concept of her ideal man. He could have adapted to, and sustained, her quest for independent self-expression. Warmth was created, if not actual heat. Jill was stimulated by some basic, inner quality of his being, but his pride may have clashed with her wilfulness, or she may have tended to grate on him, and *vice-versa*. There may also have been a struggle for supremacy. Although she would have been likely to favour him, he may have flattered her, or have led her astray, through over-confidence, tending eventually to a lack of good faith. She was likely to have become the leading player in their relationship.

There was sympathetic appreciation between them and they could have worked harmoniously together in terms of a mutually compatible response to everyday situations. Their relationship tended to be easy-going. Jack may have made special efforts to accommodate Jill, and in return, she may have indulged him after he had provided her with opportunities to display generosity.

Jack acted to steady Jill and to have deepened her thinking, generally by providing solid, practical advice. But she could have provided extra points, or a different view of things, for him to ponder over. As a result, he may have become intrigued by her novel way of looking at things that she would have brought to their relationship. However, there may have been a basic difference of approach to mental problems, as well. An element of challenge here, may have led to arguments and/or disagreements. They may have become too critical of each other. Her ideas and abilities may have been exploited by him, who may have been out to capitalise on their relationship as much as possible. Also, her sensitivity and imagination may not have blended well with his logical thinking. It may have been difficult for her to appreciate his logic, or for him to accept her readiness to indulge in flights of fancy. Misconceptions may have abounded due to a lack of clarity, or to a lack of spiritual appreciation.

A congenial link was formed between them, which encouraged the formation of a happy companionship, and of an affectionate consideration for each other. Likes and dislikes between them would have clashed rarely. If Jack had placed a high value on integrity and dependability, then he would have appreciated her serious side. This helped a long-term build-up of affection between them, but it hardly promises ecstasy. She may have been tempted to demand too much from him. Also, her relative coolness may have restricted his feelings of harmony for, and unison with, her. <u>However, and crucially, there was a capacity for ecstasy – signifying sexual stimulation, but which was not necessarily a stabilising factor for a relationship. He found her to be 'extra-special', whereas she was susceptible to his charm and attractiveness.</u> At first, he may not have realised the extent of the attraction he held for her, so he was able to view the association with somewhat more detachment. But both partners were insufficiently mature at the time. After break-up, his thoughts may well have been that, <u>"It was better to have loved and lost, than never to have loved at all."</u> Jack may have been provoked into acting unwisely, thereby taking unnecessary risks, perhaps by her air of complacency. Yet they may both have appreciated each other's sense of responsibility, and both would have felt that they could have relied on the integrity of the other. Each should have been able to pursue practical aims and ambitions, without clashing with the other. After all, this was a stabilising factor for the relationship. Also, there was a hypersensitive type of awareness between them. If they had been engaged in welfare, or artistic, activities, and had been capable of acting maturely, then a useful collaboration could have developed between them.

<u>Additionally,</u> Jack acted to steady Jill's charitable inclinations, drawing attention to the more practical side of life, and providing advice. Also, she tended to steady his charitable thoughts in the same way, but his spontaneity should not have become hampered in the process. Moreover, Jill provided good examples of charity, as a focus of interest for Jack to follow. However, in order to convince her, regarding points of charity, he would have had to strike a chord in her subconscious mind. In the attempt, he may have found that his

own charitable ideas had been transformed. A new dimension may have been added to his charitable inclinations, provided that his charitable ideas had not become brain-washed as a result.

Re-organisation of the Interpretations of Jack's Planetary 'Relocations' to the Houses of Jill's Natal Charts, i.e. Mainly Jack's effect on Jill.

There was something in Jill's personality that tended to convince Jack that he could depend on her. She may have developed her sensitivity more effectively, whereas he could have made demands on her patient understanding, and have tested her powers of endurance. Nevertheless, their relationship could still have been a lasting one. Jill would have been aware of Jack's charm, whereas his personality would have struck an harmonious chord in her psyche. She would have felt very much at home with him, and have enjoyed his company, while he was likely to have encouraged her to be her natural self. There was a similarity between Jack's essential self and the way that Jill was seeking to project herself outwardly. Also, he would have been encouraged to be his own natural self, she would have appreciated his individual worth and would have had a high regard for him. However, some confusion, as well as deception and secrecy may have developed along with an affectionate link. In addition, a struggle for supremacy could have developed, in which his showiness, extravagance and imprudence could have counted against him. Moreover, disclosures, upheavals and new starts could have occurred with trouble and unpleasantness.

Jack may have had a special talent for detecting any shortcomings in the way in which Jill handled her financial arrangements, so that she could have made a more realistic assessment of her own earning powers. He may have been able to offer her advice, which enabled her to cultivate a more realistic sense of values, to increase her material resources, so that she may have lent him money, without apparent risk, but she would have needed to be wary here. There was a tendency that Jack would have been able to communicate freely with Jill regarding her charitable activities by bringing news, data, or by operating as a go-between for her. Educational activities of various kinds could have been involved. However, the advice he gave her probably would have worked to her disadvantage, even though the outlook initially, had seemed favourable.

Jack may have been the means of giving Jill an entirely new slant on life, putting her in touch with new sources of information that gave her the opportunity to develop quite different mental perspectives. He may have been fascinated by the way in which her mind worked, and by the way she tackled her mental problems. Thus, a high degree of mental rapport became possible, but his way of thinking may have seemed to be too abnormal to merit her serious attention. However, this could have changed later. Also, an emotional factor may have intruded that prevented accurate understanding of the ideas each may have wished to communicate.

In some way, Jack may have been able to bring an influence to bear on Jill's domestic scene, implanting helpful suggestions that she would have recognised instinctively as relating to her own situation. Similarly, he may have provided her with suggestions for improving her charitable activities, but some snags may have arisen as a result.

Jack was attracted to Jill by the way in which she deployed her talents, by the way she projected herself and by her general attitude to the whole area of creative and pleasurable activities. Emotional involvement and display of affection would have tended to result in a happy association. Jack may have provided Jill with ideas that acted as a spur to her creative imagination. They may have met first through both being interested in some hobby (tennis?), or through activities connected with education, or children. Jack may have been responsible for making Jill aware of some latent creative talents, which she may have developed with dramatic effect. Yet Jack's relationship with Jill could have become somewhat less than cordial, despite good companionship initially. It may have been difficult for Jill to enlist Jack's support for any enterprise that she had wished to undertake. Sympathy could have been lacking here. Jack may have adopted a too critical attitude to Jill's creative efforts, thereby hindering, rather than helping, them. On the other hand, Jill had to learn to create for the sake of the result, and not in order to gain approval, although that could have come later.

Jack took pleasure in rendering Jill services, but he himself may have needed her care and support at some time, by return. Jack's know-how may have helped Jill to get things done, and have helped her with fitness, diet and stress issues. But possibly his advice may have proved to be rather unsettling. Jack may have been able to offer Jill some kind of service, but he may have called upon her to return the compliment, especially as he valued her services. This situation could have been more marked in a casual relationship, or for one of convenience. There may have been no emotional involvement here, although any reticence was unlikely to have come from Jack.

Jack was likely to have had an instinctive awareness of the areas in which Jill needed support. He may have been the means of making her aware of a neglected facet of her being, either as an asset, or as a liability. Jill would have tried to build on a strength, or have transformed a defect, or have guarded against it. Jack would have had her best interests at heart. He would have been pleased to supply practical help, and would have made suggestions to improve her general efficiency and physical well-being. Thus, he could have offered her services as a 'do-gooder', i.e. to show that he was capable of sympathetic attention to the needs of others. This may, or may not, have proved soothing. Jack may have taken a special interest in the way that Jill did things. If her technical knowledge had been inadequate, then she may have feared that her association with him, would have become a continual challenge. She may have started to feel like a 'probationer'. She may have had to revise totally her attitude to working in a subordinate capacity, as well as her attitude towards those, who may have had to serve her, in a similar capacity. Jack may have 'suggested' that she follow his good example. This could have proved to be an unpleasant challenge, at best.

Jack and Jill's relationship may have called for a great deal of tolerance, and a willingness to make sacrifices on Jill's part, if it was to have prospered. If not, then this would have been compounded by his reservations about her perceived weaknesses, combined with his ultra-cautious attitude regarding those areas of her psyche, over which, normally, she had little control.

<u>Reorganisation of the Interpretations of Jill's Planetary 'Relocations' to the Houses of Jack's Natal Charts, i.e. Mainly Jill's effect on Jack.</u>

Jill would have wished to make things easier for Jack, so that he could use his creative faculties in the best possible way. She would have helped him to find the most effective means of self-expression. She may have been able to provide him with ideas that acted as a spur to his creative imagination. For example, her charity interests, connected possibly with children and education, may have acted as a serious spur to his. She would have enjoyed giving him pleasure, perhaps by providing him with opportunities in this direction that he might otherwise have been denied. Simultaneously, she would have valued his support, and his good opinion of her. He may have gained real pleasure through her companionship, especially at social functions, and at places of entertainment. Romantic friendship, with much mutual affection, was possible. They may have met first through activities connected with children, education, or through a favourite hobby (tennis?). However, she may have adopted a too critical attitude towards his creative efforts, or that her ideas may have hindered, rather than helped, him to realise his creative goals. Thus, the relationship may have become less cordial than initially.

There was a tendency that Jill may have been in a position to offer him some kind of service, but occasionally, she may have called upon him to return the compliment, especially as she was likely to have valued his services. She may have felt that she had a right to expect some service from him. For her part, she would have expected to be fully recompensed for any service that she had given him. But although critical, her ultimate aim would have been to make him more self-sufficient. She may have been instrumental in keeping him busy, or she may have occasionally hindered his progress.

Jill was likely to have taken much pleasure in rendering Jack various services, and in showing him how to perform his chores more easily, but she may have needed his support and care, later. She may have been able to provide him with valuable know-how about the best way to get jobs done, how to improve his diet, fitness and exercise and how to help him to cope with any stress. She may have been able to suggest effective, new ways of doing things and have introduced him to labour-saving devices that would have helped to make his work easier. Also, she may have expected him to overhaul his methods, so as to improve them. Overall, and as a result, he may have sensed that her attitude towards him was rather critical, and so she may have set his nerves on edge. There may have been a lack of care from her, concerning his health.

Jill would have tested Jack's powers of co-operation, and his ability to cope with the give and take of partnership. In some ways, she may have been responsible for widening his circle of associates. She hoped that by collaborating with him, she would have strengthened her own position by his compensating for anything that she lacked. Whereas some degree of physical attraction was present, and while they both may have enjoyed a good row, he could have suffered more mentally. Disruptions of harmony may have been diminished if he had been careful to respect her independence and to have paid due regard to what she considered to be her personal rights. However, compassionate understanding between the two of them, could have helped to dissolve any barriers present between them.

Although Jack may have felt that Jill was his ideal partner, he may have feared that he had allowed himself to become somewhat deluded by a mirage of unattainable bliss, coupled with the wonderful union that may never have been fully realised. Usually, there was considerable physical attraction, and instinctive appreciation, between them. Also, financial transactions between them would not have led to any problems. Yet Jill may have been the means whereby Jack became aware of some hitherto neglected facet of his being, which may have operated as either an asset, or a liability, to him. He would have concentrated on enhancing the asset, or have attempted to transform, or eliminate, the liability. In either case, she would have had his best interests at heart.

Jill may have played some definite role regarding Jack's career. She would have encouraged him to develop a realistic approach to his responsibilities. Her appraisal of his performance was usually calculated to assist him to gain a higher level of achievement, and of self-development. Also, Jill may have been instrumental in making possible improvements to Jack's status, perhaps by putting him in touch with influential people, or through her wise advice based on her own professional experience. She may have given him a taste for success by her good opinion of him, or have given him the extra incentive to succeed, so that he wouldn't have let her down. All this, because she appreciated the aims that he had in mind. But she may have caused him to aim higher than that of which he was capable, either by giving him poor advice, and/or have weakened his resolve by making his path too easy.

Jack may first have been attracted to Jill because of her conversational abilities, and by the quality of her intellect. She may have been able to understand the ideals he held dear, and have been able to put him in touch with those who had similar ideals. She may have been instrumental in introducing him to societies and organisations dedicated to the furtherance of some ideal that he cherished, or to have put him in touch with a wide variety of friends. She may have had to be prepared to meet him more than half-way. She also may have been able to help him make a more realistic assessment of his best way to achieve his hopes and wishes. In times of emergency, she may have reacted surprisingly, and have offered her help, when he would least have expected it. Unfortunately, however, her suggestions, at times, may have proved to be more of a hindrance than of a help to him.

Jill may have been able to encourage Jack to develop interests that would have helped him to gain a general and greater understanding of life as a whole. His association with her may, in some subtle way, have enabled him to adjust more easily to life's problems, and so have encouraged him to develop a more relaxed attitude towards them. She may well have been able to imbue him with the spirit of, "Thy will be done", and so have avoided his "self-undoing". She may have been able to arouse his most charitable and kindly instincts. She may even have been able to change his views about the sick, the suffering and the underprivileged. There may also have been a mutual interest in psychic matters, either pleasantly, or the opposite. The main purpose here may have been to sharpen his intuitive recognition of those really in need of his sympathy and support, as well as to guard against exposing his weak points to others. She could have been the person to whom he would have most likely turned, in times of trouble. His problems may have seemed less troublesome as a result of her friendly advice, and so have done much to restore his faith in himself.

However, there just may have been some hidden enmity that gnawed at the roots of their relationship. She may have become very interested in what made him tick. Instinctively, she may have had a tendency to be able to recognise his problems and to have sensed his weak points. She would have been likely to adopt a forgiving attitude towards him, and she would have been anxious to protect him, if she had felt that he had been in a situation where one of his vulnerable points was likely to have become exposed to attack. However much she may have overdone this, he, in the process, would have become aware as to whom he could trust with his welfare.

The experiences Jack shared with Jill, may have made him uncomfortably aware of elements in his character that were apt to play him false, when he was under pressure. There was a possibility that Jill may have been able to exploit Jack's 'Achilles heel'. She may have started to think that he was unreliable, or a bad risk. There may have been a tendency for difficulties to develop in their relationship. She may have expected him to be reliable and self-sufficient in those very areas where he was likely to have been most vulnerable. She just may have involved him in some underground activity. And so, he may not have felt particularly at ease in her presence, in which, occasionally, he may have brought one of his weaknesses to light disconcertingly. She may have had to compensate for him, and in the process he would have made testing demands upon her sympathies and forgiving instincts.

Figure 13: Jill Hillside – Epoch Chart.

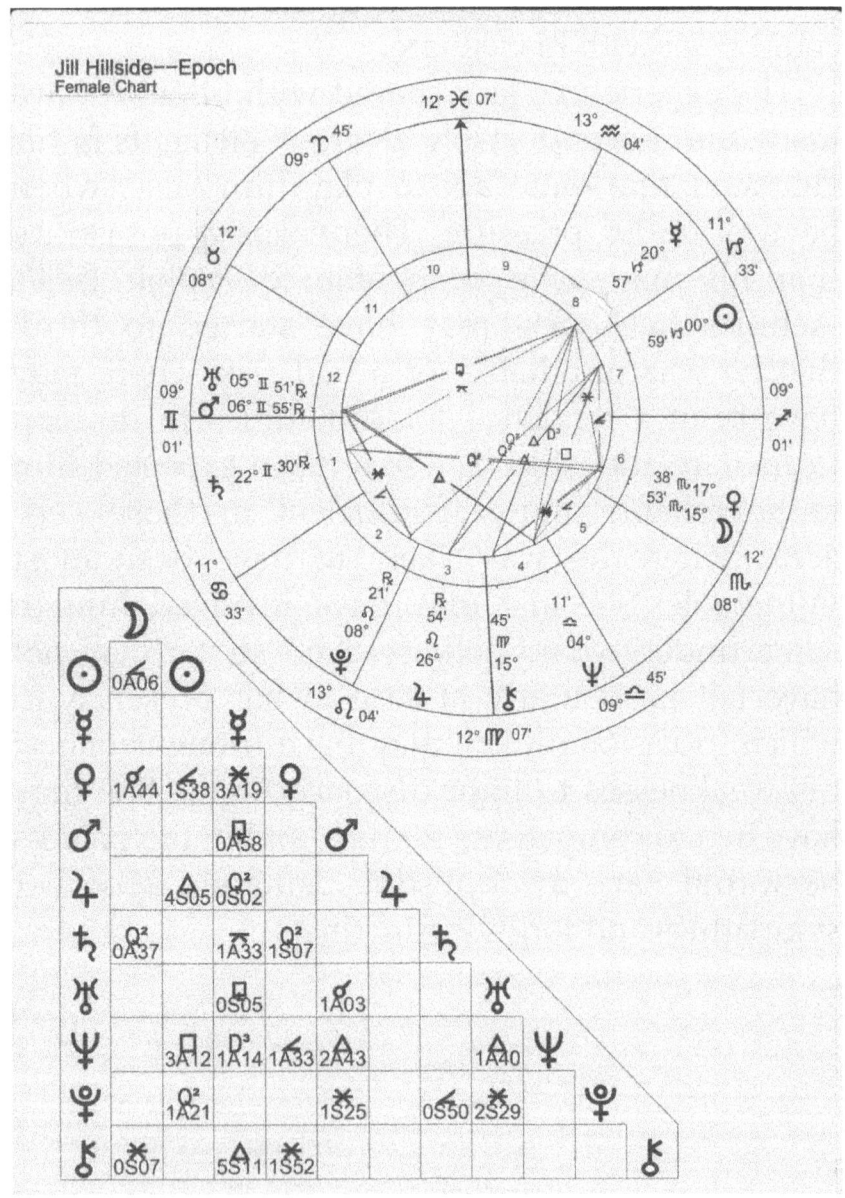

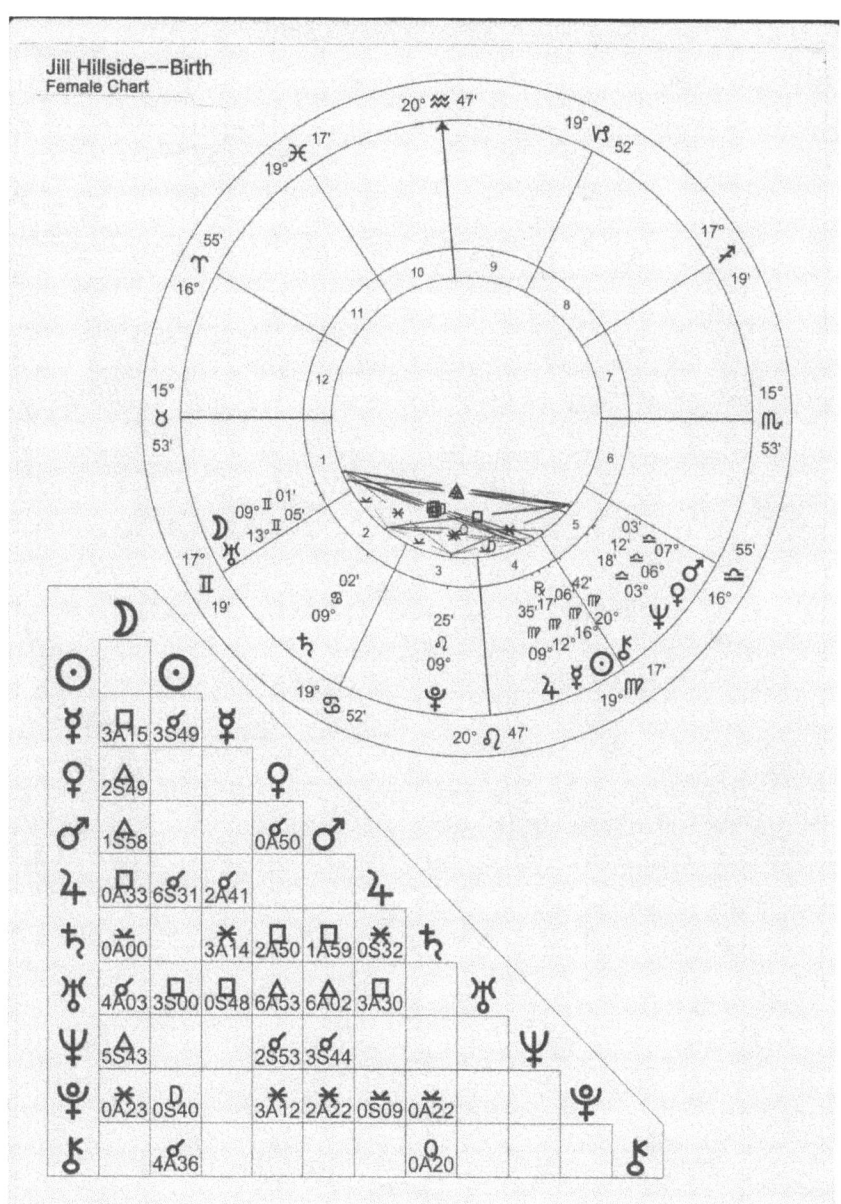

Figure 15: Jack Sprat – Epoch Chart:

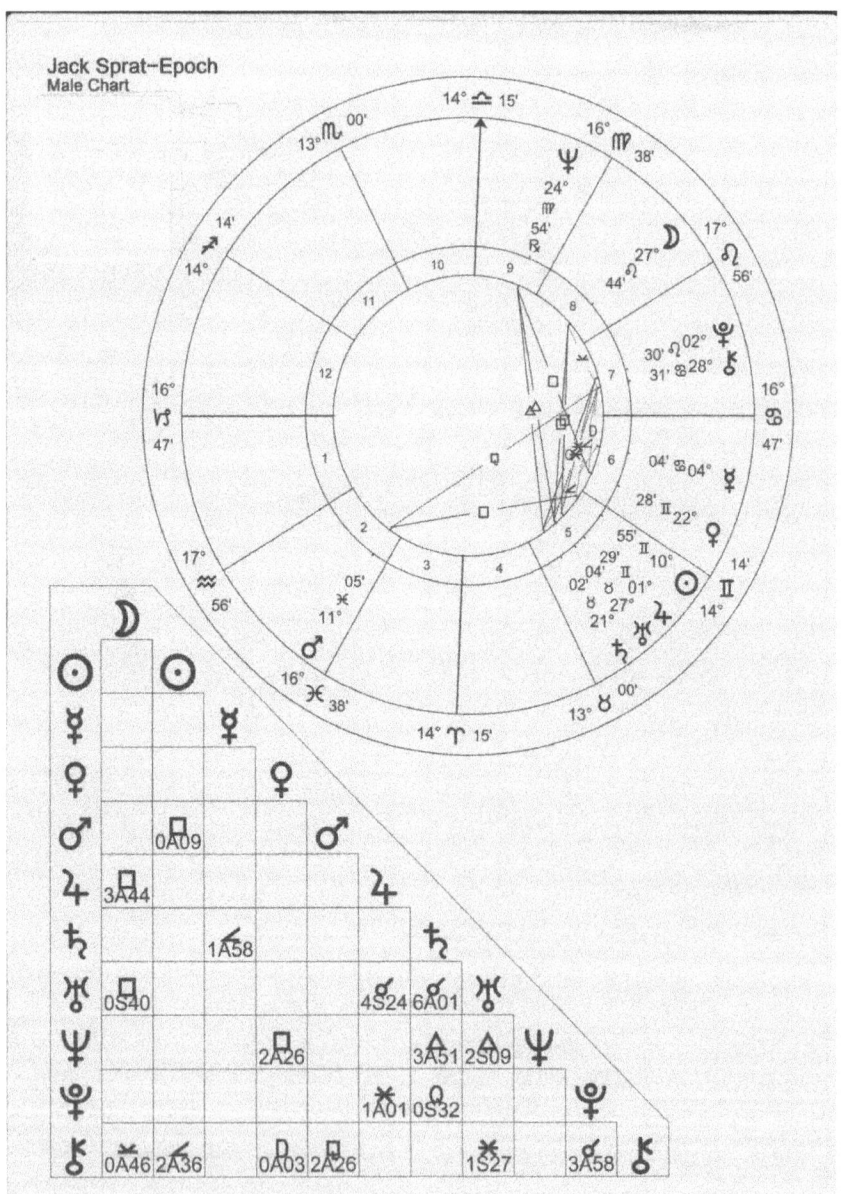

Figure 16: Jack Sprat – Birth Chart.

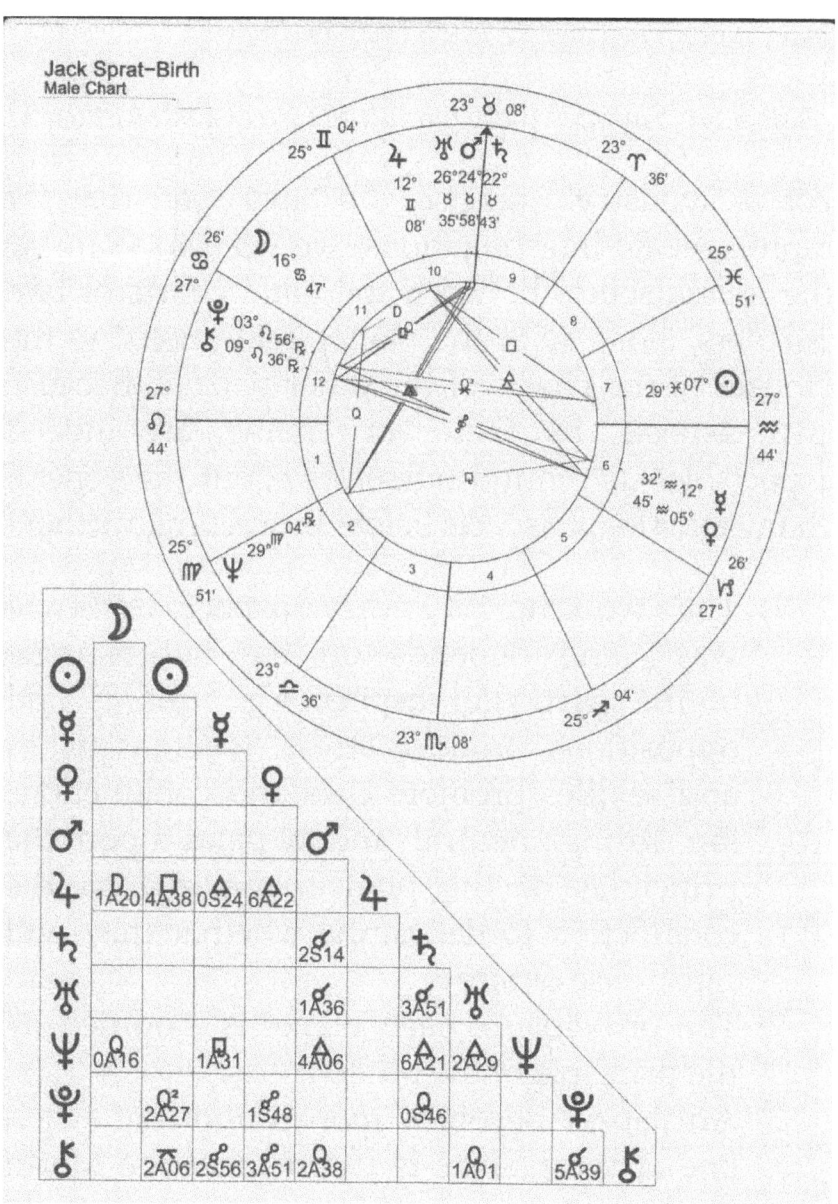

CHAPTER 6

Love

Astrology Supplies Biology with the Precision of Physics

For a 'synastry' exercise, we have seen that for more specific interpretations, we need to examine the cross-aspects between the natal charts of two partners, along with the planet 'relocations' to the Houses of the charts of the other partner. Because cross-aspects, by their very name, are indeed aspects, let us remind ourselves about the general characteristics of aspects before proceeding further:-

1) The working of every aspect is "two-way", and depends on the nature/angle of the particular aspect, e.g. squares and oppositions produce stress, whereas trines and sextiles promote ease and conjunctions are strong, neutral and depend upon the principles of the planets making up the conjunction to determine whether they will cause ease or stress.

2) The principle of each planet is modified by the principle of the other.

3) An aspect becomes more important when one of the planets is the ruler of the Morin Point, the Sun or the Moon, or is particularly prominent for any other reason, e.g. it

conjoins the Morin Point, the centre of the 10th House, or is multi-aspected by many of the remaining planets in its chart.

4) Aspects should be judged against the general character of their particular chart.

5) Two aspecting planets may be further modified by other aspects, e.g. both planets in a conjunction may receive aspects from other planets, which can alter their interpretations noticeably.

6) An exact aspect is considerably stronger than a wider one.

7) A planet that is approaching exactness when making an aspect with another planet (i.e. 'applying' to exactness) has a stronger effect than when that planet has passed the point of exactness for the aspect with the other, and so is 'separating' from it*. [*Two other properties of aspects have been omitted here. These descriptions are a) 'dexter' and 'sinister' (see R. C. Davison, "Astrology: How to Cast Your Horoscope" p 125) as well as b) dissociated (see C. E. O. Carter, "The Principles of Astrology", p 28). 'Parallels of Declination' have also been excluded, ibid.]

With these considerations in mind, let us examine the various, essentially exact, cross-aspects that have been identified for the four 'synastry' exercises. Table 5 summarises the relevant data.

Table 5: Exact Aspects for the Four 'Synastry' Exercises.

Synastry Exercise	Aspect and Type	Applying or Separating	Distance from exactness in mins of arc.	House location of her planet	House location of his planet
JS and JH (4)	$^{Her}Sa^{E}$ conj $^{His}Ve^{E}$	App	2	1	6
Control	$^{Her}Ju^{E}$ squa $^{His}Ur^{E}$	Sep	10	3	5
	$^{Her}Np^{E}$ squa $^{His}Me^{E}$	App	7	5	7
	$^{Her}Me^{E}$ trine $^{His}Sa^{E}$	App	5	8	5
	$^{Her}Ur^{E}$ trine $^{His}Ve^{B}$	App	6	1	6
	$^{Her}Pl^{B}$ conj $^{His}Ch^{B}$	App	11	4	12
	$^{Her}Ju^{B}$ s-sex $^{His}Ch^{B}$	App	1	5	12
	$^{Her}Me^{B}_{Rx}$ squ $^{His}Ju^{B}$	App	9	5	11
JS and GG (3)	$^{Her}Np^{E}$ squa $^{His}Me^{E}$	Sep	5	1	7
Control	$^{Her}Me^{E}$ s-sex $^{His}Sa^{B}$	App	2	7	10
	$^{Her}Sa^{E}$ trine $^{His}Su^{B}$	Sep	6	10	7
	$^{Her}Np^{E}$ sext $^{His}Pl^{B}$	Stat	3	1	12
	$^{Her}Ch^{B}$ quin $^{His}Sa^{E}$	App	3	1	5
	$^{Her}Ju^{B}$ quin $^{His}Ur^{E}$	App	11	1	5
RB and ET (2)	$^{Her}Ur^{E}$ squa $^{His}Ju^{B}$	App	9	6	8
	$^{Her}Su^{E}$ quin $^{His}Su^{B}$	Stat	2	8	6
	$^{Her}Ju^{E}$ trine $^{His}Ur^{B}$	Sep	12	9	10
	$^{Her}Pl^{B}$ trine $^{His}Ur^{E}$	App	2	11	1
	$^{Her}Ur^{B}$ quin $^{His}Sa^{B}$	Sep	2	7	6
	$^{Her}Ve^{B}$ quin $^{His}Su^{B}$	Sep	7	8	6
Du and Duc (1)	$^{Her}Su^{E}$ s-sex $^{His}Sa^{B}$	Sep	5	12	9
	$^{Her}Su^{E}$ squa $^{His}Ju^{B}$	Sep	10	12	5
	$^{Her}Ve^{E}$ oppo $^{His}Ma^{B}$	App	8	1	2
	$^{Her}Sa^{B}$ s-sex $^{His}Su^{E}$	Sep	6	6	2
	$^{Her}Me^{B}$ squa $^{His}Ch^{B}$	Sep	2	1	8
	$^{Her}Np^{B}$ conj $^{His}Ju^{B}$	Sep	10	1	5
	$^{Her}Mo^{B}$ trine $^{His}Pl^{B}$	Sep	7	5	5

In the Table Stat stands for stationary or relatively unchanging.

Now let us proceed in reverse order, taking the 'exact' cross-aspects for 'synastry' exercise 4, a young love control, first. Because Jack has no planets in his 1st House, either at Epoch or at Birth, he cannot obtain any personal 'relocation' influences there from a partner. On the other hand, Jill receives two different 'relocations' of Venus from Jack's charts to her personal 1st House, but that her planets, Uranus and Saturn, become 'relocated' to Jack's 6th House, which isn't really associated with love. His Venus at Birth is fascinated by her personal Uranus (conjoint Mars) at Epoch but, at the same time, his Venus at Epoch is stabilised by her personal Saturn, also at Epoch. In terms of love, the temptation here is to suggest that Jill's effect on Jack was significantly stronger than Jack's effect on Jill, even though he was supplying Jill with a double dose of cool (Aquarius and Gemini) harmony to her 1st House by means of his two Venus 'relocations'.

Secondly, considering 'synastry' control exercise 3 –an adult love, we find that Gill, having several planets (Neptune at both Epoch and Birth, and Chiron, Jupiter and the Moon also at Birth) in her 1st House, can receive 'exact' personal 'relocations' from Jack's planets. The adverse, square cross-aspect between Gill's Neptune and Jack's Mercury both at Epoch would have made it difficult for Gill to appreciate Jack's logic and conversely, for Jack to take a sympathetic view of Gill's poetic imagination. Sometimes, she may have deliberately misrepresented him, and so have damaged his reputation. However, Gill's Saturn at Epoch is favourably in trine to Jack's Sun at Birth in his

7th House, perhaps enabling him to enhance her reputation. She will have assessed his worth as a partner, and if he had managed to live up to her standards, then he would have had a friend for life. Gill's Neptune at Epoch is favourably cross-aspected by Jack's Pluto at Birth, which suggests the possibility of a useful collaboration. Jack may have been attracted to Gill by a potentiality in her, not immediately apparent to others. His association with her may have enabled him to adjust more easily to life's problems.

Thirdly, concerning the 'synastry' exercise 2, on Richard Burton and Elizabeth Taylor, we see that her Sun at Epoch is quincunx his Sun at Birth. Their relationship may have arisen through the necessity of both of them having to have earned their living in the same establishment. As Elizabeth's Uranus at Birth is quincunx to Richard's Saturn, also at Birth, both partners may have had difficult problems to solve before they could have felt truly at ease in each other's company. Possibly, Richard would have felt ill-at-ease when faced with Elizabeth's independence and lack of conformity – a noticeable lack of sympathy may have developed between them. Elizabeth may have shocked Richard's sense of propriety, and yet may have succeeded in helping him to adopt a more modern, original life style. In time, he may have lost confidence in his sense of timing, and she may have felt that her talent for on-the-spot improvisation was being wasted. Richard may have wanted to assess Elizabeth's worth, but his method of testing her could have proved rather irksome. He may have become demanding, but would have displayed integrity in the partnership, and his reliability would have challenged her to show a reciprocal dependability. On the other hand, he may have felt that his methods were cumbersome and less effective than hers, thereby causing him to try to overhaul his methods to see if he could have made improvements. Something about her presence may have proved unsettling to him and he may have sensed that her attitude towards him was rather critical, even though not verbally expressed. Thus, there may have been a tendency for Elizabeth to have set Richard's nerves on edge. The quincunx link between their Suns can pose problems as it indicates that one partner may have to nurse the other, or shoulder some of the other's burdens. One, or both, partners may have been challenged to transform some of their long-established attitudes and habits. Elizabeth may have become uncomfortably aware of a character defect that could only have been rectified satisfactorily by some kind of transcendent change in herself. Conversely, she may have challenged him, perhaps unwittingly, to have become conscious of some hidden motive for action that he had not been aware of previously. And so, he may have found that she had been the means of effecting some kind of transformation in himself that had made him a more complete and integrated person. However, the element of change may have become a crucial issue in their partnership, and an agreement upon the drastic elimination of those factors that were mutually irritating, may have become essential, if the partnership was to have survived. At the same time, we see that Elizabeth's Venus at Birth is also quincunx Richard's Sun at Birth. On occasion, she may have led him on, only to withdraw favours at the last minute. Hurt feelings and emotional disappointment could have resulted from Richard's wounded pride, while Elizabeth may have felt that Richard was too dictatorial.

Stressfully, Elizabeth's Uranus at Epoch is square to Richard's Jupiter at Birth. This suggests that she may have resorted to erratic action to break-up his irritating air of complacency, provoking him into behaving unwisely. Although considerable attraction was indicated, any unduly experimental attitude on the part of either, may have led to undesirable complications. Alternatively, Richard may have been in a position to render Elizabeth valuable service, and have taken pleasure in such an activity. In addition, he may have been able to introduce her to societies and organisations dedicated to the furtherance of some cherished ideal, or to have put her in touch with a wide variety of friends. Yet, at some other time, he may have had cause for concern regarding her health. Generally, he would have been likely to have taken an interest in her welfare and well-being.

Conversely, she also was likely to have taken much pleasure in rendering him various services. Richard may even have been willing to allow Elizabeth to assume a senior status, who would then have acknowledged some sort of obligation to see that his interests would have been looked after.

Additionally and favourably, Elizabeth's Jupiter at Epoch is trine to Richard's Uranus at Birth. She would have encouraged any originality and inventive ability that Richard displayed and would have been tolerantly disposed towards any manifestations of independence that he may have shown. He may have supplied the creative originality, while she could have afforded the required finance. Possibly, then, Richard would have become the sudden recipient of Elizabeth's bounty. She may have been able to make improvements to his status and have given him a taste for success. Besides, she would have appreciated the aims he had in mind. In return, Richard may have proved instrumental in causing Elizabeth to review her whole philosophy of life. Also, he may have stimulated in her, a greater interest in foreign countries and in travel abroad.

Moreover, Elizabeth's Pluto at Birth is favourably trine to Richard's Uranus at Epoch. She may have found herself attracted to Richard by some potentiality that he seemed to possess that would not have been immediately apparent to others. Elizabeth could have assisted Richard to express his originality more dramatically. Overall, she may have supported his objectives and spurred him on to greater efforts.

If these two talented, intelligent people, could have understood themselves, and each other, somewhat better and impartially, and had made determined allowances for each other, then surely they could have created a more lasting and significant partnership. Clearly, they had become very close to achieving this.

Finally, concerning the 'synastry' exercise 1) for the Duke and Duchess of Windsor, we see that Wallis's Sun at Epoch is square to his Jupiter at Birth. Often a Sun/Jupiter cross-aspect is found between the charts of marriage partners. Good fellowship, generosity of spirit, much mutual respect, appreciation and encouragement is promoted even when the cross-aspect is a stressful square, as in this case. Here, each would have recognised the good intentions of the other, and would have wished to put-forth their best efforts on their partner's behalf. They would have been more tolerant towards his/her shortcomings. The Duke may have known how to enhance Wallis's self-esteem, and she was likely to have shown him favouritism. Her Sun, 'relocated' to his 5th House, would have been good for friendship and Wallis would have had the capacity to bring joy into the Duke's life. She would have taken pleasure in his affectionate responses. He may have been the person to whom she was most likely to turn, in times of trouble. For example, there may have been some difficulties in their relationship, since he may have expected her to be reliable and self-sufficient in those very areas where she was likely to have been the most vulnerable. Then he may have worked behind the scenes to strengthen her position. He could have been able to show her how to cope with any deficiencies in her character that may have involved her in disconcerting situations. He would have restored her faith in herself. However, their partnership may have had to guard against scandal.

At the same time, Wallis's Sun's semi-sextile connection with his Saturn at Birth, as well as Wallis's Saturn at Birth being semi-sextile to his Sun at Epoch, i.e. they both shared this cross-aspect and type, although the House 'relocation' positions are different. Hence, the institution of marriage would have seemed attractive to both of them as they both may have lacked sufficient independence of spirit to contemplate with ease, the task of facing the World alone. In both cases, both of their roles could have been to provide a reliable anchor for each other's ship. She may have felt indebted to him, which could have been repaid most suitably on a material basis. She may have been the means of showing him how to build-up and to improve his resources. On the other hand, her cautious and fearful advice may have caused him to lose good opportunities. Conversely, she may, at times, have needed to shelter him, thereby making testing demands on her own sympathetic and charitable instincts. Additionally, she may have been a source of inspiration to him in his search for a vital philosophy of life. In this regard, she may have set him a good example, and have become a mentor to him. Alternatively, the Duke may have been able to offer Wallis some kind of service. She could have rested assured that she could have relied on his aid, even though he may have called on her to return the compliment because he was likely to have valued her services as well. His whole-hearted support may have encouraged her to function as efficiently as she could.

Wallis's Venus at Epoch was in opposition to the Duke's Mars at Birth. This cross-aspect is a primary indicator of compatibility at the physical level. In marriage, the contact between these two planets indicates a ready response to each other's animal magnetism. There is mutual reception between these two planets to strengthen this bond. However, he may have tended to force the pace too much, while she may have been too highly selective about bestowing her favours, so that some stress may have occurred in the relationship.

The Duke may have been able to keep Wallis on her toes. He could have proved a courageous advocate for her cause, but he would have expected her to display some degree of independence and self-sufficiency. However, his activities may have made too many demands on her through his continual sense of urgency that led him always to be pressing for quick results. And yet, she may have had a particularly beneficial effect upon him, not only in relation to material things, but also emotionally and spiritually. Her sense of values would have made her particularly aware of his good qualities, giving him a feeling of well-being. She would have been likely to have gone out-of-her-way to assist him. A very good understanding would have existed between them.

Wallis's Neptune at Birth was conjoint the Duke's Jupiter at Birth. This particularly felicitous aspect means that each would have sympathetically appreciated the aspirations of the other, so that Wallis could have brought a feeling of rich fulfilment to the Duke, which could have extended to the material plane resulting in financial benefit. As both planets are expansive in action, they can lead to exaggerations when operating in the realm of human relationships. The Duke would have been encouraged to "show-off" in front of Wallis, and Wallis to "play-act" before him. Wallis's personality would have encouraged the Duke to take a benevolent interest in her resulting in the formation of a rewarding friendship. She would have received favours from him and his company would always have put her in a good humour, so that she felt completely relaxed with him. They would have shared common aspirations and a respect for each other's qualities. She may have done him a favour by providing an outlet for his altruistic instincts. Also, she may have been able to increase his artistic vision and have added a subtle new dimension to his creative powers. She may have inspired him to display his personality more dramatically, and have brought a new sense of idealism to those activities nearest to his heart. She could have challenged him to live up to the highest romantic ideals. He may have developed a greater intuitive recognition of the fact that he was the object of someone's affection, and have taught him to elevate and to refine the nature of his own affection.

Finally, Wallis's Moon at Birth was trine to the Duke's Pluto at Birth. The Duke would have had a hypnotic effect on Wallis, and she would have recognised some deep quality of being in him, which attracted her, since the two planets are in harmonious cross-aspect. Her womanly instincts would have become intensified. The Duke may have understood Wallis's moods and feelings instinctively. However, this could have proved a very damaging weapon, had he ever chosen to use it.

Wallis would have been attracted to the Duke by the way he projected himself, and by his general attitude to the whole area of creative and pleasurable activities. Emotions would have become involved and affections displayed. Wallis was likely to have proved to be an appreciative audience for the Duke, encouraging him to show his talent, and enjoying his sense of humour. In turn, she may have been able to appeal to his sense of the dramatic, and to have assisted him in the process of his self-dramatization. Usually, this link is the signature of a happy association and so the Duke may have become able to cultivate an ability to evoke a sympathetic response from an audience.

The Duke may have been able to make Wallis aware of some latent creative talents that he may have enabled her to develop with dramatic effect, either by example, or by suggestion. If Wallis had found that her passions were becoming unduly involved (with others as well as with the Duke) then she may have become compelled to transform her whole attitude and approach to affairs of the heart.

Interestingly, Wallis has eight planets in her 1st Houses (of the person); four at Epoch (Mars, Venus, Mercury and Chiron) and four at Birth (Pluto, Mercury, Neptune and Venus). We find that there are seven cross-aspects from the Duke's planets to Wallis's 1st House planets at Epoch, and eight of them to her 1st House planets at Birth. This means that there are fifteen 'relocations' of the Duke's planets (out of 22 in all) to Wallis's 1st Houses. In fact, every different planet in a chart (11 of them) has been 'relocated' into her 1st House at least once. The Duke's Jupiter, Pluto, Venus and Saturn are 'relocated' there twice. Surely, all these 'relocations' to Wallis's 1st Houses must have comprised an overriding factor when considering his love and devotion for her, which may well have been more than enough for him to have preferred abdication rather than to have given Wallis up. Conversely, the Duke has three planets (the Moon twice and Chiron) in his 1st Houses, to which Wallis's Mars, Sun and Saturn make cross-aspects with his two Moons, and so can be considered to be 'relocated' to the Duke's 1st House. However, only three of all these cross-aspects to 1st Houses can be taken to be exact (see Table 5). Nevertheless, their cumulative influence/strength must still have been considerable.

From the results of the four 'synastry' exercises, we can conclude tentatively that there are several related ways for love to form. There are, for example, the general considerations of the separate natal charts being favourable enough, there are the favourable cross-aspects, and there are favourable 'relocations'.

For the 'synastry' exercises for Richard Burton and Elizabeth Taylor, plus that between the Duke and Duchess of Windsor, we see that the exact cross-aspect interpretations almost provide a reasonable précis for the longer, more complete descriptions presented in Chapters 2 and 3. Presumably, the results of further 'synastry' exercises (acceptable and natural birth data permitting) will modify and improve our conclusions here, but the author submits that we have made a useful and promising start.

APPENDIX

Seven Person Summaries/Character Portraits/Personalities

- -

EDWARD, DUKE OF WINDSOR

*"I have found it impossible to carry the heavy
burden of responsibility and to discharge my
duties as king as I would wish to do, without
the help and support of the woman I love."*
Broadcast, 11th December, 1936.

Edward VIII was King of the United Kingdom
and the Dominions of the British Empire, and
Emperor of India, from January, 1936 until his
abdication in December that same year. He was
created Prince of Wales on his sixteenth birthday,
nine weeks after his father succeeded as king.
As a young man, he served in the British Armed
Forces during World War I and undertook several
overseas tours on behalf of his father.

Edward became king on his father's death
in early 1936. He showed impatience with court
protocol, and caused concern among politicians
by his apparent disregard for established
constitutional conventions. Only months into
his reign, he caused a constitutional crisis by
proposing marriage to Wallis Simpson, an
American who had divorced her first husband
and was seeking divorce from her second. The
Prime Ministers of the United Kingdom and
the Dominions opposed the marriage, arguing
that the people would never accept a divorced
woman with two living ex-husbands as queen
consort. Additionally, such a marriage would

have conflicted with Edward's status as the titular head of the Church of England, which, at the time, opposed the remarriage of divorced people if their former spouses were still alive. Edward knew that the British government, led by Prime Minister Stanley Baldwin, would resign if the marriage went ahead, which could have forced a general election and would have ruined his status as a politically neutral constitutional monarch. Choosing not to end his relationship with Wallis Simpson, Edward abdicated. He was succeeded by his younger brother Albert, who chose the regnal name of George VI. With a reign of 326 days, Edward was one of the shortest reigning monarchs in British history.

After his abdication, he was created Duke of Windsor. He married Wallis Simpson in France in June, 1937, after her second divorce had become final. Later that year, the couple toured Germany. During World War II, he was at first stationed with the British Military Mission to France but after private accusations that he held Nazi sympathies, he was assigned to the Bahamas as the islands' governor. After the war, he was never given another official appointment and spent the remainder of this life in retirement, in France.

- -

Edward was the first son and child of King George V and Queen Mary (of Teck). He was born on the

23rd June, 1894 NS at 21:36, in Richmond, Surrey, U.K. (see Figure 2). His Epoch occurred on the 6th October, 1893 NS, at 03:08 (see Figure 1).

Character Portrait

<u>General:</u> Edward's nature was at one with itself – there was no rift. He had practical ambitions combined with a self-controlled, good disposition that was patient, persevering, dignified and orderly. His strong spiritual and refined tendencies brought balance and harmony. He showed poetic and musical ability and either his artistic, or moral nature, would have had many opportunities for development. There was an intense love of beauty and dancing as well as great enthusiasm in pursuit of an ideal. He was inclined to good-living and greedy for the good things of life. Interest was shown in the sea, in mysticism and in hidden things, which would have been pursued with energy and with a desire to experiment in new ways. Truly, he was sympathetic, dreamy, quiet, humane and very hospitable. His pleasing personality and convincing manners were both agreeable and entertaining.

Edward had a strong emotional nature that contained strong feelings and impulses. His emotional response tended to be galvanic and intense. There was independent behaviour, a love of freedom and a hatred of interference. His moods tended to be changeable, suddenly resulting in an ability to throw off the static and start new receptive ways. Also, he was fond of sensation and of novelty. Certainly, he had much energy but it was apt to sway first one way and then another. However, he expressed it with gaiety, fun and humour, although this could have been teasingly caustic. He was not likely to have passed unnoticed!

On the other hand, Edward's general nature was also soft, yielding and passive and so more likely to suffer than to act, to be timid, retiring and given to forebodings. Although constant, methodical and compassionate, he was also a person who tended to consume without producing.

More negatively, at times, Edward was assertive, then pugnaciously aggressive and finally explosive so likely to end conditions and force new beginnings. Possibly vindictive, he was also very proud, stubborn, jealous and even deceitful. Being excessively self-willed, he showed blind zeal in unconventional and expansive ways. His situation could well have been big and free enough for all this to have found vent, but if not, then he would have rebelled resentfully. He showed tendencies to squander gains, to be extravagant and to trust to luck too easily. On the other hand, there was also limitation to his self-expression, possibly through his father, resulting in his becoming separative and possibly even cowardly.

<u>Mentality:</u> Edward's mind was powerful, courageous, active and enterprising yet also sensitive. He was mainly subjective with a strong inclination to spiritual things that sometimes made his nature too idealistic. His personality could have been a studious one, fond of learning, of knowledge and devoted to books and reading. However, he had feelings of inadequacy in affairs connected with communication and with general mental interests. In any case, quick wittedness and adaptability would have been outstanding characteristics. Generally, Edward's mind was jovial, optimistic and contented with a good nervous system. There would have been width of mind rather than a good grasp of detail, in which mental inflation may have led to some conceit.

Edward would have been accustomed to basing his philosophies of life on the ideas of other people. Thus, he learned unconsciously to become separated from his own truth while his philosophical values and ideas became strongly influenced by those who surrounded him. He absorbed ideas from one individual after another, without fully understanding what was true for him. Restless while taking in other people's truths, he would have become anxious to redistribute every piece of information he had learned, to those he was about to meet. He gave out much information, along with misinformation, because he did not take the time to sort it out for himself.

Edward was able to overcome his natural caution, but not always, during which he became highly introspective. In between these two periods, he lived through a high degree of frustration amounting almost to paralysis in action, because he kept questioning the value of all that he would like to do, measuring it up against the great scope of his wisdom/experience. He kept feeling the impetus towards action for action's sake. Thus, he was either not acting, but wishing he was, or, acting and wishing he wasn't.

Edward had latent genius, a clever mind and some original talent. His high standard of intellect would have shown intellectual interests and would have been particularly attracted by new and unusual theories. He would have had refined tastes with clear discrimination. This refinement combined with his adaptability would have allowed him to express his emotions through intellectual means. However, his fixed opinions were not easily altered, his intuitions could have been fanciful so that he would have seemed eccentric, sometimes undecided as well as vacillating.

Edward was enormously inventive and usually could have displayed rare genius in the understanding of how to do things that no-one else around him could comprehend. Ideally, he was learning lessons of self-discipline so that all of the inner inventiveness he felt, could have been put to use in the present world he lived in. He had to have learned how to be different without upsetting the structures he ultimately wished to improve.

Edward's occult, mystical and clairvoyant faculties may have been awakened. His tendencies towards the intangible resulted in strong imaginative capabilities such as visions, ideals and boundless aims. These would have been of the most ethereal and inspirational kind but strength would have been needed from elsewhere in his character to actualise them. Edward's receptive mind and responsive nervous system produced mediumistic tendencies with a desire to obtain this kind of knowledge. His psychic faculties were capable of development and he would have developed an internal knowledge of the public mind and its requirements. He could have reached an awareness of the world within himself. He didn't kid himself, or live in illusions, but rather took great pride in seeing things the way they really were. However, his vivid imagination could have been gullible and confused so that his mind may not have been that well-directed. Resulting touchiness would have induced escapism and his mind may have schemed in an involved way. Action may have come from intuition rather than from reason. Even though his memory was good, his mind was subject to his emotions. He had to have tried to play down these emotions, and to have relied more on evidence before he acted. Fortunately, his mind threw off worries and began new thought but unfortunately, over-violently and explosively so resulting in great nerve strain that, in turn, led to irritability and disruptive behaviour.

<u>Lifestyle:</u> Edward had a great capacity to enjoy life, basically because he was well-integrated. It was reassuring for him that he could always have found enjoyable ways of satisfying his needs. He was impulsive and enthusiastic where his own projects were concerned, but this would have been found to be for appearances only. He would have been almost entirely self-motivated and very difficult to move, either by persuasion or argument, being in reality, surprisingly stubborn except where his own enthusiasms were concerned. He <u>was</u> impulsive, but his impulses came from within, and would not have been the result of contact from without (but see Career: Vocation).

During Edward's life, he had to have learned to focus his ideas and likes, and to observe how other people used them. Often he was an observer of other people's lives flowing through him. This caused him frustration until he had learned to settle into a practical outlook on life. However, he did not live the philosophy of that he spoke. In his communication with others he did not like to commit himself to such a philosophy. Also, he became uncomfortable when someone tried to pin him down to any specific philosophy. He would have become defensive of his ideas and attitudes because he had been struggling long and hard to build them. He liked being in control, and actually had to be, in order to live out his ideal state of standing for what he believed, regardless of any opposition.

His entire life could have stood for one attitude or idea that had come from some shining achievement early on in his life.

Edward desired to present an honourable image to the world, while at the same time maintaining his complete freedom of thought and action. Often, he would have changed his direction rather than exert himself because of his great need for expediency. He saw clearly the conflict between what he thought the world expected of him and how he himself would truly have liked to have been. This caused him to become a creature of extremes, vacillating between too much and too little self-assertiveness.

Edward sought an inner sense of identity, which afforded him a uniqueness of character within the framework of the society in which he lived. He experienced the conflict of compromising his individuality in order to keep himself in a position from which he could ultimately have expressed it more. Of course, he would have had problems, but he could always have found ways to resolve them satisfactorily. Yet overmuch careless optimism when caution was calling, would have produced unhappiness and guilty conscience. Similarly, overmuch limitation of what he conceived to be his way of self-expression and self-gratification brought exaggerated depression, possibly leading to tragic results.

In whatever Edward did, he was an extremist, never settling for a middle-of-the-road approach to life. His energy level was high and quite intense, because when he knew the truth, he wouldn't have been about to let others dissuade him from whatever independent course of action he had chosen to embark on. He assimilated the immediate needs of his environment and from this was able to understand how to cope with all that was going on around him. Still, there was a tendency for him to be a little out-of-time synchronisation, particularly when future needs met with the qualities of the past. In blending these two, he needed to do much work to gain a balanced perspective in time.

Edward understood much of what the rest of his society didn't even know existed. Ideally, he was living his life in order to play a very active role in shaping the world he lived in. He was not about to sit back and complain about all that he saw that was wrong around him; but rather, he would have been one of the leaders in transforming human consciousness. But he had to have had enough room to follow his creative instincts without having to be forced into pressures of responsibility. Yet he handled responsibility beautifully, when he was not aware that he was doing it!

Relationships

<u>Others:</u> Edward presented a favourable image and most people found him to be easy to know, and to be comfortable with. He was happy when he was a host. However, he judged people by their physical assets, paying little attention to their human qualities. But possibly, he was also hurtful to others. In fact, this may have extended to a headstrong disregard for their feelings. He would have been too pre-occupied with himself and should have directed some of his energy towards others, with whom he had to have worked to establish a place for himself in society. He had to have been appreciative when others had helped him to achieve his goals. Also, he had to have decided how much he owed to others, and how much he owed to himself; but he hadn't to have compromised, unless there was no alternative, either. Additionally, he had to have distinguished between the truths expressed by others; those he should have adopted from those which he should have disregarded as not being applicable. Most of all, he had to have learned not to force people to think as he did, because his biggest problem was his tendency to believe that his attitudes worked best for those he thought he had to teach. On the other hand, he hadn't to have deprived himself of something because others had made him feel obligated to them. That was slavery, not loyalty.

<u>Friends</u>: Edward made much effort to obtain companionship so that new friends were made often. He became popular and had many friends because he was sociable, hopeful and generous.

<u>Family:</u> Edward's home matters were happy. They were harmonious and delightful, and family relationships were smooth and loving, especially with his parents. He showed to advantage in the family circle more than he did in public life. However, his relationship with his mother became uneasy. There may well have developed a cleavage in his life relating to his parents, or to his early childhood, leading to a lack of harmony in his home. Pleasure should have been taken in domestic matters but inharmonious parental relationships would have developed, contrary to his wishes. He showed feelings of inadequacy in affairs to do with siblings and close neighbours, and there may have been trouble through his brothers. Yet his family ties may have remained so strong that they deprived him of a life of his own.

Edward had a desire for the unusual and unconventional in his own home. Pleasure would have been taken there in furnishing, decoration and in the arrangement of pictures and flowers, etc.

[Edward would have hoped to encourage his children to take advantage of the opportunities he provided so that they, too, would have reached their goals. He knew that his children would have benefitted greatly, if he had shown them how to take advantage of the resources he had worked so hard to provide. His children would have been inspired by his accomplishments.]

<u>Lover:</u> Edward's love tended to be intense, sexual, sincere, secretive and passionate, but also inconstant. He was wary of people who showed a romantic interest in him and he studied these contacts carefully to learn people's motivations for wanting to become aligned with him. He knew that he had to resist those who tried to control him, but he didn't want to hurt his loved ones. On the other hand, he offered kindness and even gifts to those who showed an interest in him, especially when he was attracted to a particular person. He would have done anything to win the love of someone who seemed sincerely interested and he would have been able to keep his partner's attention.

On a personal level, Edward went through many sexual changes in his life. During one period, he may have been seeking all kinds of excitement that he had not yet experienced, while during another, he may have turned to complete celibacy.

Edward's sense of lack intensified his shyness and prevented an easy response to what could have brought happiness. Duty, or some form of limitation, stopped the full expression of his love and harmony, but the duty appeared to be acceptable, or less heavy, because of some happiness that it brought. His partner would have been often older than he was, and his marriage may have been long delayed.

Edward was slow to make partnerships but reliable once settled. He would have been steadfast in love, but overly possessive. Although he was not inclined towards marriage, and may have preferred a celibate life, it was difficult for him, as a person, to remain single, so that he was apt to marry too much in haste, and then repent afterwards. His need to share his life would have made him vulnerable to anyone who gave him attention.

Career

Early: Edward's destiny was in his own hands and he would have been lucky. His fate was affected by marriage, or love affairs, which would have played a major role in his life, and may have brought him a rise in his social status. However, there would have been loss and trouble through misconception, through errors in judgement, through removals and fruitless travel, and through education. Also, dishonour, loss of credit, difficulties with superiors, scandal, ill-repute and trouble with his profession are all indicated.

Edward was more talented than the average person, and developing his talents into skills should have been the main priority of his early years. He had a positive outlook on life and he asserted himself in exploiting his creativity so that he could have succeeded, if he had applied himself with determination. Security was his most important consideration, and he put a lot of energy into acquiring the necessities of life, to have an advantage over those who lacked them. Once he had established a goal, and had committed himself to reaching it, nothing could have deterred him from it. He believed that there was no limit to what he could have done, if he had put his mind to it. He worked at developing his creative skills so as to attract attention from the right people. He would have succeeded in earning a comfortable living by using his skills creatively with imagination. He was an admirable worker, and when allowed to go his own way, would have managed things excellently, putting his 'heart' into all that he did, and he did everything in a way that could only have been described as 'thorough'.

However, it would have been difficult for Edward to get started, so that there may have been considerable delay before he could have realised his ambitions and have gained the security and stability he wanted. The basic problem was that his emotional nature frequently distracted him; he assumed that others were more qualified than he was, which was not true at all. It wasn't easy for him to gain the career position he wanted, because he wasn't really sure that he could have achieved it on his own. Any nagging doubts about his ability to succeed should have been resolved as soon as possible. Breaking ties with his past would have been difficult, but necessary, if he was to have become self-sufficient. He was a late starter because of his lack of organisation and self-discipline. Instead of dawdling, he had to have invested some of his time and energy that was needed to derive the maximum yield from his creative output. Because he didn't really believe that he could have failed, he may have neglected to develop his creativity to ensure success. But developing his creativity would have helped to raise his credibility. With training, he would have learned to appreciate his enormous creativity, which would have allowed him to succeed in his professional and personal relationships. He owed it to himself to have invested in his own development. Even though he knew the importance of education for his career, he may not have been willing to apply himself, and to have worked hard. There were many lessons to learn, and there were no free rides. Realising that his rise to prominence would have required a great deal of creative effort, he tried to utilise all his talent to achieve it.

Edward had to have been wary of people who suggested that he was destined to serve the needs of others, thereby neglecting his own top-priority needs. He should have become established in his career before he had thought about a permanent relationship. He could not have afforded to deal with emotional distress while trying to stay focused on the demands of his career. He had to have learned to stand on his own with the positive affirmation that he could and would have succeeded. He could have profited by developing his talent to gain his objectives. Also, he had to have broadened his perspectives, and have learned that there were other facets to life besides money and material assets. He had to have taken advantage of his creative ideas and not to have underestimated their value. He may have expected others to open doors for him, but with the proper training, he could have opened them himself.

Edward had a wealth of ideas that only needed to be promoted to be useful. He wanted to invest in his ideas because he knew that they would have brought him excellent returns for a long time. He was wise enough to get advice about investing for the future, and he prided himself on achieving his goals ethically. With his dramatic sense, and if he had made certain of his information before expressing himself, he would have won the trust, the support and the assistance he needed, to fulfil his desires and goals. He could have become financially successful and so eventually have achieved independence from those who fulfilled his needs.

But probably, Edward had some emotional insecurity about his effectiveness and was concerned that the public wouldn't have appreciated what he did. The two great deterrents to his success were smug satisfaction and the fact that he would rather have indulged in pleasurable activities than to have applied his energy to the outward expression of his creativity. Edward required lots of money to satisfy his desires. Although life was rigorous and/or hard, lessons of duty and self-control were learned. He came to over-value the practical, and had a tendency to meet hardships. Instead of feeling sorry for himself, he had to have uncovered his hidden talents and have put them to good use. Also, he should have learned to like himself for his achievements.

<u>Vocation:</u> Edward had a strong sense of lack, or of a need, or of a problem to be solved, or of a task to be achieved, in the social and intellectual world around him. He had a self-driving individuality, i.e. an executive eccentricity, which was neither queerness nor unbalance, but rather was of power. He was moved more by external factors in his environment (but see opposite interpretation under Lifestyle) than from within. His desires were towards achieving good through unusual objectives. The combination of initiative with will-power, in unusual ways, could have produced unusual results. He may have changed his direction many times until he had found that special niche where truly he would have been able to express himself.

Edward would have been happier if he had been self-employed, so that the pressure of competition could have been deferred until he had gained more self-confidence. Communication would have taken place in affairs connected with day-to-day work, especially if secretarial, commercial or educational, or also in matters of health. Then he would have thrived on proving that he offered a better product, or service, than his competitors. His connection with the sea could have resulted in work as a ship's engineer, etc. He would have tended towards success in businesses connected with liquids, particularly.

Edward's self-worth was determined by his effectiveness in serving the needs of others. He wanted the kind of career position in which people would have sought his professional services. He was stimulated and encouraged by knowing that others relied on him when they needed assistance. He would have been good for a career in advertising and mass communication, through which he could have had his versatility along with the security he needed.

Edward's energy could also have found good expression in financial affairs, and possibly in agricultural ones, too.

Middle: Edward's superiors and colleagues thought well of him and depended on him to solve their problems. He got along with them because he didn't threaten them, and because they were usually impressed by the way he used his abilities to help them to achieve their objectives. They knew that they could have depended on him to give everything to his job, because, in general, he liked his work. On the other hand, he was wary about forming close attachments with his associates.

Edward was impatient to achieve and often was more interested in the final results than in the steps that would have taken him there. He was ambitious, and he knew how to cultivate friendly relations with important people to win promotion and increased earnings. He hated to back-track over ground he had already covered, and yet, at times, particularly in relation to his career, he had to have done so in order to have picked up the incomplete pieces of what he had left behind.

When Edward was allowed to live and work on a day-to-day basis, he did much better than when he was confronted by any project that involved a great amount of long-range plans. Yet he was very capable of developing such plans, as long as he didn't see these as boxing-in his future. He was fortunate in his material results because opportunities arose for the use of enthusiasm and energy. His major problem was getting involved in matters that were beyond his ability to handle, i.e. too much at a time. 'Prudence' should have been his watchword. Although much may have been achieved, his tendency was to over-strain through over-doing. Success may have been achieved but at much cost of hard work, or of personal hardship, and may have been long-delayed. On the other hand, he was especially gratified when his creative talents were appreciated and when he could have applied them as he thought best.

Edward had to try and get away from his daily routine, now and then, to replenish his energy and enthusiasm. His career took a lot out of him both physically and mentally, so he had to have learned to stay within his limits. He had to have learned to relax and to take time to unwind from the demands of his occupation. He owed it to himself to have developed good living habits and to have got enough exercise to keep his body in top condition, at all times.

Late: Edward should have thought about becoming independent so that he could have sustained himself during his later years and to have reached the goals that he had chosen. He had to have found time to accept reality and to have learned to use his creative imagination to build tangible assets for his later years.

Appearance and Health

Appearance: Edward would have been of average height, strong and well-formed with a square build of figure tending to stoutness/plumpness later. He would have had a fearless demeanour, bold and free, but not elastic movement. Also, the lower portion of his body may not have been well-shaped, so that he was somewhat clumsy in movement, with an indifferent walk and possibly with feet pointing apart, reminding one of a fish's tail. He would have had a long but round face and round forehead with a good, dark complexion but also possibly soft and unfavourable, with a strange opalescent, or mother-of-pearl, taint and lustre. His features may not have been perfectly formed, e.g. his mouth may have been generally loose and ill-finished. He may also have been good-looking! His eyes would have been soft, dark and mild with hair that could have been anywhere between light and dark. His voice would have been powerful, but also, just possibly, discordant.

<u>Health:</u> Edward would have had good health in general. Although his nervous system was strong, hence good eyesight, hearing and sense of touch, there was a liability to nervous disorders. A tendency to excessive irritability must have been controlled, if psychological ill-health was to have been avoided. He could have become pugnacious and ill-tempered. His explosiveness would have resulted in nervous stress. There was also some liability to hysteria. Overmuch worry could have caused intestinal trouble. His bowels were likely to have given trouble, causing him to suffer from spasms, colic, dysentery or chronic constipation. There was a liability to dropsical complaints and to other chronic irregularities of his system. Also, there was a liability to blood infections, paralysis and to accidents. However, he would have been a good sleeper!

- -

Reference: 'King Edward VIII. The Official Biography', P. Ziegler, Harper Press, London, U.K., 2012 Edition.

- -

WALLIS, DUCHESS OF WINDSOR

*"You have no idea how hard it is to
live out a great romance."*

Wallis was an American socialite, who lived with her mother, Alice Montague. Edward, Duke of Windsor, formerly King Edward VIII, abdicated in order to marry her.

Wallis's father, Teackle Warfield, had died shortly after her birth in 1896. In 1916, she married Earl Spencer, but divorced in 1927. In 1928, she married Ernest Spenser, but divorced again in 1937, whereupon she married the Duke of Windsor. She remained married to him until his death in 1972.

Their decision to marry had created a constitutional crisis in the United Kingdom. Edward had been created Duke of Windsor by his younger brother, and successor, King George VI.

Wallis was born on 19th June, 1896 at 05:05 E.S.T. at Blue Ridge Summit, U.S.A. (see Figure 4). She was an only child. Her Epoch occurred on 11th September, 1895 at 07:36 E.S.T. (see Figure 3).

Character

General: On balance, Wallis came across as a mixture of opposites. She had great potentiality based on a robust and capable personality. Her energy levels were high, but with gaiety, fun and humour; but these could tend to be teasingly caustic. At times, she was likely to be very assertive, aggressive, impetuous, courageous and pugnacious; hence anything but affable, and so hurtful to others. She could seem to be self-sufficient and sensation seeking with a craving for adventure, but also foolhardy, avaricious and hard. Her unusualness was expressed in emotional ways, and with an independent strength of feeling, that tended to be both dramatic and galvanic. Still, much of this could have been controlled.

On the other hand, Wallis displayed reserve, along with a lack of enterprise, but she had good critical and judicial ability. Her manner appeared to be cautious, and seemed to be more limited than she really was. Duty, conscience and orderliness were important, and there may have been a tendency to be timid (if not shy and retiring) through a feeling of personal inadequacy. She may have shown a rapid, elusive smile, together with many quaint conceits and she may have been fond of nonsense verses and leariques. Her self-expression, though limited, occurred in a noble, dignified, loyal, high-minded and good-hearted way. She tended to respond well through the reception of ideas and influences. However, at her worst, she may have been exposed to temptation, to escapism, to deceitfulness, or to have become the object of treachery.

And yet her moods and ways could be changeful in an acceptable way, since new phases in life were liked. The sympathetic side of her nature, her love of approval and her general adaptation became accentuated. As an amiable, optimistic personality, she delighted in the company of both friends and casual acquaintances. Affable, cheerful, good-natured, humane-loving, musical and really artistic, she was fond of society and amusement, showing herself to be refined with fine comparison. She had a good, balanced outlook with a sensitivity that was receptive to harmony, rhythm and beauty. She always tried to be pleasant, because she truly enjoyed people. Her very good disposition placed a high value on honesty, but detested mean, or unjust actions. Thus, she was loving, free, just and merciful. Friendship and hospitality became marked features.

Mentality: Being both objective and subjective, with a quick and active mentality, Wallis had good, general ability that brought forth keenly, all her mental expressions. She had good, common-sense and nervous force. Her personality was quick-witted, able and swift to learn, seeking knowledge wherever it may have been found. Literature and science would have been equally attractive. She was naturally curious and eager to be involved in a variety of situations. Interesting, magnetic, rebellious and original, she was also poetical and musical but always with wit and fluency of speech.

She was very intellectually disposed but this often showed in an imaginative, artistic, or somewhat psychic direction, rather than as pure intellect. There was much foresight, sharpened perception and developed comparison with inclinations to be greatly imitative.

Yet Wallis's self-expression was somewhat hurtfully limited. Her tendency was to express herself through her affections, beauty, art and gentle ways. Through her receptive foresight, she had opportunities to blend head and heart, reason and intuition. Even her philanthropy was given a good balance, easily. Yet, basically, Wallis's mind was directed towards herself. Her communication was expressed in personal affairs rationally and coolly, but also with charm of speech and manner. She clearly enjoyed friendly discussion, and all beautiful objects of contemplation. In fact, she was often inspired and imaginative, but her intangibility could result in vagueness and muddles. With her mental intuition and receptive sensitivity, she was apt to create illusions, rather than to accept reality. She would have found it difficult to express herself here, and so would often have withdrawn to avoid unpleasantness. She had many ideas but poor fulfilment. She may have become deluded as to the realities of life through too much living in the clouds, lovely though this may have been. There became a tendency to avoid the concrete by day-dreaming. Even though her ideals, ideas and 'hunches' came easily, and were kept in bounds and given shape so that they became useful in this material World, yet mental limitation was still felt through difficulties that were hard to grasp, and so to come to terms with, or had to be kept hidden.

To help here, Wallis's mind threw of worries and began thought anew with good results in relief of nervous tension. Her deep concentration and inventiveness was used to satisfy her thirst for experience along with her search for novelty. Her obsession became mobility with a compelling need to achieve comprehension. She became egotistical, suspicious, inscrutable, sceptical, shrewd, mathematical, ingenious and dissimulating. As an idealist, she abhorred the injustices that prevailed in society.

Lifestyle: Wallis was extremely adept at acquiring anything that she might have set her mind upon. She was mostly at home when expectation ran at its highest. Even then, she tried to emphasise positivity to move herself on, into the future. But she also experienced her naturally negative, magnetic quality, through which she was expecting to be the receiver of love. She was restless, eager and when stimulated her aggressive nature sprang into action. It was the thrill of competition that made her accept challenges. She thrived on sensationalism and conflict. Yet she was also a lover of morality and respectability. Courteous, civil and obliging, she was one who delighted in doing-good for others. She loved justice and virtue in all their forms, so that there would have been gentle kindliness. She was very fond of learning, and of good company, so that generally, she was a fluent, eloquent and agreeable speaker, but although she was talkative, times of quiet and withdrawal, would also have been needed. Overall, her somewhat intensified sensitivity sought fulfilment, but, at the same time, she remained utopian.

When her thought was focused on the expectation of self-progress, she became impatient, with a tendency to jump to conclusions, which later needed correction. Then her behaviour took on a child-like quality, as many of her energies were redirected inward to a focus on herself. Not fully understanding how to focus her mental energies outward, she became a part of all that she thought that she projected. Thus, she experienced difficulty knowing where she ended, and where the outer World began. Like a child, she needed attention, but she didn't always know what to do with it, once she had it. She stampeded into situations only to retreat into herself, once she was there. Hence, her biggest problem was finding out who she really was, for she was sifting through a fate of constantly questioning her self-identity. And again, like a child, she was highly impatient to find out. Never waiting for the understanding of the World to come to her, she rushed out into it, to know all she could, yesterday! Yet still she had difficulty, measuring what she knew, even when she had found out what she thought she had been looking for.

Wallis had a mind that could take varied patterns, as wax takes on an imprint. Hence, her imagination would have been fertile. At times, she felt herself to be out-of-balance with her delicate need for centring. At other times, when she experienced a little of the past, along with the present, as well as with slight hints that in the future, she would be coming back to where she was now, she would have been more in harmony with her basic qualities. However, these spells would also have led her to her experiencing a strong feeling of non-direction.

Indecisiveness, in her thought processes, made her keep tipping the scale from one side to the other, so that people close to her, hardly understood what she stood for. Simultaneously, because she was not sure of the directions her decisions would take her in, she was always interested in knowing how people in her past would have approved, or not, of the decisions that she had made at that present time. Hence, she could have become extremely contrary, and possibly dishonest, i.e. she could well have tended to value tact and diplomacy above truth.

Still, she confused her thinking and feeling levels, and could have become fearful of self-expression. Often, she thought that by expressing herself, she would not have been accepted by those whose love she wanted. This could have led her to see the World through rose-tinted spectacles, with a leaning towards the avoidance of being personally responsible for her own thoughts. Overall, and as a result, she had difficulty knowing her own identity. But, interestingly, this is exactly what enabled her to become of great assistance in balancing others, as she, from moment to moment, put herself in one person's place, and then into that of another, so as to understand a situation from all possible points of view.

Relationships

<u>Others:</u> Wallis was popular because she attracted others, or the public in general, by sheer innate charm. She was genial, warm and affectionate. She always tried to be pleasant because she truly enjoyed people. Possibly, there was a tendency to be over-friendly, and to put too much trust in others, which could have led to trouble, if not restrained. Generally, her life was bound-up with others, even though she may have been a stranger in her own home through her own peculiar magnetic conditions. Her natural identity was to seek out the needs of others quietly, and in some fashion be useful enough to realise them. She won the approval of those around her by conceding to their desires, if she could. She was encouraging and helpful to others, as well as equable in affection. Concerning herself, however, she was one who

required to be treated courteously, because she was easily offended and then somewhat resentful.

On a very deep level, Wallis was not-at-all sure of what she really wanted for herself. She was in a constant state of change, trying to tune herself to whatever seemed fulfilling to others. Highly aware of the psychological games that society plays, she was, in fact, herself, one of the most skilful players. She liked others to let her live her own life, yet she could have become overly possessive of others, because she feared being left alone. This conflict could have caused many problems in areas of relationships (and even in marriage). There may well have been harshness from others. Her need for harmony, combined with her expression of unity within herself, could not tolerate being crossed for any great time period. Her greatest key to happiness would have been based on realistic self-acceptance.

<u>Friends and Acquaintances:</u> Again, warmth and enthusiasm entered into Wallis's relationships of affection. There was a keen delight in social intercourse, loving all that pertains to the social side of life. Her activity was rooted in the balancing of her value system through her relationships and only when she was sure of this, would she settle down, and truly stand for, the ideas she lived the most. She cultivated good relations with her friends because she was genuinely concerned about them, and she hoped that the concern was mutual.

Indeed, friends could have contributed much to her success in every sphere of life.

Friends and acquaintances were many, and much enjoyed, but somewhat limited. Wallis had an ability to make friends, but who lost them by being too pushy, or quarrelsome. Also, she tended to be brought into contact with those who were young and immature, so that there was a very basic, elemental direction to her self-development.

Family: Wallis was much concerned with relatives, especially brothers and sisters, uncles and aunts, or cousins. She lived sympathetically with family and relatives, and may have married a relative. Probably, she had a rare closeness with those she loved, in that she participated with them in their interests. This was sure to produce a tightly knit family group that appealed to her in every way. Probably, she experienced conflict with her parents, and, as an adult, kept thinking that she had to create harmony with them (in fact, she tried to do this with everyone she met). Wallis would have wanted the best for her children and she would have encouraged them to develop their own creative potential.

Lover: Wallis's partnerships were beneficial and very successful. Her love affairs were numerous and very happy. Once more, warmth and enthusiasm entered into relationships of affection in sexual life. She was sensuous and insouciant.

She was attracted by many, rather than 'the one'. Her ability to love, and to enjoy sexual life, and all things of beauty, was strengthened and made more robust, but less delicate. Inconstant in love, she had many 'dualities', love episodes, and was likely to have married twice, or to have carried on two amours simultaneously. Thus, her affection was changeable and often for more than one at a time. However, expression of it was charming and fluent. She had an attractive personality that liked to be 'spoilt', have plenty of amusement and social life. However, her intensified, easy charm may have been overdone. Troubles may have been caused by too many love affairs, and too much love of the beautiful, the easy and the pleasant, at any price. Her desire for partnership may have been overdone coupled with a restless lack of ability to be happy alone. Her unusualness was apt to be fascinating and compulsive, but less pleasantly. Partnerships were unconventional and likely to be broken, because of insistence on freedom. Hence, affections and partnerships were subject to disclosures, upheavals and to new starts. Partnerships may not have been what they seemed, and conditions, often, would have been kept hidden. Thus, partings were likely, through unhappy causes.

Wallis's love nature was polarised towards the higher emotions and was elevated to the plane of the mind. She was not necessarily a great giver of love, but she could have absorbed much love from others. She needed this to boost her self-confidence. She needed much attention and yet never quite felt fully fulfilled. There was much egocentricity as feelings of self-love ran much higher on the conscious, than on the unconscious, level. Underneath her constant seeking for more attention, she had much ambivalence about herself. Although she thought of herself as a creature of love, she tended not to understand just how much love to give out to others. She gave either too much, or not enough. Generally, the amount of love she experienced, in either giving or receiving, was inappropriate to the situation. In her love experiences, she kept emphasising her positive, or her negative, nature, more according to how she felt, rather than on, whether or not, circumstances, in her relationships with others, actually warranted these kinds of response.

For Wallis, there was gain and honour by marriage. Marriage and partnerships were likely to have brought her great material benefits. Her mate would have understood her hang-ups better than she did, and may have compensated when she had felt overwhelmed by difficult situations. He gave her strength when she weakened, courage when she faltered and encouragement when her enthusiasm wavered, and for this, she should have been grateful. By applying herself to the responsibilities of her career, she would have won her partner's respect.

At home, she came to feel more needed. Her concept of love was romantic, and depended more on ideas, or on things that people represent, than on the fulfilling of her own physical tastes and needs. Just possibly, she may have experimented with lesbianism, for unconventional reasons – and, in fact, there was usually an unconscious contrariness in nearly all that she did. She would have convinced herself that certain people couldn't have lived without her, when, actually, this was a projection of her own need, in reverse. She could have been happy by fulfilling herself with nearly anyone who suited her unconscious tastes, because truly, she never related to others, but merely divided herself in two, and then, using the other individual as a mirror to that part of her she wanted to identify with, at that moment, wound up making friends with, talking to, and yes, even making love to herself!

Career

Early: Wallis's destiny was very much in her own hands. Her fate depended upon her philosophical attitude, which decided, whether or not, she would have become a mere imitator, or copier, of others, or one who awakened her spiritual tendencies, which were latent within. Also, her fate was affected by friends and close associates so much as to make her a slave to them, and to their attachments. Additionally, there was a tendency to a lucky journey through life, and to success in her objectives, through meeting good opportunities and helpful people. She knew that she could control the general direction of her destiny. There was a tendency too, either to cultivate clairvoyance and her artistic abilities, which she did, or to a lack of continuity, i.e. to indolence and/or indecision. She had amazing sources of inspiration, but she did need training to exploit these creative talents for optimum results. Moreover, she had the ability to adapt to circumstances, either good or bad, which would have persisted throughout her life. Thus, changeful happenings, even though violent, were turned to good account. Though she may have gone to extremes, she also had the sense of purpose to change conditions in her environment, which would have improved her chances of success. Yet her creative potential could have failed her, unless she had realised how important it was to develop her talents. She would have profited by this and so have gained her objectives. Yet still she may have neglected to take advantage of her own potential by over-indulging in pleasurable activities.

Wallis was set-off against a definite part of the World; a complete half of experience, from which she was excluded in some subtle fashion. Her total power of achievement arose from her instinctive realisation that she was so set-off. Not only did she hold something; but also placed whatever it was, into a relationship with an equal, empty consideration. Thus, what she held, reveals her activity and organisation, whereas her excluded half became a challenge to her existence, or the need, and emptiness, to which she had to direct her attention. There was a marked sense of what was self-contained, contrasting with what her self could not hold, and this would have taken on an everyday form in an advocacy of some cause, the furtherance of a mission, or an introspective concern over the meaning of experience. Always, she had something to give to her fellows: whether literally or psychologically, or constructively or vindictively, because her orientation to the World arose from division, i.e. from frustration and uncertainty. She was self-expanding, or self-self-seeking (in her case), and practically interested in what things mean and what they are.

Wallis had highly individual, or purposeful, emphases in her life, in which her temperament jutted out into experience according to her own very special tastes. She made her own anchorage in existence because her individual character showed rugged resistance to pigeon-holing, either in the neat, conventional compartments of nature, or in the idea pockets of her associates. She could not have been limited to any single, steady point of application. Thus, Wallis's temperament was particular, yet she was impersonal in her interests.

Wallis was good at starting new enterprises. Quick and stirring in action, she had the energy, now all she needed was training and education. An education was essential because it would have given her the ability to understand the people with whom she was to be involved, and she herself knew how to use her experiences to benefit her continuing development. She would have been able to sell herself more effectively, when she had come to know what people expected of her. But also, she had to have learned how to open the doors of opportunity herself, without waiting for others to do it for her. It would have been essential for her to make a self-inventory to see, whether or not, she was wasting a lot of energy.

There could have been a loss of opportunity in Wallis's life, arising from irresolution. Yet this brought her into an eminent position, which may not have been retained. She couldn't have relied on faith, or luck, to see her through her lean years; she needed skills, so that she would have gained the self-confidence to reach the outer limits of her potential. Hence, her ability to accumulate the material necessities of life depended largely on whether or not she was willing to invest in her higher education. She had an immense thirst for knowledge, and because she became so well-informed, she felt that she would have succeeded. She was insatiably curious and eager to be involved in a variety of situations. However, not being able to come and go as she pleased, was painful for her, but this should have motivated her to get her education. Again, she preferred to work independently, but to realise that privilege, she had to get as much training as possible. Effort was made to attain her ideals in unusual ways, but tension could have snapped, causing much tragedy. Yet through some ingenious method, she acquired the education she needed to achieve her goals. But these tended to come at the cost of hard work, personal hardship and long delay. Overmuch careless optimism, when caution was calling, could have produced unhappiness and guilty conscience. Similarly, overmuch limitation of what she conceived to be her way of self-expression and gratification could have brought on an exaggerated depression, often with tragic results. Necessarily, she needed to have lived purely.

Vocation: Wallis's achievement had to have been public in nature, and it had to have been rooted in her sympathy with the affairs of men and women generally. Mental diversions and occupations would have attracted her. She was a pioneer and her work would have been concerned with the outer side of life. She had the talent and the temperament for becoming a true professional in the career she had chosen. Her ability to absorb diverse kinds of information may have qualified her for many different professional positions. She could have accomplished anything she wanted provided that she understood the responsibilities that went along with it. She needed to aim for less, and to do what had to be done, rather than have simply talked about it. Her future was hers to use well, or to dispose of. She could have changed her occupation, or to have followed two at once. All of her hidden talents and resources would have come to her when she needed them, and, at times, she would have wondered how she had solved a particular problem. Probably, she would have wanted to exploit these hidden talents, but she might have experienced some problems in attempts to translate them into cash. However, she was fortunate in material results, because opportunities arose for the use of her enthusiasm and energy.

Finding the proper vehicle for putting her talents to work, would have been a matter of some concern for Wallis. She had to determine how she could have made her best contribution without having to ask for suggestions. She reserved the privilege of seeking her future in any way she deemed fit. She wanted to find a way to earn what she needed without sacrificing the freedom she valued so highly. She also tried to avoid any occupation that could have forced her into boring and dull routine. Her love of people, and her high ideals, gave her a responsibility to use her creative talents for the benefit of others. People were eager to discuss their problems with her because they had confidence in her abilities. With her concern for the problems of society, she could have applied her skills to help find solutions. When she helped others with her creative resources, her accomplishments became unlimited. Once she had been trained to use her talents wisely, the lives of everyone she contacted would have been improved immeasurably. She could have left a lasting impression on others by means of her sacrifices. Serving others was what she did best, but she shouldn't have neglected herself.

One of Wallis's principle deterrents was being distracted by romantic alliances, or by other personal pleasures, which drained her financial resources. She appreciated the pleasures of the good life, which she could have gained easily by taking advantage of her gifted imagination. Self-discipline would have been essential to derive all the benefits from her potential; once developed, this would have yielded constant gains.

Wallis was fitted for receiving a good education with inclinations for music, dancing, painting and languages. She could have followed some scientific, or professional career, in which intellect was more important than practical business ability. Yet she could have succeeded in business because she was well-informed about all the details, and she handled them with complete control. She may have had to travel in her business, which she would have been willing to do, if success and future growth of the business had depended on it.

There was a good possibility that she could have expressed her gifted imagination through writing. She had a good blend of feeling and the ability to express it. She thoroughly enjoyed any opportunity to demonstrate her creative talents because of the attention she got that stimulated her to improve her skill in expressing her creativity. The fruits of her imagination would have been used for works of art, literature, acting, mimicry, psychism, or intuition, in both every-day, and in professional, life.

Wallis would have done well as a clerk, reporter, editor, or in any literary capacity; in educational pursuits, or as a secretary, agent or traveller. She would have been a busy worker and a most useful servant, if and when managed judiciously. She may have found a career in vocational training, or in recreational enterprises. These certainly were compatible with her nature and with her ability to deal with pressures. On the other hand, she might have considered a career in financial management, or investment.

Wallis had ambitions to be charitable, which she was to the utmost of her ability. However, her career may have made her philanthropy difficult to express, and so difficult to achieve.

<u>Middle:</u> Wallis's point of application would have consisted of long-term communication, profound mental interests and travel. This was where and how she sought to carry out her mission, or to gain her every-day justification for existence. Wallis continued to feel that she would always have had the privilege of indulging herself as she chose, and yet she still expected to be well-paid for her professional skills. But she mustn't have assumed that she could have asserted herself in any way she needed. She mustn't have thought that she could always have realised her ambitions tomorrow. She had to have broadened her perspectives and

learnt that there are other facets to life besides money and material assets. She also needed to build substantial character values that would have helped her to gain the security she needed. Wallis tended to live for the moment and so often tended not to plan for the future, which she considered to be too abstract. If she had experienced problems in finding a suitable outlet for her creative talent, then, probably, it was because she had lacked sufficient information to make that decision. An education would have given her the knowledge she needed to realise her ambitions.

However, a great liability was a lack of restraint in Wallis's spending. Whether or not she reached her goals, depended on how much ingenuity she applied in making full use of her resources. If she had persisted in this effort, then she certainly would have become financially independent. Otherwise, she would have had to accept obscurity, or the limited income that went with it.

People lent on Wallis heavily for support, but she believed that most of them could have succeeded on their own, just as she had. But she had to have been appreciative when others had helped her to achieve her goals. Otherwise her efforts would hardly have been remembered. However, when someone appreciated a service she had done, then her vitality became regenerated.

Wallis did need to become more organised to derive the full benefit from her resources. On the other hand, fulfilment in Wallis's career did come through making a determined effort and through mobilising her resources efficiently. Her energy was expressed by keenness towards taking trouble with every minute detail. Also, she was inclined never to be content with her knowledge, or accomplishments, and so tended continually to seek to learn more about the World, so that she would have been ready to assume a more responsible position. Additionally, she was inclined to maintain the highest ethical standards regarding her affairs. Moreover, she knew how to keep the lines of communication open to associates and competitors alike, which gave her an advantage over them. There would have been some compulsion to achievement, but also trouble could have arisen through escapism, by treachery and in craziness about '-isms'. Change would have been expected in financial ways, and money would have been earned unusually.

Wallis had a good common-sense approach to her personal philanthropy. Her imaginative, balanced and creative communication made it easy and successful. Similarly, successful charity was conducted in unusual, but harmonious ways.

<u>Late:</u> Wallis became quite pre-occupied with acquiring the material resources that would have sustained her later on. As she was insecure regarding financial affairs, she dwelt on finding the best way to free herself from material anxiety during her later years.

Appearance and Health

Appearance: Wallis was good-looking, of medium to tall height, erect, slender, well-composed, and with perhaps a tendency to stoutness in middle age. She would have had a long face, nose and chin that were also even and rounded. Her arms and fingers were also relatively long. Her hair would have been brown with a somewhat luminous, ruddy to dark complexion. Her quick-sighted, expressive eyes could have been blue, hazel or brown. She would have been dextrous manually, with a quick, light and graceful walk. Her speech might have been slightly drawling, soft and attractive, but her vocal range would have been great, now high, and now low.

Health: Wallis would have had good health. However, as her chest and lungs were her most sensitive parts, she may have suffered from bronchitis, asthma and even consumption. Kidneys (but Bright's disease not that likely) or bladder may have caused her to suffer from debility, and possibly ulcers, but spinal trouble and diabetes were not so likely. Possibly, her muscular system (weakness in her back?) was affected by some liability to feverish and inflammatory complaints. Possibly also, her generative and nutritive systems may have been affected. In addition, she may have had some susceptibility to unusual diseases.

Mental overstrain was risked. She may have been predisposed towards melancholia, weird fancies and possibly obsession. There was some tenseness that was hard to relax and may have led to nerve storms. In all tensions, relief could have been found in the attempt to let the energies free themselves in happier ways, e.g. for Wallis, through her lover/partner/husband, and through her general philanthropy. Although her sleep may have been heavy, she needed to relax, and to make sure that she got sufficient rest.

There may have been a tendency to falls, chills and orthopaedic troubles, to burns, colds, accidents, disasters and to bad luck. Escapism was possible through the use of drugs or alcohol, and there may have been some danger from gas, poisons and anaesthetics. Her health would have depended a great deal on her general surroundings.

RICHARD BURTON CBE

*"She was, in short, too bloody much, and not
only that, she was totally ignoring me."*
Burton's first impression of Elizabeth Taylor.

Character

<u>General:</u> Richard's personality was rather too quick for his slow, steady individuality, but concentration was added to his impulsiveness. On the other hand, he was somewhat overly restless, which tended to diminish his concentration. But there was also an inclination to let matters remain as they were, and to put up with them. Often, he would have become conditioned to trying circumstances. He tried to express himself outwardly in order to prove to himself that the World would have accepted him, one day.

Richard's energy was apt to sway one way and then to another. He wanted to do everything right away because he never knew what would have happened tomorrow. His inclination would have been towards beauty and ease, but too irresponsibly and easily. He desired emotional outlets but there was limitation to his self and to his expression, possibly through his father, and so, perhaps, he became even shy and retiring. There was a tendency for him to become very worldly (e.g. he would have liked to travel, and to acquire foreign languages). Knowing that he could have applied his talents effectively, would have made him very happy. Neutral traits that he would have shown, included tenacity, persistence and endurance, but also a tendency to retire.

Not knowing when to be silent, was Richard's greatest liability. Potentially, he was quarrelsome and irritable. He appeared to be arrogantly self-confident but, in fact, he couldn't have borne to be upstaged by anyone. Although caution and limitation were expressed as strong reserve and secrecy, there were inner struggles within which he felt a compelling desire to achieve through violence in bursting away from existing conditions. Here, results often caused further bondage. He was too much at the mercy of changeful emotions. There tended to be too much reliance on luck and he was showy, exaggerative, conceited, imprudent, extravagant and overly expansive. Further negative traits would have included being superstitious, complacent, careless, parasitic, dogmatic, rash, violent, boastful, presumptuous, taciturn, self-important, selfish and too assertive.

But Richard could also have been forceful and dynamic. He was charming of speech and showed pleasantness of manner. He was vital, with gaiety, fun and humour, although this could have been teasingly caustic. He was very changeful, but all with good intent. He tended to be optimistic, hopeful, cheerful and contented with his own surroundings and ways. Additional positive traits would have included being kind, affectionate, charitable, friendly, calm, talented, elegant, pleasure-loving and popular. Moreover, he was generous, organising and powerful. He had a strong will, and became independent, determined, authoritative, interesting, dramatic and magnetic. Being self-reliant, he was also dignified and ambitious.

Mentality: Richard was somewhat more subjective than objective; his intellect was profound and was combined with a good balanced outlook. He showed an interest in the arts. He had religious, or psychic tendencies, as well as considerable literary ability. There was a great deal of pride, much passion and a liability to become very sarcastic, carping and bitter in speech. Similarly, his philanthropic tendencies could have been energised to the point of overstrain. Breakdown was possible, as a result of bad temper. Emphasis was on "the values", "the intangibles" and on everything rhythmic, such as the sea, music, dancing and colour harmonies. All this was mixed with kindness and philanthropy.

Richard's mind worked in a "far-flung" manner. He was restless because he was far-seeking. But he could have been satisfied by knowledge. His personality was quick-witted, seeking knowledge wherever it may have been found. Literature, or science, would have been equally attractive. If he had been inclined towards spiritual, rather than to physical matters, then these may have become a joy and a happiness. His mind led him to an expansive and pleasant existence, but vague, albeit well-intentioned ideas, could have led to an inflation of self-approbation and to idealistic notions about his own organising powers, and the governance of countries. Generally, loving kindness would have been shown while organising. All these foregoing increased his higher mind and brought out his imagination, love of beauty and those faculties that work through music, acting and painting. Similarly, his emotions and feelings generally, whether artistic, religious or humanitarian, were brought out too. As a strongly artistic personality, he showed an interest in the psychic, the mystical and the occult. His mind was imaginative and intuitive, and so could have been used for the study of hidden, or occult, matters.

There would have been a tendency to be impractical in that he concentrated on visions of the future, rather than on those of the present. He operated largely on a sub-conscious level and tried to avoid any unpleasant truths about himself. With a little honesty, he could have become free from fears about his hang-ups. Everyone has some of these unacknowledged problems, but he had to have taken advantage of his hidden talents, and then to have utilised his creativity better. He was apt to become severely self-critical and very dissatisfied with his own achievements, not from diffidence but from a desire for perfection that was never achieved. His speech became quick and decisive, but tended to lack a little in concentration. Yet he had a keen, internal aspiration to become a channel through which good forces may have flowed. However, a tendency only, to a vivid imagination, may have been gullible and confused, so that his mind became poorly directed. Touchiness induced escapism, and his mind may have schemed in an involved way, yet his actions still tended to come from his strong intuition, rather than through reason.

Richard's mental interests would have been of the scientific kind, possibly in aviation, and of those deemed to be for the good of humanity, but also to a linking with other minds similarly motivated. Scientific thought, originality, and with a tendency towards genius, would have led to leadership and to success in flashing thought. His communication took place in ways in which, again, his mind would have worked through swift intuition, rather than by ordered reasoning. His imagination was rich with ideas but he may have had some difficulty finding a suitable field in which to apply them. He was contemplative and serious, and rarely shared his innermost thoughts with other people. Yet his skill in getting the co-operation he needed, attested to his communicative ability. Even so, he would have been likely to have kept his communicativeness hidden, unless otherwise brought out. Idealistic, clever, original and prophetic, he sought new and interesting ways even if this meant letting go of the old. Although constructive in a narrow, one-track way, his ordering would have become rigid discipline and dreary planning. Mental loneliness then resulted, because of fear and apprehension, leading to a lack of poise, forced, brusque speech and writing.

Lifestyle: Richard had an ability to adapt to circumstances, either good or bad, which would have persisted throughout his life. He would have dipped deeply into life, and would have poured forth the results of his experiences with unremitting zeal. He would have been ambitious and aspiring, particularly for rule and authority. His personality would have been out-of-the-ordinary and tended to be eccentric. He was unusually inventive, and so could have displayed rare genius in the understanding of how to do things that no-one else around him could have comprehended. He was learning lessons of self-discipline, so that all the inner inventiveness he felt, could have been put to use in the present World that he lived in. His effort was made to attain his ideals in unusual ways. But he had to have learned to be different, without upsetting the structures that he wished to improve ultimately. However, he would have been too ready to alter his life at short notice.

Richard would have expressed power, vitality and self-expression intensely, passionately, secretively and penetratingly, as well as perhaps resentfully and revengefully, in affairs to do with service, in work (especially if it was of the detailed, practical type) or to do with health and hygiene. Long-term results could have been good, if patience could have been used and his character strong enough to bear what had to be borne. Life was rigorous and hard, but lessons of duty and self-control would have been learnt. He tried to make the most of his everyday circumstances by setting out a plan for developing his creative skills. He was serious, thoughtful and resourceful in everything he did, especially in his daily career routine. He had plenty of successful opportunities in life, and so a feeling developed that 'good luck' was to have been expected. Force, magnetism and determination conduced to results through dramatic bigness of personality, and belief in himself. Thus, there was a tendency towards genius. However, there was also a compulsive desire to achieve through violence in bursting away from existing conditions. Results, often, would have caused further bondage, but all this latter was mitigated by the availability of easy distractions/deviations. Life, on or by the sea, was liked.

Richard had experienced long, continuous trauma with either one, or both, parents and family crises never seemed to have ended. While trying to put an end to all that bothered him, he never really vibrated away from the source of his difficulties. Richard had spent his entire life trying to recreate a rebirth in his memory system, so that he could unlock from his consciousness, all that had shaken him previously on an emotional level.

Unfortunately, he had the tendency to fix himself right at his trauma points. Hence, each new person, or circumstance, in his future, was only symbolic of a past that he had not yet left behind. The more effort he exerted in killing his past, or even of hiding from it himself, the more he focused himself back into it. The more understanding he sought to create within himself, the more he was drawn, like a magnet, back into the reasons that had made him seek understanding in the first place. Thus, he was on a treadmill, until he had learnt that the power of memories dies in time, if it's not continuously re-powered negatively. There became very little of him left to be sure of emotionally. He tended strongly to thought-project unconscious dependency onto all those around him. He underwent much inner suffering, internalising and personalising his full consciousness, and tried to find a substitute security in the other World of material possessions.

There was a residue of an animal-self needing to be overcome. In order to transform himself, he had to have studied his inner motives, and have realised that most of what he was holding onto, and seeking, had little basis in the reality of what truly would make him happy throughout his life. He had placed much emphasis on accumulating possessions because they gave him an artificial sense of power. The key to end the suffering of past, unpleasant memories, was not to regenerate them by seeking reminder symbols, but rather to view each day as a new birth of freshness.

Richard experienced much inner turmoil as he questioned constantly, the different rôles in which he saw himself. He may have resented himself on a very deep level, and was truly trying to find reasons for accepting himself, and the society he lived in. Often, this took the form of actually crusading for some sort of personal expression that society, in general, did not approve of readily. In this way, he felt that he was able to prove himself worthy of his own personal existence. He would have reached happiness, when he had stopped trying to topple the World, and have accepted himself as just part of it.

Richard was living through bondage. Either he was chained to society's values, or to his own life-obsessive thoughts, which had to be brought to the surface, in order to be eliminated. It didn't really matter what bound him. What was important was his reaching the understanding that he had to destroy his past value systems, if he was ever to reach happiness. Initially, he had not seen the World clearly. He tended to blame external factors for depriving him of all he thought he needed. He had to have learned the difference between his wants and his needs. Although he rarely got what he wanted, he would always have had what he needed. He would rather have seen the World bent to fit in with his own needs. As a result, he lived in his self-created bonds, silently scorning all who disagreed with his ideas. He had identified with Hollywood movie stars, with crowns, chandeliers, velvet chairs and many of the movie-set symbols, in order to create more power in his own self-image. He identified with power. At the very least, he needed to experience the appearance of achievement. For his own self-growth, he had to have raised his consciousness to the point that he saw this need in terms of his true spiritual goals, rather than of the symbols of beauty he was able to amass on the physical plane. He should have taken the enormous power of his positive belief system, got in touch with it, and have helped to create the better World his Soul had dreamed of.

Richard sought an inner sense of identity that afforded him a uniqueness of character within the framework of the society he lived in. He experienced the conflict of compromising his individuality in order to keep himself in a position from which, ultimately, he could have expressed it more. He may have changed his direction many times, until he had found that special niche, where truly he was able to express himself. He had to have had enough room to follow his creative instincts without being forced into the pressures of responsibility. Yet he handled responsibility beautifully when he was not aware that he was doing it. He assimilated the needs of his immediate environment, and from this, was able to understand how to cope with all that was going on around him. Still, there was some tendency to be a little bit out of time synchronisation, particularly when he tried to relate more to qualities of the past. He had work to do in gaining a balanced perspective in time.

Relationships

<u>Others:</u> Being too subjective in his general outlook, Richard had to learn to become more conscious of other people's feelings. Until he could have done this, he would have distorted his perceptions, since the World is really more impersonal than he would have liked to believe. He had hoped that success would have allowed him to afford fine clothes, and the other trappings of wealth. However, his lack of self-assurance made him put others on the defensive, to distract them from his weaknesses. But he could read character. He understood that everyone had some weaknesses, or flaws, which usually he could have overlooked, if their positive traits were outstanding. Generally, he tended to enjoy people who weren't afraid to speak their minds, provided that they had something worthwhile to say. It became important for him to impress others. But what he failed to realise is that this never quite brought him the satisfaction that he was seeking, because he himself, was just as easily impressed by others, who were doing the same thing to him. He may have become deceitful, or possibly he himself may have become the object of treachery. Yet he met helpful people, particularly women. Generally, he got what he wanted by impressing people in important positions that he

could have accomplished almost anything, if given the opportunity. However, his values would have been challenged by people with different opinions, and by those harassing him because they envied him his accomplishments. If he hadn't wanted to be involved personally in developing his ideas, then he should, at least, have communicated that fact to those who could, and would, have developed them. Regardless of his motivations for acquiring possessions, he risked incurring other people's resentment, if he had used his assets to enforce his will – naturally, people feared someone who used this kind of advantage. But because he was secure in the righteousness of his own motivations, he feared no adversaries.

Generally, Richard was willing to help others with their problems. Throughout his life, he may have dreamed of not having to concern himself with anyone else, and he wondered if he would ever retire, since there was always someone who needed his help, and he hated to refuse. He was deeply sensitive to others' needs and was always ready to offer assistance, but people may have taken advantage of his generosity. Thus, he had to have been alert to the possibility that others could have done this. On the other hand, he could have depended on support from others, when he needed it.

Richard acted instinctively to the needs of people in distress, and immediately got the wheels turning to give them the help that they required.

People knew that he could have been trusted to handle their affairs, or to have provided them with services. He brought his Worldly understanding down to the Earth's plane, where it could have become of practical use to others. This was difficult to do personally, but as long as he could have been a servant, without being a slave, then he would have tried his best to live the life of a dedicated humanitarian. It was sometimes difficult for him to determine what had the greater priority - his own needs, or those of other people. Giving material gifts was not the best way to win people's approval. Instead, his willingness to help others, when they needed it, would have earned him their appreciation. Those who had benefitted from his services would have remembered him, and would have been grateful for it. Often, he may have been helped by others, but possibly, there was also trouble through opponents.

Friends:- Much effort was made to obtain companionship, but possibly with little result. Richard knew how to win friends and influence people with his charming manner and winning ways. Even his beliefs tended to increase the number of his friends and acquaintances. He made friends among those in positions humbler than his own, and was greatly affected by the death of some particular friend, or subordinate. Richard had the support of his friends, who admired his courage and aggressiveness. He got help from his friends, associates and learnt from his competitors, because they could have catalysed his success. But Richard was easily intimidated by his friends' achievements. However, they had applied themselves, and were only getting what they deserved. His future could have proved as satisfying as theirs, if he had accepted the fact that there was more to life than indulging in pleasures.

Family: Richard may have been difficult for others to live with. He was lacking in peace in the home, but he himself was happy in domestic conditions. He had a love for clean, hygienic conditions and possibly in fussy, interfering ways. He knew he had to apply himself diligently to achieve security for himself and for his family. His parents had taught him this, and he was grateful to them for encouraging him to accept responsibility. Generally, he was responsive regarding home, family and ancestral matters, as well as in change of residence. In all of these, he was addicted to precise attention to detail and readiness in the way of working regarding them. It may have been hard for him to loosen his family ties, but as his competence grew, so this should have become easier. His brothers and sisters could have helped him to get started but he'd rather have done it alone. It became essential that he cut those ties so that he could become free to take advantage of opportunities. But he had to have felt right about making decisions without parental approval, based on what he had hoped to achieve. His highly subjective vision made him feel guilty when he took any action, of which he thought his parents might have disapproved.

A partner (and family), who had depended on him, would have stimulated him to derive the most from his considerable potential. He worked diligently for those he loved, especially his children, to give them every advantage that he hadn't had. He hoped that his children would have obtained a formal education, and would have gone on to fulfil their own identities. As they succeeded in their own way, he would have felt grateful for having had the opportunity to support them. Although it may have been difficult, he would have managed to satisfy his responsibilities to his children, and still have had a career that satisfied his desire to achieve recognition for his services. Possibly, one child would have been either difficult to raise, or hard to reach, in terms of that child's own personal sense of individuality. In some cases, that child would have tried to become its parents' teacher.

Lover: Richard was sincere and stable in affection, but conventional. In choosing an associate, friend or lover, he would have been selective, preferring someone who was mature and willing to make a substantial contribution to the relationship, so that it would have endured. He was willing to make sacrifices for those he loved, if he knew that they would have reciprocated. He willingly indulged anyone with whom he was romantically interested, in order to create a happy relationship. Similarly, he developed his creative talents, so that he could derive the yield he wanted. Communication was expressed in affairs to do with partnership of any kind, or in any matter that implied reciprocity, or rapport, with others. His genial outlook on life, coupled with his drive, could have proved overbearing. Possibly, he was too practical and strict with loved ones (and with younger people). Also, his affection was difficult to express. Any partnership brought responsibility, with sorrow and loss through his affections. In his personal life, he could have become highly possessive, unbelievably stubborn and amazingly resistant to any encouragement that tried to get him to fit in with the World around him. His affections and partnerships were subject to disclosures, upheavals and new starts but also with trouble and unpleasantness. Feelings could have been strong and would have caused, and received, hurt. There was a cutting harshness that entered into relationships of affection. Sexual relations could have been intense, but not without quarrels, but there were also harmonious conditions in his sexual relationships. Any further difficulties he had in forming relationships, probably resulted from his parents' suggestions that he could have made a better choice. This would have gone on and on. He had to have asserted his independence by picking his own mate. Moreover, he had a tendency to free himself from bounds, or ties, with an easy elimination of the unwanted. Overall then, and as a result, Richard's life tended to be solitary.

In addition, there was development relating to early life misuse of the creative process. Often, this had occurred in sexually routed thought projections. He had to have enjoyed his sexual fantasies as a safety valve because his libidinous energy would have found other outlets, if not released. Fear of this energy, made him apprehensive about getting too close to people, except in social application of his duties. Later, he would have had to learn how to give free psychic space to those around him. As he had learned to do this, so he could have found himself with an abundance of new energy to be directed into new areas of creativity and accomplishment.

Richard had to have deliberated long and hard before he committed himself to a permanent marital relationship. Probably, he would have chosen his life-partner because of her versatile mind. His partner should have shared his dreams, and he should have listened to his mate's suggestions. Possibly, there would have been trouble through marriage.

Career

Early: Richard's destiny lay in his own hands, in the hands of others and depended on circumstances. There was a tendency to a lucky, successful journey through life, with prosperity and happiness, as well as good opportunities and the meeting of helpful people. There was gain through his partner's money, inherited property and/or possessions. Also, there was gain by marriage and sometimes through opponents, inferiors and through his own industry both in employment and in business generally. There were opportunities, of which, seemingly, he felt compelled to take advantage. The special direction of his energies was strong and he would have responded to an immediate promise. Additionally, he had the internal power necessary to rise through merit and adaptability. On the other hand, he kept having to deal with upheavals in his past, so that his advancement became hindered. There was some liability to loss, and to wrong employment.

Richard's basic survival instincts, and the foundation of his experiences early in his development, were at odds with his drive to achieve in life. Initially, he tended to have a do-nothing attitude about making an important investment in his future goals. Sometimes, he felt that the World owed him a living and that he didn't have to apply himself, if he didn't want to. It wouldn't have been easy for him to have been realistic about making his own way in life. But if he could have accepted responsibility for finding a way to make a good living, then the financial rewards would have given him security and so have compensated him for any emotional anxiety he had felt. Perhaps parental conditioning had led him to believe that he was not qualified to make his own way in life. But once he had understood this, he needn't have felt that he had to have proved himself to their satisfaction; only to his own. Consequently, acquiring the appropriate skills to establish his authority in his chosen field was an absolute must for his own sense of worthiness. But he had derived many benefits from his ability to cope with frustration. His success then became all the more precious to him. Thus, his rise to success may have followed severe limitations early in his life.

Richard planned carefully because he knew that that was the best way to achieve his goals. He had ability to do good work, for example, in connection with the army and navy, research, butchery, passion, sexuality, detection, pharmacy and psychology. His burden to bear, or his responsibility to take, would have been through his work, which he would have taken seriously, but also, there may have been feelings of inadequacy in matters of service and work. Satisfying his ambitions honestly was important to him. However, his keen imagination would have helped him to become independent.

Richard wanted to become the best in whatever he did. He was thoughtful and serious in everything he did, and he rarely acted upon impulse. He felt that he had a moral responsibility to serve the public as best as he could. To live up to this commitment, he had to get as much education, or training, as possible, so that he could better understand how to live up to the public's expectations, and to become fulfilled personally also. If he had chosen to use his creative talent imaginatively, he could have earned a place of respect in the World, but he might also have wasted his efforts in non-productive, self-gratifying activities. Once he had understood that achieving depended on being competent, he might have considered getting more training through education. He came to realise that the best way to take full advantage of his creativity was to have obtained such training. Also, he realised how important it was to become well-informed about many subjects, and that this would have improved his chances of achieving lasting success. Developing his skills should have had a high priority, because others may not always have been available to help him. Training would have taught him how to use his potential to accomplish his goals. This would have been an investment in his future, because it would have enhanced his ability to meet competition successfully. He would not have become afraid of competition in his field and he would have gained the self-confidence to meet any challenge successfully. He would then have been ready to make a contribution that would have established his value to the World, which would have satisfied an important social need and because he knew that being well-trained impressed others. They would have been attracted by his resourcefulness and dedication.

There was an inner frustration between Richard's inclination to follow the line of least resistance, with his awareness that he must assert himself in exploiting his creativity. This resulted in difficulty in dealing with persons in authority as he mistakenly assumed that they were somehow determined to obstruct him. Hence, his most persistent adversary was often himself. If he had been gainfully employed, and had been making some contribution to society, then he wouldn't have needed to apologise to anyone, least of all to himself. He had to have defined his goals, and to have established their priority. Then he had to take whatever action was required to achieve one goal at a time. He hadn't to have been too hard on himself when he suffered set-backs – experience would have taught him how and why they had happened. Getting his plans and ideas into shape, would have helped him to achieve his goals, but he needed more self-discipline to mobilise his efforts. Constantly, he was searching for ways to improve his skills, and getting additional training on-the-job may well have been a good way. He tried to make the most of his everyday circumstances by setting up a plan for developing these skills. He had high expectations, so he took advantage of every opportunity to show his talents. He didn't doubt that he would have achieved his goals and ambitions, but he was troubled when the demands of his career limited his freedom to come and go as he pleased. Still, having his efforts recognised more than compensated him for any inconvenience he had suffered. He was focused on the real, tangible World, where he could have derived everything he needed to succeed. With his gifted imagination, he could have become whatever he wanted, if he had persisted. And so, he had little difficulty finding suitable employment that allowed him to increase his skills in diverse fields.

Richard knew how to use his resources effectively/imaginatively to earn a comfortable living and gain a feeling of accomplishment. Although money was important to him, the way he earned it, and the skill required in his work, were equally important. He came to believe in himself and he knew that his dedication in conducting his career responsibilities would, one day, result in deserved recognition, as well as the satisfaction in making the most of his potential. He became very concerned about getting everything he could from his efforts. Knowing how much hard work was required to accumulate a nest-egg, he refused to indulge in risky ventures. He tried to operate as efficiently as possible to derive the most gain, while expending the least effort. Few people were as competent as he at managing financial resources. He became competent in everything he did, and he felt that if something was worthwhile doing at all, then it was worth doing well. In fact, he became impatient with those who failed to live up to that idea. Probably, he became continuously in demand by people who needed his services. He expected a lot for what he did, but he knew that he was worth it.

However, he could not have afforded to neglect the trivial details that he met in his career, even though they seemed to be a waste of time. Through dealing with them, he could have become independent of the people he would have relied on otherwise. This was the only way that he could have gained complete control of any situation that developed, in his career. On the one hand, he didn't mind working without recognition while developing his talents, so that he could have shown them to the World, later. On the other hand, it may also have bothered him to work without recognition, but he would have had to accept this situation, until he had become more confident about his abilities.

Richard's success in striving for significance depended on how well he used his creativity. Self-development had become the key. He could have become a credit to himself by building a sound mind in a sound body. There was a tendency that he had to base his fortune on his ability to think for himself, even though he had some anxieties about being able to make the best use of his resources. Although his ideas were rich and varied, they still needed to be developed, if they were to become useful to him in earning a living. He had to have promoted his ideas at every opportunity. More often than not, his suggestions would have been accepted.

As a splendid leader in the affairs of the World, with vision and readiness to change old ways, he would have found it awkward, if he was not in a position to lead. However, if he could have reached out to help less fortunate people, then he would have learned how competent he was in coping with the World. With his sympathetic understanding, he could have done a great deal for others. The appreciation of those he served, gave him a warm feeling of satisfaction. He hoped that he had shown them how to face the future with greater optimism and self-confidence. If they had remembered him for his efforts, then he would have felt that those efforts had been worthwhile.

Vocation: Richard's career should have involved working with the public in some way, for he was qualified to solve many kinds of social problems. Especially, he wanted to know that he had made an important contribution to society, so he sought a career that would have involved him with the public. Social Science may have been an attractive field for him, and it would have given him the freedom to come and go as he chose, in performing his duties. Temperamentally, he was well-qualified to deal with the public in his career.

Richard had an overwhelming desire to be of service to others because he was intimately aware of the problems that were likely to have been troubling them, and his compassion cried out to extend a helping hand. His healing ability could have helped to mitigate the unacceptable social conditions that diminish man's dignity. At times, though, he should have thought about the probable outcome of his assistance, because he may have been interfering, when people should have helped themselves. However, his overall influence was beneficial, and when he needed favours later, he could certainly have counted on the people, whom he had helped in the past. He was very good at advertising and mass-media communication, through which he could have used his versatility, and still had the security he needed. Working with the public, and offering services that were in constant demand, would have allowed him to earn a comfortable living. It would also have provided him with the feedback that assured him of his competence.

At his best, Richard could have become a real instructor and inspirer of others (but at his worst, an agitator and/or malcontent). There were many fields in which he could have succeeded including: social services and crafts, masonry, carpentry, plumbing as well as electricity. He could well have developed his own company and have offered these services. Self-employment would have been ideal for him because it allowed him the growth potential he needed.

He showed some fitness for a public career in connection with religion, philosophy, law, or in any one of the fine arts. He had a certain inclination for politics, in which he could have succeeded, if he had received training in government and law. His keen perception tended to tell him what was right, or wrong, with current politics, so that he could have become involved in this field. He may also have been drawn to speculative investment. He could have succeeded in finance because he understood money and had a flair for making it serve those who had it. His intuition was helpful in making investments. He knew what people expected of him and he capitalised on this. He could have been turned towards artistic work, or to imaginative writing. Balance rather than worry was evident so that, as a writer, or speaker, he would have benefitted in this way, but ease rather than strength would have been gained. His enthusiasm for the arts could have led to good results obtained with high ideals. Work would have been done to achieve these, even though visionary and unattainable.

He would have been interested in art, in science and in all sociological schemes. He was good for being a doctor, a chemist, or for one who was inclined towards making scientific discoveries (similarly, women of his type made good nurses).

As his imagination and subtle impressionability became well-developed, so all forms of mediumistic and psychic ability became open to him. For example, telepathy and psychometry would have been suitable. Additionally, he was easily interested in assertive charity, connected with "the values", or "the intangibles".

Middle: The special direction of Richard's energies was intense. There would have been a particular, and rather uncompromising, direction to his life effort. He was interested in a cause, and with an executive drive, but was less concerned about end results, and with no basic desire to conserve himself, or his resources. He would have been far more likely to adapt his allegiances to lines along which he could have made his efforts count for the most. He would have been more of an asset to society if he could have accepted his obligations dutifully, and had not have minded working behind the scenes, where the problems were. He had a tendency to good fortune with material results because opportunities arose for the use of his enthusiasm and energy. He reached his goals by carefully implementing his ideas without letting them intimidate those around him. Practical planning and determined self-will united in an unusual way to produce brilliant results as and when suitable opportunities arose. Unfortunately, he had to be first and foremost in everything he may have been engaged in, so that there was a tendency for him to be subject to upsets, and to forced new phases.

Richard needed organisation and planning in order to use his talents, and to get the most benefit from them. When he was allowed to live and work on a day-to-day basis, he did much better than when he was confronted with any project that involved a great amount of long-range planning. Yet Richard was very capable of developing long-range plans as long as he didn't see them as boxing-in his future. Richard alternated between being pre-occupied with money, and then considering it to be a cross to bear. Because of that attitude, he may have found himself on the fringes of poverty. There was also little wrong with remembering his past, unless this denied him the freedom to participate in today's responsibilities and tomorrow's plans. He had to let his pre-occupation with the past yield to a program for improving his future.

Generally, Richard's constructiveness forced to a patient working-out of what had been begun, but not with ease. His results had to have been battled for. The narrowness engendered tended to produce selfishness and egocentricity. Hardship was endured and sternness given. His energy was expressed in hard and unstinting work so that there became no substitute for it. Yet he still considered it necessary to test public opinion before taking any action that might have reflected badly on his credibility.

Richard had good relations with workers, but difficulties did come through them, or through services given to others. On the other hand, he would have had little difficulty with superiors because they would have delegated to him the necessary authority to satisfy their objectives. He had the savoir-faire to use his skills effectively, and so could have obtained the limits of his potential. Probably, he would have succeeded because he was not afraid to take chances in showing his ability, which he did with dramatic flair. He knew that it wouldn't have been easy to keep his position, unless he had striven continually to provide better services. Additionally, he prided himself on being able to succeed without resorting to questionable practices, or to unethical behaviour. He deplored the fact that some people bent the law to reach their goals, but he knew that this could jeopardise the gains that had been made. If accomplishment had become easy, then brilliance could have been shown in management, in science and in unusual ways.

Richard was a true "Angel of Mercy". His dissolving qualities were offered to others as a mission of healing service and of great personal sacrifice (many in the medical and nursing professions, as well as faith healers, act like this). He sought opportunities and situations, where he would have been needed. Most of his dreams and ambitions were dedicated to how creatively he could serve the society that had given him so much. He could have lived a life of service, and the more he served, the more he freed himself. In the back of his mind, there was a desire to help others to build a future for themselves. Using his own life as a model, he could have shown others how to adapt their skills to take advantage of opportunity. Since common-sense control was well-combined with optimism, and with the desire to expand both his viewpoint and his circumstances, there was success in material ways. Extremism was kept in bounds and fortunate results accrued. With his creative inspiration, he was usually able to solve most of his problems, so that he was more likely to be considered for promotion than those who were less innovative. Probably, he enjoyed his work, and added vitality to even the most ordinary job situations. But it was not his ideas that got results, but rather his ability to use his creativity with skill and competence. At times, he seemed almost inspired in his ability to solve day-to-day career problems. With his creative talent, he could easily have handled the most difficult job situations. However, Richard showed a compulsive desire to achieve through violence in bursting away from existing conditions. Often, this resulted in further bondage. But strong mitigation was also present here. Changeful happenings, even though violent, could have been turned to good account.

<u>Late:</u> Richard knew that he had to be sure to plan for the future, when he would have retired. Usually, he could have found a way to make the kind of investment that would have assured him of some financial independence in his later years and have prevented a lack of security. He hoped that he would have had enough time and money to help to

solve the problems of society. Probably, he would have got involved with social programs, and have made a fine contribution to society. An easy death was indicated.

Appearance and Health

Appearance: Richard would have been of average height, well-erect and evenly composed. He would have had physical strength and endurance. He would have had a rounded, long face with nose, chin, arms and fingers to match. He would have shown a somewhat sanguine complexion, dark hazel eyes, quick sight and an active walk. He was neither handsome, nor agreeable, by any means. There was apt to be much impulse in speech, together with an inclination to be abrupt. He could have been eccentric, cantankerous, wantonly peculiar, irregular, given to unnatural tastes and generally unsatisfactory – but capable of modification.

Health: Possibly, Richard had good health, but there may have been trouble through rheumatism, difficulties with his generative organs, ruptures and abscesses. His sex glands would have affected his voice (and singing). Because he was of strong character, petulance, worry and the refusal to accept necessity, would not seriously have affected his health. However, he became conditioned to trying circumstances, which implies strain. Probably, his chest and lungs were his most sensitive parts, so that he may have suffered from asthma, bronchitis, consumption and nervous disorders. Nervous tension was likely, since freedom and limitation do not combine easily. Similarly, self-will and self-control do not blend and are apt to alternate. If possible, he should have avoided acting hastily, or on impulse. More likely, there was great nervous tension leading to irritability, disruptive behaviour and breakdown, causing tragedy. Throwing off worries also led to stress. In fact, he tended to function largely on nervous energy. Physical overstrain was risked leading to unnecessary exhaustion.

There was a tendency towards incurable and uncommon disorders, chiefly affecting his nerves and psychic aura. Unfortunately, his recuperative power was not good. Similarly, a sluggish circulation, made him liable to gout, impure blood (leading to boils, etc.), brain fever, bunions and ailments arising from cold, or damp, feet. He needed to be abstemious on the one hand, and to avoid hypochondria, on the other. But relief was possible following easy chart paths indicated. Also, there were generally beneficial results due to an harmoniously working nervous system.

Richard was somewhat accident-prone, leading to falls. Possibly, there were burns and scalds also. In addition, he had a tendency to avoid the concrete by day-dreaming, by the use of drugs and by the use of alcohol.

- -

ELIZABETH TAYLOR DBE

When people say: "She's got everything".
I've only one response:
"I haven't had tomorrow".
Elizabeth Taylor

Character

<u>General:</u> Elizabeth tended to be an idealist. She had a very mental nature that was given to intellectual action. She was studious and fond of expressing her thoughts, yet there was a danger of extremes, i.e. of becoming too independent and also too changeable. There was a tendency to a robust, courageous manner, although overly direct at times, and overly quick in response. She showed a strong, eccentric and possibly erratic self-will combined with a rebellious inability to conform to any conventions. This would have made life disruptive and unpleasant both for herself and for all others in her life. Her nature was lacking in calmness, self-control and perseverance. In fact, she was combative and disobedient. Thus, her self-expression was shown energetically, forcefully and initiatory. She was also interesting, dramatic and magnetic. At her worst, she showed an almost criminal personality, seeking fulfilment of personal aims, without regard for the feelings of others. She tended to be too hard and selfish, along with some morbid inclinations and indiscreet actions. She would have been too ready to get rid of the

old and to begin the new. Her reaction to explosive, expulsive ways would have been strong. But, changeful happenings, even though violent, could have been brought to good account. Consequently, an accompanying weak spot would have been the haste with which she jumped to conclusions, while only having to re-evaluate her judgements later. Negative words to describe her could have included: self-willed, precipitate, explosive, utopian, irresponsible, perverted, exposed to temptation and to base desires.

Yet Elizabeth was also optimistic, sensitive, and mainly objective. She had an amiable side, delighting in the company of friends and casual acquaintances. There was evident enthusiasm for the arts, dancing, psychic sensitivity, or for any form of idealism. Her interest in the sea, in mysticism and in hidden things was pursued with energy and with a desire to experiment in new ways. If her life energies had tended towards spiritual, rather than to physical pleasures, then these would have become a joy and a happiness.

Mentality: Elizabeth kept dealing with upheavals in her past. She tried to create a rebirth in her memory system, so that she could unlock from her consciousness all that had shaken her previously, on an emotional level. This tendency fixed her right at her trauma points. Each new person, or circumstance, in her future became only symbolic of a past she had left behind. The more she tried to kill the past, or even of hiding from it herself, the more she focused herself back into it. The more understanding she sought to create within herself, the more she was drawn like a magnet, back into the reasons why she had sought understanding in the first place. Thus, she was on a treadmill, until she had learnt that the power of memories dies in time, provided it isn't repowered negatively and constantly. While trying continually to put an end to all that bothered her, she never really vibrated away from the source of her difficulties. The World War II years had left very little for her to be sure of emotionally. Hence, she tended to thought-project her unconscious dependencies onto all who were around her. There was much inner suffering, which was the reason why she internalised and personalised her full consciousness, thereby trying to find substitute security in the World of material possessions. The key to ending the suffering due to past unpleasant memories, was not to regenerate them through seeking reminder signals, but rather to view each day as a new birth of freshness.

Mainly objective, but also subjective, there was difficulty in communication. She could not have put her thoughts into words that she knew that others would have understood. Part of the problem was that too many of her ideas were formulated in black and white, and she hadn't realised that many shades of grey would have existed in between. Because she tried overly hard to get her thoughts across to people, while inwardly believing that they were not as receptive as she would have liked, she experienced great difficulties in all of her relationships. Often she blocked her conscious mind from being sensitive to the signals that came from deeper parts of her. Thus, her personal nature tended to block the impersonal awareness of her higher mind. Hence, she was not fully integrated within herself. As a result, she could have become more out-of-touch with her true nature than she knew.

Elizabeth went through conflict between the input and output of information. She had spent so much time earlier, learning how to learn, that she had actually become a victim of habits that led her to fulfil herself with more information than she really needed. She had to have learnt how to develop a clearer priority of thoughts, throwing away all that was unimportant, while learning to express better that which was meaningful. There was so much importance attached to each thought that she had, that she actually weighed herself down with one question after another. Interestingly, she had already pre-programmed the answers. This hampered her learning process, for what she sought after, would only have substantiated that which had already been formed solidly in her belief system. Those parts of her that she was able to understand consciously were in great measure a façade of thoughts, of rationalisations, and of the constructed ideas that she had found to be acceptable socially. There was thus a tendency that her mental and nervous powers would have become limited. Although her mind would not have wandered, but would have ordered and controlled in practical, cautious and methodical ways, concentration and power were possible in a mind lacking width. Her mind may not have been resilient, but it would have turned towards practical and pleasant things. Possibly, there would have been good fulfilment in the arts, in spiritualism and, more simply, in love of the sea. Through apprehension, prudence would have been increased, but depression would also have become more likely. All current life thought forms would have become crystallised very strongly in her case.

Unable to experience the full freedom that she would have liked, her imaginative processes were focused on a World too small to allow her full expression. She saw the whole by viewing all of its separate parts. While this made it easier for her to crystallise her impressions, it put her through many detached steps than would have been needed normally. However, she was able to confine her infinite imagination to the practicality of the real World, and, as such, could see the relationship between that which was within the realm of the five senses with that which lay beyond. Hence, a great deal of clairvoyance could have been shown.

At a personal level, Elizabeth was thrown back and forth between the present and the future, and then, as she was living the future, realised that she would spend much time later, reflecting over her past. Crucially, this future experience touched both her future and her past, while she was living in the World of outer experiences. In fact, it was her outer experiences that made her past and future come together in her inner reality. As long as she did not confuse her microscopic view of her World with what she understood macroscopically, then, literally, she could have walked in two Worlds at the same time.

Overall, she saw and knew that there was more to her World than what was apparent immediately. At the same time, she understood that she must make her practical, realistic bargain with the reality of her presence in day-to-day living. She would have done well when she could have synchronised her intuition with what was practical and realistic, filtering out, in the process, all that which was unimportant. She went back over the pictures of all she had already been through, in a more subtle reality, so that all she did not need to carry with her into the future, became loosened.

Elizabeth had great insight into the full, Worldly reality. She was able to see the whole of things without having to dissect it. Her vision was detached and impersonal because she could have easily dissolved past experiences by not holding opinions of them. It was then that she became able to attune herself to her own true Worldly identity.

But in all intellectual matters, Elizabeth would have become very powerful. Positive, lacking in both sympathy and feeling, there was a liability for her to live too much in her head. There was success in inventive, flashing thought, with a tendency for it to have been scientific. She was receptive to ideas and influences that, after modification, may well have been given back out. Her philosophical views of life would have differed from those around her, and it would have become important for her to learn that things could be different without being valued as better or worse. Her higher mind was stimulated by a need for exploration. She was highly curious about all that she had not yet tasted. Often, there would have been a tendency for her to have been lax about the details of life. She was idealistic, and tended to have an open-minded attitude towards life. Yet she also tended to rebel against all that would have bound her to traditional thinking. She was freedom-orientated. In some ways, she lacked practicability, and was unhappy about accepting the responsibilities associated with intimate relationships. But despite all of this, her thirst for understanding was so great that eventually she became one of the very few, who touched the truth of Worldly law. As her inflated ego began to diminish, so she became able to experience one of the most beautiful views of the World.

On a different level, Elizabeth's mind and mental outlook were improved in so far as charm of speech, pleasantness of manner and the generally good results imparted by an harmoniously working nervous system. Hence, she had a tendency to have a good, balanced outlook and to a love of beauty. Also, she was stimulated mentally by social contact with others. Social activities provided her with many opportunities for forming close alliances that would have allowed her to exploit her ideas.

Both Elizabeth's mentality and her self-expression were nebulous and impressionable, but shown energetically with a tendency to be bold, forceful and initiatory. But her intangibility tended to result in vagueness and muddles along with many ideas, but poor fulfilment. Her vivid imagination led to confusion, gullibility and misdirection. Touchiness induced escapism, and her mind may have schemed in an involved way. Action would have come from intuition rather than from reason. As a possible escapist, she may have tried to avoid the concrete by spending a good deal of time day-dreaming, or by the effect of drugs, or through the use of alcohol. Although intuitional, and tending to become confused by practical issues, her mind was very sympathetic and highly receptive to artistic, psychic and benevolent ideas.

Elizabeth would have been capable of mediumship because she could have understood the essence of things without getting involved personally. Her past was easily dissolved since she knew instinctively that it had no basis in her present reality. Earlier, her less worldly attributes had been more pronounced. She had experienced an inner sorrow that had made her a kind of collective, psychic garbage pail for everyone with whom she had come into contact. But once she had begun to sense her true essence of things, much of her own self-pity became replaced by a greater tolerance of the World she lived in.

Lifestyle: Elizabeth's manner appeared to be cool and cautious, so that she appeared to be more limited than she was really. Duty, conscience and orderliness were of importance. But there was a tendency to be timid through a feeling of personal inadequacy. There was limitation to herself and to her self-expression (sometimes through her father). Life was rigorous, or hard, but lessons of duty and self-control were learnt. There were feelings of inadequacy also regarding possessions of, or from, others. Additionally, these extended to the life-force in birth, sex, death and the after-life.

Elizabeth felt set-off against a definite part of the World; there was a complete portion of experience from which she was excluded in some subtle fashion. Whatever someone she was, was placed into a relationship within a larger consideration. Her activity and organisation were challenged by her need, her feeling of emptiness, to which she had to direct her attention. Practically, she was more interested in what things were, and in what they meant. She tended to 'scoop-up' events that initiated experience. Basically, she tended to be an idealist.

Elizabeth's ability to attract attention came from her skill at dramatizing her ideas, as well as her plans for the future. She dipped deeply into life and poured forth the results of her experiences with unremitting zeal. Earlier, she had had a need to experience freely many diverse situations, in order to expand her understanding of life. She may have been continuing to seek a goal that she had been chasing for a long time. Often, her goals seemed unreachable, as she tried to think beyond human possibilities. This made her highly individualistic. As a result, she became discontented with the idea of settling for less than what she knew was possible.

Elizabeth was living through a mission of accomplishment, but what she achieved in the outer world, was far less important to her, than the amount of inner meaning that these achievements brought to her. She did want the best for herself, for her friends and for the World she lived in. Usually, this caused havoc, because she saw a great gap between her ideal nature, and the way things were really. Thus, she could have appeared as a rebel, trying to close this gap by literally destroying all that she saw as meaningless.

Elizabeth was trying to restore a past image of herself. She was accustomed to hard work, and she thrived on the possibility of one day looking back at jobs and projects that she had done well. Having a unique ability to lock-out interference, she, better than many, could have directed her life towards a useful purpose. This was the gift that made her capable of achieving so much. At the same time, she worked backwards, i.e. not starting before she could have conceptualised the finished product. This increased her practical approach to life. She was reserved, and often secretive, as her inner planning tried to shut out external directions that might otherwise have swayed her from her own, self-appointed direction. Especially, she was good at picking up pieces from the past that society had overlooked, and making a great life's work out of such seemingly useless fragments. This was because she could not bear to tolerate waste.

Elizabeth's excess energy, force and initiative were controlled, whereas her inertia, caution and patience were enlivened. These results could have been depressing when she felt energetic, and hurtful when she felt slow and solid. Success may have been achieved but at much cost of hard work, or of personal hardship, and may have been long delayed. Overmuch limitation of what she considered to be her way of self-expression and self-gratification brought on depression with possibly tragic results. On the other hand, overmuch careless optimism, when caution was calling, produced unhappiness and guilty conscience. However, much may still have been achieved. She would have completed whatever data she had collected in her past, later in life. With her maturity, she became ready to bring to fruition, a lifetime of labour along a given path. She would have attained things in her own way. During her life, she developed an overall understanding of the true nature of her dreams. In this way she could have built a purposeful reality by knowing the reasons behind her goals, hopes and ambitions.

Relationships

<u>Others:</u> Elizabeth was popular, with an ease of attracting others, or the public in general, by sheer, innate charm. But she was likely also to have been selfish with others. She could have been abrupt with others too, often interrupting their thought patterns, desiring that she herself was heard. She was the type of individual who believed that she could teach everybody else how to live. Being highly independent, she didn't take advice well from others, but she did listen and, at some future date, would have realised the truths that had been told to her. Nevertheless, Elizabeth could have proved a real instructor and inspirer of others. An internalisation of an earlier consciousness had motivated her to the point where she could have inspired others, so that through them, she could have achieved her goals, dreams and ambitions almost vicariously. Thus, she herself escaped to transform, and could have been of great personal help to others, by not being personally bound to the World herself.

Elizabeth hadn't to have been intimidated by her father's expectations of her, or by comparison of her accomplishments with those of others. She had to have been true to herself. People were the key to her fulfilling her destiny. If she had accepted this responsibility, then her efforts on their behalf would have become recognised.

Elizabeth always had something to give to her fellows, whether literally or psychologically, or constructively or vindictively, because her orientation to the World arose from division, i.e. from frustration and uncertainty. Deriving the most benefit from her fine creativity depended on her willingness to satisfy the needs of others. But her early conditioning may have taught her that she didn't have to get involved with others, or extend a helping hand, if she hadn't wanted to. She may not have cared about others' needs, or have wanted to know how they thought, which only signified that she was determined to extract as much as she could from them, to satisfy her own desires. With these attitudes, her road to success in relationships (and in her career!) would have been paved with frustration and conflict. There was a tendency that if she had become obsessed with gaining public attention, then she should have examined her motives carefully. People would have picked up on that kind of vibration, and they may have held her in disdain for it. She had to have focused on doing the best she could, with or without publicity. What really counted were her accomplishments. When people spoke, she listened attentively in order to find out what motivated them. Often, she was rewarded with keen insight into their problems, even if they hadn't said anything was wrong. She came to understand people's needs and was sensitive to their failings. She realised that everyone had some weaknesses, or flaws, which, usually, she could have overlooked, if their positive traits were more outstanding, but generally, she became willing to help others with their problems. She became a benign influence on people and generally gave others the benefit of the doubt. Her success in reaching people, and forming good relationships, resulted from her willingness to make concessions. This endeared her to those with whom she was in a close, social environment. Such contacts could have given her the opportunity to develop and exploit her ideas imaginatively. Winning support for her endeavours wasn't difficult because she knew how to arouse the public by focusing on their desires. Because she knew how to bring out the best in others, she could have won recognition as an educator. She could have impressed her zest for life on others. However, at the same time, she tended to dwell in the self-pride of trying to live a moral life. Yet usually, people sensed that they could have told her their problems and that she would have done what she could to help them to find solutions. She became troubled when she saw that so much needed to be done for people who were unhappy, or disturbed, but she felt that she lacked the training to do anything about it. When she was deep in thought, people sometimes assumed that she was day-dreaming! Actually, with her easy-going nature, she needed to become more aggressive in making beneficial contacts, especially with people who were well-informed. She also needed to encourage contacts with people whom she admired because they too, may have stimulated her development.

Philanthropy: If Elizabeth had understood herself, then she felt that she would have gained a better understanding of the people with whom she dealt. Conservative, high-minded charity would have been helped by enthusiasm, but, on the other hand, hindered by selfishness.

The tendency was that her own responsive charity would have been given but with difficulty. Her charity could have been given easily to others but it was limited, cautious and controlled, yet with good results in relief of nervous tension. Also, there was a tendency that her high-minded, conservative and conventional philanthropy would have been made difficult by her emotional, changeful response. This philanthropy, thought about as a service, but was perhaps confused by a long-term ideal, poor judgement and possibly indiscretion.

Having a natural, self-confident nature, Elizabeth was likely to have succeeded in her charitable objectives. Harmony came from her conservative charity. Her life circumstances allowed her to develop her philanthropic faculties as she wished, and gave her the privilege/

opportunity of using her creativity to advantage. Using her high-minded philanthropy for the purpose of attaining a long-term ideal, was thought through with critical sensitivity and benefitted through protective, elimination/generation of friends and objectives.

Friends: Elizabeth's friends probably liked her more than she liked herself. She enjoyed doing things for them to show that she cared, and they reciprocated. However, there was sometimes a tendency to be overly friendly, and to place too much trust in others, which could have led to trouble, if not restrained. When her friends asked her for help, she hated to let them down. She may have been unhappy because she received from others, the repercussions of her own awkwardness as a companion. Also, her situation could have been hampered as she questioned the meaning of things, perhaps even more than she participated in them personally. On the other hand, her tactlessness antagonised her friends. Often, she appointed herself as the conscience of her friends. This, while it was motivated by a highly spiritual desire, frequently caused great friction. As a result, much of life became seen from the point-of-view of a spectator. Overall, she may have become an escapist, but it would have troubled her, if she had allowed her friends, or the World, to have taken the same path.

Friends (and/or relatives) died, or became separated from her.

<u>Family:</u> There was a tendency towards general harmony at home, with strong family links, but also mixed with a lack of peace. Frequent changes of home were likely, and so there may have been a tendency to adopt an unconventional way-of-life. Interestingly, she may have experienced continued trauma with either one, or both, parents, and family crises may have seemed never ending. She may have had to make concessions to her family, who may have pressured her to follow their suggestions. But she mustn't have tried to live up to her parents' expectations, and so ignore her own dreams for the future. This situation would have become easier as she became older, but by that time, she could have felt so conditioned as to feel guilty about doing things her own way. Thus, their influence could have persisted. She may have programmed herself to do what she thought that her parents expected of her, but that may have been completely different from their real feelings.

Elizabeth's communication was better with her father than with her mother. She could have discussed her goals, and have got his opinion, about the best way to reach them. She may have disagreed with his opinion, but she would have been sure that he was confident in her ability to succeed.

Elizabeth expected her children to take advantage of the opportunities she had given them. She hoped that they would have learned from her example, and have achieved their own goals for their own reasons. As a true disciplinarian, she treated her children fairly. Although friendly with them, usually she wasn't affectionate, any more than she was with a romantic partner. When she said that she cared, she really meant it. Perhaps her children's needs would have reminded her that she owed them her best efforts. She may have become so anxious to get the best for her family that she may have gone to extremes in her ambitions, but this was likely to have resulted in losses.

<u>Lover:</u> Elizabeth was somewhat defensive when others showed interest in her because she questioned their motives. She was unsure whether their interest was physical or intellectual. She needed to give people a chance to show their intentions before jumping to conclusions. Once she had relaxed her defence mechanisms, and realised that everyone had failings, she increased her chance of having satisfactory relationships.

Elizabeth was attracted to people who were serious, conservative and responsible. She needed to respect her partner and to be respected in return. She sought a partner who shared her perception and deep concern for people. The tendency was that she would have been drawn to a partner who was sincerely interested in her future. Being loved was important to her and would have helped her to achieve goals that would have been beneficial, and have brought security, to both her and her partner. Communication was expressed in affairs to do with partnership of any kind, or of any matter, which implied reciprocity, or support, with others. She would have been slow to make a partnership, but reliable once settled. She made many concessions, when she wanted attention from someone she desired for a close relationship, and she let that person's needs take precedence over her own. Her keen desire for attachment thus tended to break up a great deal of her selfish side. However, her jealous tendencies would have been increased. For example, she was inclined to be decidedly jealous of the conduct of others. She would have been steadfast in love, but possessive. Love affairs were numerous and very happy. Partnerships were beneficial and very successful. Her ideas on love, art and beauty were out-of-the-ordinary, hence more exciting and attractive, but there was a tendency to be, "off with the old and on with the new". A partner, who didn't understand her, could have proved to be a severe liability. There was a tendency that a cutting harshness could have entered into relationships of affection. Feelings tended to be strong, but caused and received hurt. Possibly, sexual relations were intense, but not without quarrels. In fact, she quarrelled easily with loved ones, but there were harmonious conditions in sexual relations too, even though her own desires may not have always been fully satisfied. On a personal level, she found it difficult to endure frustration in her physical desires. Thus partnerships tended not to be easy. Her affections and partnerships were subject to disclosures, upheavals and new starts, but with trouble and unpleasantness. Overall, there were separations, estrangements and romantic/possibly even dangerous, attachments.

There was an excellent indication for a happy marriage, and an ability to live harmoniously with others. Similarly, business partnerships would have run smoothly. For Elizabeth, limitation of affection, or of a happy social life, had its reward in a serious, one-pointed direction. Love may have meant sacrifice, or a life lonely, except for the chosen one. Partnerships would have been a serious matter, but successful in a practical way. It would have been important for her to know, deep inside, that her efforts were very important to the one she loved. Elizabeth believed that, usually, a permanent relationship was the best way for two people in love to fulfil their needs for each other, and that did not mean necessarily that one was using the other, except in mutual interest. However, neglecting her moral responsibilities could have destroyed everything she had gained. She hadn't to have assumed that people wouldn't have known, because they would have done, although they may not have reacted immediately.

There would have been a tendency for Elizabeth to marry early in life. The chosen person would often have been a person of strong, even dominating character. He would have been unusual, but attractively so. However, his eccentricities could have exasperated her. Her own affections, while being strong, keen and ardent, tended to be self-seeking, also. There would have been unusual conditions in marriage, or partnership. Changes in circumstances were likely in both, but could have been agreeable. However, changes could also have been hurtful and unexpected. Also, explosive temper, wilful impatience and nervous strain, did not make for easy partnership in marriage, or in business. On the other hand, her partner could have been her most ardent supporter, and would have helped her to succeed. For example, she should have discussed "being avaricious" with him, who, in turn, would have been honest and direct with her. Her partner must have had to work with her to build a future that would have been secure from want. For her part, she strove to make her physical relationship satisfying and fulfilling. Also, if she had felt that her mate had failings, then she would have tried to compensate, where and when she could. Knowing that she was needed by her partner gave her morale a boost, and strengthened the bond between them. She wanted and needed a partner, who was as eager to grow as she was.

Career

<u>Early:</u> Elizabeth was mainly objective, yet her destiny lay in the hands of others and depended on circumstances. There was a tendency towards a lucky journey through life with many new beginnings, and prominence at certain times. Although misfortunes were indicated also, with trouble in connection with money, left by will or legacy, there was also gain through her partner's money, or possessions.

Elizabeth needed to define what she hoped to gain in life, and to determine the best way for her to succeed. As painful as it seemed, she absolutely had to have got some formal education, or her future would have been limited indeed. Her goal should have convinced her to get the formal training she needed because, otherwise, her aspirations were little more than fantasies. Without it, she ran the risk of an unproductive life, and not being recognised. Even she couldn't have faced that! In fact, she had to have got the best possible education, because she often assumed that everyone else was more qualified than she. She had to have persisted in her studies, if she had wanted to derive the most benefit from them. She had to have tried neither to become distracted, nor to have indulged in day-dreaming, because these activities wasted time. She had high aspirations and a vision of herself in a position of trust and authority. There would have been many ways for her to achieve distinction through her efforts, if she had got the right education. Thus, her first priority was to get training for the career that she was interested in. However, even with a limited education, she could have accomplished more than others, who had had more formal training.

Elizabeth felt an obligation to bring her talent before the general public. She may have been motivated by a strong, spiritual commitment to serve others, in which case, her results would have been made greater than the sacrifices that she had made for them, in the first place. She came to know how to win the public's approval by her tactful presentation of herself and her credentials. These skills would have proved to be an asset as she sought to make an impression on others. Using her skills to help to improve social conditions became an important part of her destiny. Whatever it was she did, she should have used her creative imagination to the fullest. She may have become disappointed with her earlier efforts, but she would have succeeded eventually. She had to have found a way to make a meaningful contribution to society, either through individual, or through group, activities. Her talent for improving existing social conditions was much needed. Those, who had benefitted from her services, would have remembered her, and have been grateful for them. It would have been important for her to choose a career that gave her room for future growth and development. If her profession hadn't allowed her to achieve financial independence through worthwhile service to society, then it may not have been a wise choice.

Public response would have motivated Elizabeth much more than she would have expected. She could have built her life around her many exciting ideas, if she had developed and promoted them for that purpose. With her creativity, she could have made a valuable contribution to society, but she had to have accepted the responsibility for making it available. In her haste to get things done quickly, she had failed to realise that she wasn't always willing to accept responsibility for her actions. Once she had become aware of this, a vast World of opportunity would have opened up.

Focusing on achieving important status may have required some sacrifices, and her feelings of inadequacy may have caused her to lose interest. To start with, she had to have found a way to keep her personal life, and her career, separate, by avoiding intimate contact with fellow workers, and by avoiding discussion of her private life. She must not have allowed her emotions to interfere with her progress towards her goals. If her selfish tendencies could have been resisted, then honest success could have been achieved by means of a thrusting, purposeful nature and a capacity for hard work. She may have been misjudged by the World, and may have seemed too positive, hard and unyielding, but her real, inner nature was much more kindly and sympathetic than it seemed outwardly. Also, she felt it was a burden when someone asked her to show her creative skills, because she was so sure that her talents were less than adequate. If she had worked at them however, then she would have learned that they were more valuable than she had thought. She had to have been given plenty of time to get her head together to make full use of her creative ideas. Additionally, she was easily intimidated by people's expectations. When they implied that she was obliged to help them, she wasn't prepared to challenge them. She was more intimately sensitive to their problems than she had realised. Moreover, fear of competition only delayed the time when she could have met it successfully. When she avoided confrontation, she missed an opportunity to learn how to deal with challenges. Furthermore, indecision may have been a problem, at times. There was so much that she wanted to do that it was difficult for her to establish priorities. Finally, she had to guard against wasting time in fruitless, self-indulgent activity. Sacrificing personal pleasures would have been the best investment she could have made for her own future. Self-investment must have been considered to be a high priority, if she had truly expected to gain any recognition for her talent.

Elizabeth was interested in a cause, but she had much less concern over end results and had no basic desire to conserve either herself or her resources. An executive drive would have been present, but she would have been more likely to adapt her allegiances to lines along which she could have made her efforts count for the most. Her success in striving for significance depended on how well she used her creativity. Putting her imagination to work would have helped her to alleviate her insecurity about her future. Generally, her gift for conversation would have been an asset, but she may have needed some help in making decisions. The tendency was that it would have been easier for her to exploit her creative ideas, provided that she had received co-operation and support from a trusted advisor. Also, she should have sought the help of people who were already established, because she could have benefitted from their inspiration. Additionally, her dedication in achieving a high degree of competence, should have improved her chances of attracting the attention of important people. If she had understood how important she was to others, when she had helped those who had lacked her skills, then perhaps she would have gained more satisfaction. She didn't expect to receive gifts, and probably, she didn't give any either.

There would have been a particular and rather uncompromising direction to her life effort, in which the special direction of her energies was intensified. She worked hard for what she got, and she hoped that, in time, she would have received sufficient reward for her labours. Although she may not have completed her tasks very quickly, her superiors would have recognised that she was very thorough. Probably, she was not distracted by physical, or emotional, needs, so that she could have devoted sufficient energy to her career. She could have succeeded in the field that she chose because she believed in herself. She was forceful, magnetic and determined, all of which conduced to results through sheer, scintillating bigness of personality. Although she had the ability to convert her creativity into worthwhile skills, she did have some problems deciding where she should have focused her attention. As a result, she concentrated her thoughts on finding the best way to use her creative resources to derive the most benefit. She came to know how to make the most of her creativity, without resorting to deception. She sought the kind of job that required problem solving, as well as physical effort. And she was willing to work behind the scenes, if necessary. On the other hand, it may have bothered her to work without recognition, but she would have accepted this situation, until she had more confidence in her abilities.

Self-development was her key. She could have become a credit to herself by building a sound mind in a sound body. She liked to believe herself noble, resulting from having supported some powerful idea, or principle, previously. She liked to feel that everything she did in life, symbolised progress. As such, she kept spreading herself out, to increase the quantity of all that she thought was worthwhile, i.e. she was attracted to all in life that gave the appearance of reward.

<u>Vocation:</u> There was a tendency only that her willingness to do what her family thought best, may have delayed the fulfilment of her destiny. Finding the proper vehicle for putting her ideas to work, would have been a matter of great concern for her. There would have been practical and executive business ability to apply to occupations concerned with liquids, or with the intangibles, e.g. with the arts. Self-employment may have been a way to achieve greater, personal satisfaction. Her interest may have been in economics, education, financial counselling, or law; these would have allowed her self-determination and enough time to do the best possible job. She had a talent for drawing and sculpture. She was inclined to music, art and good-living. Witty and sharp-tongued, communication would have taken place in affairs connected with day-to-day work, especially if secretarial, commercial, or educational. Probably, she could have expressed her gifted imagination through writing. She had a good blend of feeling, coupled with the ability to express it. Balance rather than worry, would have been evident, and a writer (or speaker) would have benefitted through ease, rather than strength. Hence, she might have chosen a career in journalism, education, medicine, in any of the crafts, at which she would have become a true expert; in public relations, or in social services.

She would have been likely to travel, some of which, especially, by water. The broad field of the occult would have been deeply interesting to her, and her reading would have covered philosophy, religion, metaphysics and psychology.

However, the public sector was the most suitable for her talents, and as she grew in competence, so would her recognition and reputation also. But Elizabeth may well have found herself in a calling that didn't wholly accord with her real nature, and yet she would have been quite unable to change it. Similarly, she would have found that she could not have freed herself from adopted customs and habits. But no matter what field she had chosen, she would have consolidated her efforts to avoid scattering her energies. She shouldn't have had any difficulty in finding ways to earn a comfortable living.

Middle: Because a comfortable lifestyle was important to her, the best way for her, and to improve the quality of life for others, was through a career involving public service. If she had been alarmed by the predicament of people in need, she would have found ways to solve their problems. Although there was a strong desire to exert for others in kindly, self-sacrificing ways, confusion became possible when too many irons were in the fire. It wasn't always easy for her to put her ideas to work, because she sometimes doubted that they would have succeeded. Her only alternative would have been to promote her ideas at every opportunity. More often than not, her suggestions would have been accepted. The difference between success and failure would have been her ability to integrate her feelings with her will, so that emotional distress did not interfere with her ability to perform well in her career. She had always known that the public would have bought her services when she had had time to develop her ideas and to make them work. Also, she knew that she would always have been required to extend herself to serve the public's needs. In fact, she may have been required to serve others before she could have served herself. If she had looked ahead, then she would have realised that with a little planning, she could have achieved her goals, but her dream had to have been a vivid one. Very hard work may have been done for idealistic ends. Results may have been disappointing because all had been too imaginary.

Elizabeth was easily disturbed by social problems, and by the political processes that had failed to solve them. Vivid, over-imagination, without common-sense, tended to produce chaos, and irregular, over-glamorous, escapist ways brought downfall. She had to have been careful about the people she associated with, and to have avoided anyone whose motivations were suspect. She had to stop, look and listen for evidence that would have forced her to change her course. Yet she had to have remained progressive in her thinking, and to have tried not to belittle herself for past failures.

Elizabeth would have derived the most benefits from a career that required her to deal with people and their needs. She had a talent for helping people to achieve greater harmony in their lives, and to face the future with greater optimism about reaching their goals. Her services would always have been in demand because she had a talent for understanding what people wanted, and for giving it to them. If she had used her skills with ingenuity, then she would have been accepted easily by groups and individuals. She was an effective sales person, especially when promoting herself. It became comparatively easy for her to arouse and maintain the public's fascination because she knew how to work for their best interests. She communicated effectively to people that she could have handled their needs, and they became impressed when she lived up to her promises. People would have remembered with gratitude that she had worked to improve their circumstances. Her compassionate nature allowed her to focus sharply on all facets of a problem, and its probable solution. She would have made a good public speaker, because she could win an audience easily. She would have contended aggressively for rights and privileges and so may have displayed considerable power of regaining any lost prestige.

Elizabeth put a lot of effort into her work, because she expected increased benefits from her accomplishments. She maintained the highest ethical standards in her affairs. She understood much about law, politics and the ideologies that guided nations and their people. She was never content with her own knowledge, or accomplishments, and she sought continually to learn more about the World, so that she could have become ready to assume a more responsible position. She was always ready to prove herself to the World, and she pursued her ideals with devotion. She may have become deeply motivated to serve society by working with others, who were dedicated to helping people, who couldn't have sustained themselves using only their own resources. She had always known that someday she would have had the opportunity to go after the goals that she had selected early in life. However, her success may well have come through a profession that had served the public well. If she had received further, formal education, then she could have contributed to the evolution of society, which would have enriched everyone's life.

Late: There were no interpretations found for inclusion in this section.

Appearance and Health

Appearance: Physically robust as well as good-looking, Elizabeth was of medium height with a well-framed body. Although slender in youth, there would have been a tendency to stoutness later. Her face would have been a rounded square with a good complexion and regular features. She would have had dark, wavy hair, prominent eyebrows, blue, or brown, eyes and possibly an aquiline, or Jewish, type of nose and profile.

Health: Elizabeth had strong health but a liability to feverish complaints. Although she had good, perceptive faculties, her mind and nervous system could have been energised to the point of overstrain. Elation and depression would have alternated quickly. Her nerves tended to suffer through suppression and outbreak. Breakdown could have occurred with irritability and temper. Incisiveness would have become critical and carping. Over-worry could have led to intestinal troubles and brain trouble may have become possible. The lack of correct working between her nervous system and her liver could have lain at the root, at times, of poor judgement and indiscretion. Also, dream-intoxicated, strange fears, could have played upon her nerves. These could have undermined her health and there may have been a susceptibility to fish-poisoning and to harm from impure water.

Elizabeth's reproductive and eliminatory systems were liable to weakness, causing her to suffer, possibly from piles, gravel and venereal diseases. Granulation of the kidneys, or bladder, could have led to debility, weakness in her back, diabetes and Bright's disease (kidney and spinal trouble) or ulcers.

Elizabeth may have tried to avoid the concrete through the effects of drugs, or alcohol. Paralysis, accidents to limbs, and unusual diseases, were also possible.

Although an easy death was indicated, so too was an unpleasant one.

- -

GILLIAN GRAY

"Anyone, who harms a hair of yon old grey head,
dies like a dog in the dirt. March on." he said.
"Barbara Frietchie", John G. Whittier.

Character

<u>General:</u> Gill's moral nature and personality were both very strong. She was jovial, optimistic and cheerful, being contented with her own surroundings and ways. She had a great capacity to enjoy life because basically, she was well-integrated. Also, she was progressive, steadfast, hospitable and conservative. She showed considerable persistency, tenacity, endurance, self-discipline, self-denial and exactitude. Her abilities were by no means under-valued. There was plenty of reserve power behind all the courageous and enterprising force that was expended, and when she had made up her mind to carry out any purpose in life, she nearly always succeeded. Additionally, there was a love of approval and an ability for general adaptation that were both accentuated. She showed self-confidence, faith in her own ideas, pride, passion, a desire to rule and managing ability, combined with a stimulating, dramatic instinct. She may well have been an idealist and a reformer. Of course, there would have been problems but she could always have found ways to resolve them satisfactorily. More mildly, Gill's disposition was good, loving, kind,

pleasant and obliging. She was likeable, definite and yet adaptable. There was happiness along with a love of peace and beauty. In addition, there were inclinations to retirement, philanthropy and to day-dreaming.

Gill preferred her own methods to those of others, being enterprising and independent, but sometimes wilful and wrong-headed. Also, she could be moody, quarrelsome, taciturn, defiant and assertive, but although aggressive, with an explosive temper and wilful impatience, she was rigorous and brave, too. She had an intention to surmount her difficulties but with inclinations to be impulsive, head-strong and rather too dogmatic.

Gill had plenty of successful opportunities in life that gave her a feeling that "good luck" was to be expected. But because of emotional anxiety, and a fear of inadequacy, she may not have taken advantage of opportunities for meaningful, social activity.

Mentality: Gill's power, vitality and self-expression would have been spent on her strongest feelings, in sexual matters and often would have been connected with death, legacies and the intangible. There was an equable side to her mentality that inclined her to the inspirational and the spiritual, giving her the ability to weigh-up and balance the internal sense of things. There was a tendency to a good sensitivity, i.e. to receive and then to give out, but also a lack of concreteness. Her mind was sympathetic and intuitional. Although she tended to become confused by practical issues, she was highly receptive to benevolent ideas. However, her sensitive and impressionable mind could become strained so that the outcome was likely to be vivid imagination that was both gullible and confused.

Gill absorbed impressions impersonally from her environment. Usually, she thought that all the feelings she experienced were her own and that ultimately they demanded some type of action, or solution, on her part. However, the truth was that she had an opportunity to experience much of the World, while not truly being obliged to personalise it. She was highly sensitive, particularly to music and the arts, but had great difficulty dealing with the harshness in life, to which she was overly open. To balance herself, she made the mistake that she had to balance all that was around her. She should have understood that each new grain of sand she added to the scales as a balanced solution to what was there already, created yet another imbalance that then required a further solution. She may have become so frustrated at trying to centre her World around her that eventually she resorted to escapism to keep her from recognising that her own personal difficulties were coming from problems that needed no solutions.

She was so emotionally sensitive to every experience that she often lost her composure. Touchiness induced escapism, her mind would scheme in an involved way, so that resulting action came through intuition rather than from reason. Thus, her intangibility could have resulted in vagueness and muddles. She would have had many ideas but poor fulfilment. She may have become deceitful, or, more likely, the object of treachery. There may have been an inclination to avoid the concrete by day-dreaming, by the influence of drugs, or by the effect of alcohol. She had moods of dreaminess, and inattention, and could have lost herself in a World of imagination. Her highest ideals could have become eroded, if she had become fascinated by purely physical modes of self-expression. But there was no dishonour in this sort of temptation, provided that it had not diverted her from her primary goals. However, Gill could have gained a tremendous amount of insight into the mirror of herself, i.e. that part of her identity that she saw through the eyes of others. She could have learned how to integrate better with her society through this type of vision. At the same time, she would have become further removed from the basic essence of herself through others.

On the other hand, Gill's speech, thought and nervous energy could have been used assertively, cuttingly and strongly. Although she was easy and courteous in speech, her mind tended to be forceful, incisive, downright and good at debate. Her gestures would have shown this. Also, Gill was refined and concerned only with the higher emotions. She continued to expand her self-awareness through her higher mind, but she must not have appointed herself as one who sat in judgement of others. She was aware of a great deal about experiencing the outer self, and she would have given this to others, but she had to try not to scatter her knowledge too thinly. Eventually, she became highly independent with a strong sense of her relationship to the World. Yet mental inflation may have led to conceit, with width, rather than depth, on display. Indeed, she glowed when the spotlight was focused on her. But there was also an inclination for Gill to have power of concentration and drive. Through apprehension, her prudence would have tended to increase. She would have reviewed the prestige and dignity she had attained already, and this determined her current opinion of herself. She was status conscious, particularly in her peer group. Unusually, she judged herself in terms of past peer groups, and how she measured up to, or surpassed them, now.

Gill was both objective and subjective. Her perceptions were strong. Self-expression became her highest priority, and she indulged herself whenever possible. Her mentality was changeable, alternating between periods of deep response to her environment, and to periods when she projected herself outwardly. When external crises developed, she had to have learned to use them as opportunities to show her superior skill at coping. She had to have stopped worrying about problems that never materialised. She had an inclination towards strong mental action through revolutionary thought, but communication, in every way, became too brusque and independent, so that it lost good contact with others. She became strongly emotional and intuitive with a difficult touchiness that was aroused quickly. Also, there was a tendency towards a strong and awkwardly expressed addiction to the unusual and unconventional that may have led her, eventually, to become eccentric, odd and tiresome.

Yet Gill had faith in her own ideas, with an obsession towards megalomania, coupled with that compelling need to achieve fully creative self-expression. There was deep concentration, deliberation and dissimulation, coupled with intense sensitivity. However, her moods were suddenly changeable, resulting from an ability to throw off the static easily, and then start new thought and receptive ways.

Lifestyle: As a 'bowl' individual (see her Epoch chart), Gill was someone who always had something to bear. She was set-off against a definite part of her World, because there was a complete half of experience from which she was excluded in some subtle fashion. Whatever her 'bowl' held, it was placed into a relationship within a larger consideration. The occupied half of her 'bowl' revealed her activity and the organisation of her 'self' (since planets are significant according to their place by sign and by House). Her unoccupied half became a challenge to her existence, or the need and emptiness, to which she had to have directed her attention. This challenge took the form of an advocacy of some cause, of the furtherance of a mission, or of an introspective concern over the purpose of experience. 'Bowl' types tend to be idealistic. Thus, she always had something to give to her fellows, whether literally or psychologically, whether constructively or vindictively, because her orientation to her World arose from division, i.e. from frustration and uncertainty. Her leading planet here (Mars in Aries in her 7th House) provided a point of application and showed where and how she sought to carry out her mission, or to have gained her everyday justification for existence. Her 'bowl' character was definitely self-expanding, or self-seeking, so that Gill was more practically interested in what things mean, and in what they are. She inclined to 'capture' things, or to consummate various phases of life, because her leading planet was placed between her 10th House centre, on round and down, passing her 7th House centre, and down again to her 4th House centre.

Early on, she had begun to imagine herself as different from her ideas about herself. And whether she had realised this, or not, this would have been the beginning of her spiritual journey. In her life, she would have continued to sacrifice old parts of her identity, until she had truly blended with her higher Worldly nature. She would have learned that all of life is but appearance including the image she believed that she had of herself.

She lived constantly in a state of illusion. Continually, she imagined herself in different identities as she kept trying to displace a constant feeling of loneliness. Much of her life lay at the unconscious level as she kept sifting through her formless nature, trying to establish a concrete sense of belonging to herself. Like a chameleon, she was in a constant state of change, always readjusting herself to the environment she was in, at that moment.

She had a tendency to feel sorry for herself, always believing that something was missing in her that might have been found in another person. This feeling would have been overcome as soon as she had accepted the formless part of herself as her true nature, understanding that this gave her the freedom to blend with her environment, so that her true identity was more worldly than personal. She could have reached happiness when she had realised that she did not have to reach for it, but that happiness was found within, as a more, or less, permanent state of contentment with one's individual life experience, combined with the minute part that one plays within the totality of the Worldly plan.

Also, as a 'splay' type person [in which the planets lie in groups irregularly spaced around the Zodiac circle] (see her Birth chart), Gill had purposeful emphases in her life, during which her temperament jutted out into experience, according to her own very special tastes. She made her own anchorage in existence and her characteristics were marked by a rugged resistance to pigeon-holing, either in the neat conventional compartments of nature, or in the idea-pockets of her associates. Hers was a very intensive personality that could not have been limited to any single point of application. She had a temperament inclined to be particular, but generally, she was impersonal in her interests. There was a 'splay-foot' certainty to every approach that she made to the problems of life.

Gill would have had a positive outlook on life and she would have asserted herself in exploiting her creativity. Her desires would have been towards achieving good through unusual objectives. She was anxious to experience the future through her own individuality. She was highly competitive, particularly with herself, because she was idealistic and because she was uncomfortable settling for less in life than she believed she could have achieved. She wanted to be recognised for her progress. She found herself propelled into many activities at the same time, while she would have preferred to start one thing at a time. Nevertheless, she had a high level of enthusiasm for making new beginnings. At times, she had a tendency to over-extend herself, and could have leapt before she looked. This tended to make her into a pioneer, but one who was not always on steady ground. She moved through life quickly and did not like to waste energy. But she had to work at maintaining a reasonable sense of proportion, so that she did not make things larger than they were. She was continuing a lesson on the evaluation of self-truth, and so became forced, personally, to live her own philosophy.

Gill felt a need for dedication to go with her strong sense of responsibility. She had to account to herself for everything that she did. She saw her life as some sensible, formative structure, which had followed a more, or less, reasonable track from the start of her memory to the present time. She tended to be rather crystallised, so that reason and logic may have eluded her, if that meant deviating from her pre-programmed sense of duty to her self-image. The only way that she could have been swayed was by the possibility of improving her self-image in the future, as long as nothing of her past was destroyed in the process. She was trying to establish a sense of principle, which she had not formed thoroughly earlier, in areas other than in her career, in her public image and in her sense of duty to society.

Gill found conflict surrounding the decisions she had to have made, in order to have established the security of her future. Many of her goals were based on the past, and so each step forward carried with it the full burden of her destiny. She tended to feel that barriers were holding her back, but truly they were her own. Desiring to earn the esteem of her peers, she often checked and re-checked her actions to the degree that she seemed to be a 'procrastinator'. She would beat around the bush, and undergo countless activities, before taking the one step that she knew she was going to take all along.

Gill wanted the best for herself, for her friends and for the World she lived in. Usually, this caused much havoc, because she saw a great gap between her ideal nature, and the way that things were really. Thus, she could have appeared to be a rebel, trying to close this gap by literally destroying all that she saw as being totally meaningless around her. Often, she appointed herself as the conscience of her friends. This, while it was motivated by a highly spiritual desire, often caused great friction. Much of Gill's life was seen from the point of view of a spectator, and her creative process could have been hampered as she questioned the meaning of things, perhaps even more than if she had participated in them personally.

Relationships

Others: Gill's communication was expressed in affairs to do with partnership of any kind, or to do with matters that implied reciprocity, or rapport, with others. She was stimulated mentally by social contact with others. In general, she was fond of young people and children. She presented a favourable image, and most people would have found her easy to talk to, and to be comfortable with. There was keen delight in social intercourse, loving and appreciating all that which pertained to the social side of life. She did what she could for others because she felt that she owed it to them. Initially, it may have seemed demeaning, but she should have offered to do favours for people who were less fortunate than she. Her deep concern for people prompted her to commit her life to satisfying their needs. This allowed her to make the most significant investment of her talent, which would have given her the most rewarding and enduring benefits. She should have become proud of the chance to make a social contribution that would have been much appreciated. In time, she would have demanded the freedom to do whatever was necessary to make a better life for others.

Gill expected a great deal from others and manifested a stubborn desire to make others conform to her requirements. Her response in ways and manners would have been pushy, self-assertive and quickly aroused. Possibly, she was quick tempered and unthinking, and yet she stimulated others to capitalise on their own resources and so won their gratitude for her efforts.

Gill may have been tempted to take more than she gave, especially if she couldn't have controlled her desires. She tended to be more interested in other people's business, than actually, was good for her. She had always to have kept her moral and ethical standards in positive focus. It would have been so easy to assume that the ignorant deserved to be "taken" by anyone who was better informed. She had to have remembered that she had a social obligation to the public, and that she could have been held legally responsible for any deception that she had practised. And yet her greatest danger was being deceived by others. She had to have checked everyone's credentials, and to have believed only the facts that she could have checked. She should have got legal advice even for insignificant contracts.

There was a tendency that strength and freedom loving expansiveness was shown, but with uneasy expression. Wilfulness and insistence on being "different", produced tactlessness that offended others. Gill's view was highly egocentric, so that the ideas and ways of all others were scorned. "Everyone else was out-of-step but our Gill".

Friends: Gill had an amiable personality, delighting in the company of both friends and casual acquaintances. Often, new friends were made. Social activities gave Gill many opportunities for forming close alliances in endeavours that allowed her to exploit her ideas. Friends could have contributed much to Gill's success in every phase of life, but, in her turn, she was able to influence her friends also. For Gill, there was a vital need for friendship. Her need for companionship meant that she must have made many concessions to others. Generally, she waited for the other person to make the first move because she feared rejection, or a lack of interest. She took her friendships quite seriously, and identified personally with their successes and failures. Her conciliatory manner endeared her to those with whom she was in close contact, and she was willing to be interested in all subjects that pleased her companions. An internalisation of past consciousness motivated her to the point whereby she could have inspired others, so that through them, she could have achieved her own goals, dreams and ambitions, almost vicariously.

However, Gill sometimes showed an inclination to be over friendly and to have placed too much trust in others. She always seemed to have the need to make concessions, especially when a situation arose that could have caused disharmony between herself and others. Indeed, her fate could have been affected by friends and associates, so much so that she would have become a slave to friends and attachments. Gill may have become an escapist herself, but it would have troubled her if she had allowed her friends, or her World, to take the same path. She herself escaped to transform, and so could have become of great personal help to others, by not being bound to her World personally.

Family: Generally, there was harmony, particularly at home. Gill hadn't to have been intimidated by what her father expected of her, or by comparisons with others' accomplishments. Unfortunately, her relations with her mother (and with women) were not always easy. Yet much of her daring resulted from the stimulating influence of her parents.

Contrarily, Gill may have been a stranger in her own home through the peculiarity of her magnetic conditions. However, happiness came eventually through lovely children. Her desire would have become to collect and maintain family and home. She had worked hard to succeed, so that she could have given her family every advantage. She knew that her children would have benefitted greatly, if she had shown them how to take advantage of the resources that she had worked so hard to provide. She hoped that her children would follow her example, and would succeed according to their own specific needs.

<u>Lover:</u> Gill was sentimental, very emotional and very expressive of her feelings. Hence, she was easily influenced through her affections. She was ready to sacrifice herself for love, not only in an amorous way, but also in a self-abnegatory one, i.e. for a greater love for the weak, or suffering.

Power, vitality and self-expression would have been expended in sexual matters. Gill's affection would have been keen, ardent and strong, but with a tendency to be self-seeking. Her strong, physical drive made it hard for her to endure rejection by those she loved. She always suspected that she was being used to satisfy their desires, and that she could have been discarded at any time. She wanted her partner to defend her and to appreciate her efforts. She was forceful in intimate relationships, but her partner was combative, too. There were poor relations with her partner causing irritation and quarrels. She was too susceptible to the attractions of others, and so liable to deception.

Gill's easy charm could have been intense but overdone, with a restless lack of ability to be happy alone. Yet there was happiness and success through her love affairs. Her naturally romantic nature inclined her to make concessions to those she loved, in order to stimulate warm, friendly relations. Because she was unwilling to see anyone's negative qualities, she became extremely vulnerable in her love affairs. She needed to question, and to examine closely, every important contact that she made. On the other hand, troubles could have been caused by too many love affairs, too much love of the easy, of the pleasant and of the beautiful, at any price. She may also have been attracted to people, who were financially independent. She might have justified her materialistic attitude by saying that as she was always the one making concessions, that that evened the score. But this would not have been a good basis for a permanent relationship, unless genuine love was involved as well.

Despite all the foregoing, there was an excellent indication of a happy marriage and the ability to live harmoniously with others. Similarly, business partnerships would have run smoothly. Generally, Gill didn't allow her marriage to interfere with her professional life, but she enjoyed the co-operation of an understanding mate. Probably, her partner was sensitive to her long-range goals, and indulged avidly in the same kind of dreams. Her partner may have expected more from her than was fair, but she thought of her contribution as an investment that would have enriched them both.

Gill's response was changeful towards those in any intimate relationships, in a liking for women as intimates and in an expectation that her marriage partner would have been "motherly". It was important for her partner to show that he needed her. In turn, she would have done anything to make life comfortable and fulfilling for the one she loved. But she would have felt secure in their relationship only if he just couldn't have managed without her. On the other hand, she would have found it easy to accept any sacrifice in order to have a permanent relationship. However, explosive temper, wilful impatience and nervous strain, tended not to make for easy partnership, in either marriage, or in business.

Career

<u>Early:</u> Gill's destiny lay in her own hands, but just more so in the hands of others, as well as being dependant on circumstances. There was success in life through her energy, enterprise and courage, as well as in her desire to excel. Also, she would have achieved worldly success and popularity.

People tended to be the key to fulfilling her destiny; her efforts on their behalf, would have become recognised. She had many exciting dreams about what she wanted out of life, and she had the inspiration to achieve them. She should have developed her talent for artistic endeavour. She enjoyed creativity through art, through things of the theatre, through all games/happy occupations, and through any way of being prominent. With her dramatic sense, she should have easily gained the support she needed in her endeavours. Developing her creativity would have helped to raise her credibility. She was more talented than the average person, and developing her talents into skills should have been her main priority during her early years. She owed it to herself to invest in her own development. Becoming a specialist in some skill, would have brought her the financial rewards she wanted. She knew that her chances of achieving her goals would have been improved if she had received a good education. With training, she would have learned just how enormous her creativity was. This would have allowed her to succeed in both professional and personal relationships.

Gill would have had to give up some of her self-indulgent ways in order to make a personal investment. She had to have put her vanity on the shelf and have done her best to earn the position she wanted. If she had started at the bottom, then she would have learned how not to fall flat on her face. If she had suffered some setbacks like this, early on, then only a few people would have been aware of them. If she had brought all her creative resources to the surface, then she would have attracted the attention of important people, who could have helped her to move up the ladder of success. She hadn't to have been afraid to make sacrifices, or to have been realistic and not to have mixed business with pleasure, in order to have fulfilled her destiny. Once she had established a goal, she would have been committed to it, and nothing could have deterred her from it. Her faith was limitless, and her devotion to any task so complete that she could have "moved mountains". She didn't doubt that she could have accomplished nearly anything that she wanted. Clean living habits and physical exercise would have paid dividends in a prosperous and productive way of life. However, she must also have taken time out to relax, and to unwind from, the demands of her vocational interests. She had executive ability, good constructive power and the ability to organise. She knew how to make the most of her creativity without resorting to deception. Additionally, she should have learned to like herself for her achievements. Overall, she could have succeeded, if she had applied herself with determination.

Possibly, there had been a cleavage in her life relating to parents, or to early childhood. But the resulting disharmony in her nature, could have urged her to accomplishment. At first, she may have had some doubts about asserting herself as strongly as she did, but in time, she would have learned to become more restrained, and of how to avoid difficult situations. There was success and good fortune with a lucky journey through life, but accompanied by an inclination to squander gains, to be extravagant and to trust to luck too easily. Because she didn't really believe that she could have failed, she may have neglected to develop her creativity to ensure success. If she had limited herself to achieving personal goals and ambitions, then she would have denied herself the full benefit of her potential. She had to have been wary of people who suggested that she was destined to serve the needs of others at the expense of neglecting her own top priority needs. It may not have been easy for her to gain the career position she wanted, because she wasn't entirely sure that she could have achieved it on her own. But her development and success in her career, may have been limited also by the feeling that she didn't deserve to succeed. She had to have stopped making comparisons with competitors. She needed to have established realistic goals, and she mustn't have made excuses to others. Breaking ties with the past would have been difficult, but she needed to do this, if she was to have become self-sufficient. She would have encountered some tension, if she had tried to achieve her career goals, and have satisfied her romantic interests simultaneously. She had expected others to open doors for her, but with proper training, she could have opened them herself. Even though she knew the importance of education for her career, she may not have been willing to make the necessary investment. Instead of dawdling, she had to have invested the time and energy needed to derive the maximum yield from her creative output.

Gill was a late starter because of her lack of organisation, self-discipline and because of her indulgence in pleasurable activities at the expense of applying her energy in outward expression of her creativity. Probably, she had developed some emotional insecurity about her effectiveness and had become concerned that the public wouldn't have appreciated what she did. On the other hand, smug satisfaction could have proved a great deterrent to her success. Also, because of her distaste for unpleasantness, she may well have become overly compromising. In addition, she needed to be wary of misplaced affection that could have proved costly in her career. Moreover, however, a good deal of rather "bad luck" may have been experienced, of which hostile criticism, lack of sympathy, a sense of frustration, opposition and rivalry, as well as misfortunes brought about by other people, or resulting from them, would have been notable features. But Gill must not have given in to anyone who suggested that she used her skills in an irresponsible way to achieve certain of her objectives. The risk would have been too great, even for personal reasons.

<u>Vocation:</u> Gill's desire would have been to work for the care of others. Her career should have brought her into close contact with people because she needed them as much as they needed her. Through them, she could have reached the fulfilment of her potential. If she could, she should have got out on her own and built a foundation of personal security, so that she could have extended herself more positively in pursuing her goals. Gill was fitted for a position of some prominence and responsibility. Living up to her vast potential required that she applied herself to the enormous responsibility of dealing with society's needs. Her deep sensitivity enabled her to make a worthwhile contribution to society through her career because she was so keenly aware of the causes of social problems. She was insatiably curious about getting to the root of important social issues, and, as she could detect the seemingly insignificant details that resulted in social frustration, she certainly should have sought a career that involved this responsibility. The legal and political ramifications of such a course made it important for her to have had a broad education, especially in the social and behavioural sciences. With the right training, she could have withstood anything she may have had to face, and have succeeded despite it. No-one became more aware than she was, of the limitations imposed on certain groups in society, and she could have done a great deal to help those people. Her aggressive nature could have become

an asset in her profession, if it had been balanced by compromise and common sense. Provided that she could have controlled her temper, she may have avoided a great deal of bad publicity. She could have nourished the needs of society with her compassion and love.

Gill's communication was expressed in affairs connected with day-to-day work, especially if secretarial, commercial or educational. As a writer, or speaker, she would have benefitted from balance rather than worry, but ease rather than strength would have been gained. The legal profession, government service, public relations, social programs and sales, exemplified some of the many careers from which she could have chosen.

Middle: Gill's prosperity was obtained through perseverance. She fulfilled her social obligations by doing for others what they couldn't have done for themselves, which could have involved a spiritual motivation. She preferred to work on her own, but she would have considered a partnership, if that would have served her goals better. She achieved through painstaking effort. Work and energy were put into the daily routine. She was fortunate in Worldly matters that favoured energy, enterprise and the desire to excel, as well as requiring a determined self-will. Winning support for her endeavours wasn't difficult for her because she knew how to arouse the public by focusing on their desires. Because she was tuned into society's most urgent needs, she must have used that skill to help her to satisfy them. The tendency was that she had learned many skills because she had enjoyed finding new uses for her creativity. In fact, she would have gone to great lengths to become skilled so that she could have demanded a good price for her services, and have gained recognition for her achievements. She became especially gratified when her creativity had been appreciated, and when she could have applied it, as she thought best. She extended herself willingly to reach her goals, knowing that they might have escaped unless she had remained focused on them strictly. She was dedicated to her career, and she performed her duties with the required professionalism. Her superiors admired her and respected her ability to accept responsibility, and they always trusted her to give of her best performance. With even a limited education, she could have accomplished more than others, who had had more formal training.

Gill showed keenness to get to the top in material ways, but she was liable to have suffered, and to have caused hurt to others, in the attempt. Her energy and limitation did not combine well, but possibly it was good that excess energy was controlled, or that inertia should have been energised. Thus, her force and initiative were canalised and ordered, while her caution and patience were enlivened. However, these results could have proved distressing when she felt vital, and hurtful when she felt slow and stolid.

Although Gill may not have been more talented than the people she worked with, she was more innovative. She knew that those who shrank from demonstrating their skills were ignored, while opportunities were given to adventurous individuals, who weren't afraid to act on the knowledge and skills that they had acquired. However, Gill wasn't always sure that she could have carried out all her plans because she doubted her ability to live up to the enormous responsibility of success. She underestimated her ability to render the kind of service that produced results. Her constructiveness could have forced to a patient working out of what had been started, but not with ease. Her results had to have been battled for. But, in this way, she might have used up so much energy that she began to lose interest. On the other hand, her ideals and imagination would have been kept in bounds and given shape, so that they became useful in this material World, but not easily.

Gill's career life tended to gravitate backwards because earlier, she had striven to reach the top, and then later had had to retrace her steps in order to place herself realistically at levels she should have dealt with before. Her life had become a succession of by-passed steps, which had to be retraced later, as she kept trying to balance her foundations. Gill was learning how to discover her future. And always, it was by retracing and filling in the gaps left earlier that made her future more assured. As she grew older, she learned to build in ways that were more meaningful to her ultimate purpose, rather than by labouring under a previous illusion that she must have had to conquer a World that would have been too formidable for her to master.

Gill's schemes came to frustration because they were too impractical. Being restricted in a job diminished her enthusiasm. There was a subtle undermining of her power of control and of her completion of purpose. The practical became over-valued with a tendency to meet hardships. The narrowness engendered produced selfishness and egocentricity. The hardships were endured but sternness was given. Extending herself more than her competitors might have caused her to over-react, and to have become more aggressive than necessary. Gill played the hazardous game of challenging every opponent, who seemed to stand in the way of her ambitions. The tendency was that very hard work may have been done for idealistic ends. However, her results may have proved disappointing and elusive because all was too imaginary. Irregular, over-glamorous and escapist ways could have brought downfall.

Late: Financial independence had become very important to her. Gill abhorred the idea that she might have to live out her final years in an institution because of a lack of resources. She hadn't to do anything without a plan designed to reward her in later life, when security would have become so important. She wanted to have the security, so that she could have enjoyed retirement later, in relaxed comfort. Success was indicated regarding legacies, and eventually, by a normal death.

Appearance and Health

<u>Appearance:</u> Just over average height, Gill would have had a well-formed body and regular features. She would have been good-looking, slender in youth but tending to stoutness in middle age. She would have had a rounded face, a good complexion together with a good expression of countenance. Usually, Gill's type would have been of great beauty with an ethereal appearance due partly to large, liquid, dove-grey (or blue, hazel, or brown) eyes and smooth, brown hair. Gill would have had sharp eyesight, good hearing and sensitivity of touch. Her bodily communication, (i.e. walking, motoring, etc.) would have been undertaken keenly, with speed, and yet she was, generally, somewhat dove-like in figure and movement. She would have seemed gentle, wistful and melancholy, in repose. She would have had a fondness for silver-grey, or light-blue, apparel (rather than garments/clothing!).

<u>Health:</u> Gill had good health with the beneficial results from a responsive, good and harmoniously working, nervous system. Her sensitivity was such that elation and depression could have alternated

quickly. Similarly, nervous tension was likely since freedom and limitation did not blend well and they too, were apt to alternate. Over-doing impaired her vitality, tending to make her pugnacious and bad-tempered, which could have led to minor accidents. When she was run-down, her head, or nervous system, could have suffered. Also, strange fears played on her nerves, undermining her health, which became susceptible to fish poisoning, or to harm from impure water. Additionally, strain was possible when affairs in general went well, i.e. from too much of a good thing. Moreover, overly violent, explosive release from worry could have led to nervous stress. Furthermore, failure to get sufficient rest could have endangered her health. More specifically, over-worry may have led to intestinal trouble. Overall, she owed it to herself to develop and maintain good living habits and to get enough exercise to keep her body in good condition at all times. Other possibilities would have included: kidney and bladder trouble causing debility, weakness in her back and ulcers. Her blood and liver may have been affected. There may have been a liability to dropsical complaints, and to chronic irregularities of her digestive system. Poor circulation, flatulency and rheumatism were possible also.

There was the danger of accidents, such as burns, scalds and falls as well as of the limb-breaking kind. Also, sudden accidents were possible while abroad, or difficulties, while travelling.

JACK SPRAT

"Jack Sprat would eat no fat.
His wife would eat no lean.
And so between them both, you see.
They licked the platter clean."

Character

General: Jack had a strong will (with impulse and persistence added) zeal, and ardour, within a quiet determination. He was optimistic, ambitious and tenacious, showing self-discipline and self-denial. There was a tendency towards a cheerful, humorous and witty personality with success through its exercise. He had a keen, emotional nature with 'active feelings' but was not lacking in reflection; his whole nature being harmonious and hospitable. There was sweetness of character and behaviour showing kindness and sacrifice. Also, there was a tendency towards the arts, dancing, to things of the sea and to a psychic sensitivity that needed rapport for expression. However, there was too much reliance on luck; he was showy, exaggerated, conceited, imprudent and extravagant, with a tendency to squander gains. His extravagance was likely to imperil financial stability, and so there was a risk of unexpected losses, possibly arising from his own restlessness. He seemed always to be "on the go". At a neutral level, he showed self-confidence, pride, passions, desire to rule, managing ability and dramatic instinct. Also, he was somewhat ready to get rid of the old, and to begin the new. More negatively, he could be stubborn, taciturn, egotistical, avaricious, hard and even brutal.

As a 'bowl' individual (see his Epoch chart), Jack always had something to bear. He was set-off from a definite half of his World, so that there was an equal half of experience from which he was excluded in some subtle fashion. He held something, but whatever it was, was set-off against a relationship within a larger consideration. His occupied half revealed his activity and organisation (since planets are significant by sign and by House) and his unoccupied half became a challenge to his existence. This takes the form of some cause, the furtherance of a mission, or of an introspective concern over the purpose of experience. Jack always had something to give to his fellows, whether literally or psychologically, whether constructively or vindictively, because his orientation to the World arose from division by two, i.e. from frustration and uncertainty. His energy (Mars, his 'leading' planet) was directed to where and how he sought to carry out his mission, or to gain his everyday justification for existence. He was definitely self-expanding (or self-seeking) and practically interested in what things mean, and in what they are. Because his Mars lies between the 4th House centre (the nadir of the chart) then up and over to the 10th House centre (the chart's

Mid-heaven) he tended to 'scoop-up' things, in order to initiate further experience.

<u>Mentality:</u> Jack was subjective (at Epoch) and objective (at Birth). His mind and mental outlook tended to be improved as far as charm of speech and pleasantness of manner are concerned. Balance rather than worry was evident. His self-expression tended to occur through mental alertness, where advantage came through versatility. Possibly, he could be talkative, and he tended to be idealistic about his possessions. Though constructive in a narrow, one-track way, his orderliness tended to become rigid discipline and dreary planning. Mental loneliness could have resulted through fear and apprehension, so that his resultant lack of poise forced brusque speech and writing. His ideas and intuitions were strong through heightened receptivity, generating faith in his own ideas, but they might have been carried out in a perverse and cantankerous manner. He had deep concentration that was deliberating, suspicious, imprudent and possibly foolhardy, with an obsession bordering on megalomania. His mind tended to be overly tenacious of his opinions that harked back to authorities of the past, rather than of reaching out to those of the future. Additionally, he had a psychic faculty consisting of a receptive sensitivity that could also give out, in which harmony, rhythm and beauty were combined. His spiritual ideas were chaste and calm, his imagination was strong,

he was liable to be critical in psychic matters and his economy was increased. However, the vivid side of his imagination tended to be gullible and confused, so that his mind was not very well directed. Touchiness induced escapism, with a tendency to mental retirement, to philanthropy and to day-dreaming. Then his mind would scheme in an involved way, and action came from intuition rather than from reason.

Lifestyle: Jack gave the impression that he was in complete command of his situation but, in fact, he was quite unsure of his ability to succeed when faced with a challenge. He had ambitions and a power-seeking personality that would have burned for success. His creative imagination was second-to-none but he needed to develop it. By playing down his creative gifts, he derived less benefit from them. Unfortunately, his personality suffered somewhat because there was insufficient firmness in his background to support his creative and pleasurable inclinations. Thus, there was likely to be too much impulse, excessive will and a "too clever by far" attitude. Hence, he fluctuated, at times, between being very self-confident and hopeful, working well and achieving much, but then often felt that he had greater powers than he could express outwardly. Indeed, there was a need for him to try to achieve fully creative self-expression. He understood, but was slow at working out. The moral guidelines he lived by were more universal in concept than those specified by his social environment, or by custom. His moods and ways could be changeful in an acceptable way, since new phases in life were liked. Also, there was a weird tendency with a love of display, though accompanied by abundant sympathy.

Jack's ambitions were tempered by a plodding persistency that inclined towards conservative and orthodox conditions. He was a self-controlled personality capable of achieving success through hard work. Usually, his practical abilities were combined with a shrewd mind and inner stability. Also, there was benefit through the easy casting-off of old contacts and ways, and a readiness to start anew. Thus, he showed firmness and reserve, but he relaxed in social life. There was a galvanic desire for change, working through a static medium, implying sudden outbreaks from a smouldering intensity. He became very restless when denied the opportunities to show his talents. Conversely, when he turned down a chance to improve his skills, he really diminished the rewards that he could have expected.

Jack's fulfilment was linked intimately with the public, as well as with the people, to whom he was close. He depended on others for opportunities to use the skills he had learned, and when people were satisfied with his accomplishments, he knew that he was effective. Although he was reasonably aware of his capabilities, this kind of feedback gave him greater self-confidence. Without this response from those he served, he found it difficult to make progress in his career.

Relationships

<u>Others:</u> Jack had a vital need to co-operate, and he was not likely to have passed-by unnoticed. Business partnerships tended to be beneficial and successful. Yet it wasn't easy for him to start a conversation, but he could contribute meaningful ideas. He expected others to accept the strict moral code that he used for himself. He could be helpful, but otherwise he could have been resentful and rebellious. His enemies were secret and ruthless.

Jack had a tendency towards popularity, and an ease of attracting others, or the public in general, by sheer innate charm. He was ready to give a helping hand to make life go happily. He knew how to deal effectively with people at the social level, and he enjoyed it. People liked him because he seemed to understand their needs. He had a strong desire to exert for others in kindly, self-sacrificing and humanitarian ways, even though his efforts, sometimes, were liable to become confused, so that muddles were made. People were almost always interested in what he had to say, whether as individuals, or as the general public. They might even have been interested in his charitable activities. He was a benign influence on people, and generally gave others the benefit of the doubt. He helped them to exploit their creativity by convincing them that they had potential to develop. They were inspired by his belief in them.

Jack attracted people who had significant deficiencies, for which he was glad to make-up. Anyone with a hard-luck story won his compassion and help. He tended to give others more credit than they deserved, while underplaying his own abilities, in order to avoid competition whenever he could. But with self-determination, he could have avoided putting-up with people who abused his generosity. As a result, he should only have helped those who needed it genuinely.

Jack was fully aware of his impact on those around him, and he let everyone know that he was a person of substance. It could have been painful for him to know so much about people, because it suggested that he had an obligation to use his creativity to help to solve their problems. He could have known more about people psychologically than they knew about themselves. This ability gave him many opportunities to enrich people's lives through his efforts. He tended to feel that he had to concede to people because concession seemed to be the only way to win their approval. But when he did this, he was avoiding the responsibility for asserting himself, because he feared disapproval, or rejection. Yet he was good at getting others to work harmoniously, either as co-workers, or as employees, but delusion was possible. He had to allow enough time to provide the services that people needed and expected from him.

<u>Friends:</u> Jack's friends and acquaintances were many and much enjoyed. He tended to cultivate friends in unlikely places, but, in the long run, they may have helped him. He seemed to attract the kind of friends who always needed something from him. It was fine to be helpful, but he had to think about his own current and future needs, and save some of his energy and resources to acquire a nest-egg of his own. There were frequent breaks with friends.

<u>Family:</u> Jack had a love of home and family; affection, sympathy, kindness and companionship were marked. He had a strong attraction for his mother, and a resemblance to her, as well as a long association with her, and benefit through her, or through her side of the family. Much of his daring resulted from the stimulating influence of his parents. [His brothers and sisters would have helped him to get started, but he'd have rather done it alone, which he had to do because he didn't have any siblings].

When Jack's children were young, he taught them to be self-reliant, so that they wouldn't fear competition, as they made their own way in life. He may have got vicarious satisfaction from his children's self-expression, which he encouraged. He wanted his children to take advantage of the benefits he'd provided, and had felt very fulfilled when they had appreciated his efforts. He impressed them deeply. However, his children may have been a great burden, by not allowing him to develop his skills fully. Thus, responsibility to family and loved ones may have diverted him temporarily from his goals. His children were unusual, and there might have been separation from them.

Lover: Jack's affections were keen. He was a romantic. But he was not especially romantic, preferring a partner who is a dutiful friend, rather than a lover. Taking responsibility in a romantic relationship was painful for him, and he didn't really want to make a permanent tie. He was wary of expressing his feelings until he was sure that he wouldn't have been rejected. But his sparkling conversation did attract romantic partners. Communication was expressed in affairs to do with partnership of any kind, or of any matter, which implied reciprocity, or rapport, with others. But there was confusion in love affairs and even deception. Secret partnerships may have been formed. His affection could have been changeable, and often for more than one at a time. Expression of it was charming and fluent, but also possibly inconstant, involving all talk, rather than any real feeling for another. Love affairs tended to be numerous and happy. However, affections and partnerships were subject to disclosures, upheavals and new starts, along with trouble and unpleasantness. Thus, partnerships were disappointing and not dependable.

When thinking of marriage, he was attracted to people who are mature, straightforward and self-sufficient. There was attraction to older people, and his feelings were controlled, serious and steady. Although elopement was possible, love was unemotional, detached and too cool in affection. Friendship was preferred, rather than emotional ties. There may have been an ungenerous and unresponsive-to-beauty, attitude, with dull feelings. However, there was self-expression in affairs to do with marriage, and he could have been possessive, with a strong affection for those possessed. For him in marriage, compromise worked better than force. A successful marriage was indicated, and the resulting happiness was all the thanks he needed.

Probably, he would have attracted a partner, who was in constant need of affection, and expected him to yield to her demands. Probably, she made heavy demands on him, as the price for sustaining their relationship. However, if that potential partner, had established her credentials with him, then he would have chosen the right one. His partner could have made a valuable contribution by supporting him in his endeavours. He wanted a partner who was as eager to grow as he was. She tended to be the catalyst that made him excel in his efforts. She would have given him support when he met problems, and appreciation when he did his job well. His devotion inspired his partner to assist him, so that they both benefitted in the life they shared.

Career

<u>Early:</u> Jack's destiny lay mainly in his own hands, and he tended to have a lucky journey through life. His fate could be under his control through his reason, and illuminated by his intuition. There was success in his objectives in life, in foreign lands and in sudden, good fortune.

It was essential for him to get as much formal education as possible, so that he could avoid getting locked into a job situation that seemed to be going nowhere. If his goals had been clearly defined, then all he needed to do, to realise them, was to get an education. He certainly knew that without training, his objectives and future goals, were greatly limited. In fact, he strove to increase the knowledge he had gained by getting more formal training. One of his goals should have been to attain a reasonably independent lifestyle with substantial monetary rewards for his efforts. Security should have been an important consideration when he chose a career. His creativity merely needed to be developed so that he could gain skills and be able to compare himself favourably with others. Only self-discipline and hard work would teach him the skills he needed to succeed. Even a moderate amount of feedback would have dispelled any of the anxieties he may have had about his abilities. From that moment on, there would have been little to impede his continuing progress.

Jack must have based his future on his ability to think for himself, even though he had some anxieties about being able to make the best use of his ideas. He underestimated his creativity, which he had had to develop, so that he would have had the freedom to choose an independent base, on which to build continuing fulfilment. At first, he considered himself to be less proficient than his competitors, and had had to extend himself to win their approval. But he was underselling himself, for he was more competent than he realised, and certainly equal to any challenge that he may have encountered. He worked hard to develop his skills because he knew that he could make a good living by applying them in his chosen field. Caution, patience and care were used in practical ways. He had a great respect for knowledge, knowing that it could open doors that his shy nature kept him from opening otherwise. He was happy in work so long as it was neither ugly, nor dirty. He was attracted to occupations that brought him into contact with persons who were polished and refined. But he was apprehensive about his future security. He borrowed now and then, to tide himself over, until conditions improved. But it was a mistake to do so, even though there was economy in small matters, unless he had been absolutely sure that his low economic situation was only temporary.

Work and energy were put into a day's activities. Jack showed keenness to get to the top in material ways, although, possibly, he was liable to suffer, and to cause hurt to others, in the attempt to do so. He took pride in his ability, and he knew when his efforts were no longer producing the results that he wanted. The tendency was that he realised that he had unusual creative gifts, but he may have put-off using them, until he had found a vehicle that would dramatize them. His imagination and psychism were brought to concreteness for money-making purposes. Then his energy was expanded in keenness to become involved with both educational, and with literary, pursuits.

Vocation: There would have been some literary ability, perhaps in the direction of fiction, etc. As a writer, or speaker, there were benefits from balance, but ease rather than strength was gained. Probably, he would have made a good teacher, because he used his mental skills cleverly. With his keen abilities, he could have succeeded in social-service programs, or in some area of medicine, such as in surgery, pathology, in obstetrics, or in diet and nutrition. Wouldn't it have been better if he had worked with people who had problems, as a vocation? He would have been doing what he enjoyed, and getting paid for it. Religious and charitable influences too, were congenial, and he would have benefitted through hospitals and charities, etc. Indeed, there was an inclination towards charity, but perhaps too irresponsibly and lazily. Also, he might have found satisfaction in construction and associated services, which would have provided a good income, in a field where there would have been a need for his competence.

Travel tended to be wandering, and without planning. Life, on or by the sea, was liked.

Middle: Jack's work would have been plentiful and lucrative. His contacts with workers remained good. But he should have investigated what motivated his associates in his dealings with them. He played the hazardous game of challenging every opponent who seemed to stand in the way of his ambitions. However, by paying close attention to reality, he may have been able to rise to considerable prominence. His ability to visualise the results of self-development inspired him towards his goal of successful prominence. His superiors were content with his performance, since he always gave them what they required, and sometimes more than what they expected. He may have felt that he wasn't being paid as well as he deserved in his career, but the best way for him to have corrected this, was by doing the very best job that he could. There was gain in house, property, land, or investments. However, if he had to have invested, then he needed to have sought the services of an advisor. He must never have formed an alliance without getting legal advice to make sure that his interests were protected. Although much may have been achieved, Jack's tendency was to overdo. Limitations tended to be through maze-like worries, but these tended to clear-up in the long run, through patient endurance and quiet keeping out of the limelight.

Jack's energy and limitation did not combine well, unless excess energy was controlled, or that inertia should have been energised. Force and initiative were canalised and ordered, while caution and patience were enlivened, but these results could have been depressing to the energetic, and hurtful to the slow and solid. Yet the combination of initiative and will-power, in unusual ways could have produced unusual results. However, until Jack was sure that he wouldn't be rejected, he was very wary of revealing his creativity. Similarly, the tendency was that practical planning and determined self-will could have united in an unusual way, to produce brilliant results, too. Jack knew how to capitalise on his creativity to derive the most benefit. Again similarly, his ideals were carried out into actuality by an unusual power of leadership in practical, scientific and advanced ways. Also, his ideals and imaginative intuitions tended to be kept in bounds, given shape and form so that they became useful as well. Moreover, intuitions could have been used advantageously in serious study, and for work to be published.

Jack attracted people who have problems because he had the talent and skills to offer them solutions. In this way, he should have been able to earn a comfortable living and so have reached the goals he had set. He wanted to be appreciated by the people he had helped, and that he'd been somewhat helpful to those in need. He was eager to show his skills, so that the public would have requested his services. Yet he underestimated his ability to render the kind of service that produced results. It may not have been easy but he had to have made some concessions in his work, and have accepted full responsibility for his gains and losses. Working with the public and offering services that were in constant demand, would have allowed him to earn a comfortable living. Also, it would have provided him with the feedback that assured him of his competence. He fulfilled his social obligations by doing for others what they could not have done for themselves, which could have been a spiritual motivation. Through service to others, he could have made his greatest contributions.

Jack had interesting hobbies. He was interested in the sea, in mysticism and in hidden things, which he pursued with energy and with desire to experiment in new ways, with good results and with high ideals. Work was done to achieve these, even though they might well have been visionary and unattainable.

Middle (Charity): Jack's inclination would have been towards a sensitive and protective charity but too irresponsibly causing him some small distress. Independent and self-reliant philanthropy was given but he was more interested in this for home and family. However, he would have been stimulated by charitable contacts with others. Such activities would have provided him with opportunities for forming alliances. His charity was ended easily, and was begun anew.

Perhaps Jack would have exploited his charitable inclinations more easily with co-operational support from a trusted advisor. He may have needed help in making charitable decisions. In these cases, charity would have been forced, perhaps somewhat unwisely. He had to try not to be envious of other philanthropists because they were not more resourceful than he, but some stress was involved here, also.

Generally, Jack's mind opposed charity. Perhaps there was a tendency that kindly, self-sacrificing emotions would have been sapped by his partner's sensitive and protective concerns.

Late: There was a tendency that Jack looked forward to getting out of the rat-race, and turning his attention to social issues.

Appearance and Health

Appearance: Although above average height, with large bones, muscles and shoulders, he would also have been bony and thin, in parts. He would have tended towards a square build in middle age with a round, full-sized head but also hatchet-faced in profile. There would have been a tendency to a ruddy complexion, grey eyes, long nose, thin neck, long chin, medium to dark hair – not plentiful, thin beard and a tendency to baldness. His walk would have been upright.

Health: Generally, Jack had good health and a vitality of spirit that could have been almost too intense. There were general, beneficial results due to an harmoniously working nervous system. However, nervous tension was likely, since freedom and limitation do not go easily together. Self-will and self-control do not blend and are apt to alternate. Danger was possible through accidents of the falling, crashing, limb-breaking kind. Violent and explosive change could have led to nervous stress, irritability and disruptive behaviour. He could have become pugnacious and bad-tempered. There was disappointment, frustration and/or delay in what should have brought happiness, such as in games, sport and love. Guilt feelings about his inadequacies could have contributed to health problems. He had a tendency towards hypochondria, but there may have been unusual diseases, also.

JILL HILLSIDE

"Jack and Jill went up the hill,
to fetch a pail of water.
Jack fell down and broke his crown,
and Jill came tumbling after."

<u>Speculative Only</u>

Character

<u>General:</u> Jill was cheerful and contented with her own surroundings and ways. She had a good, balanced outlook, as well as good critical and judicial ability. There was happiness in domestic conditions and an interest in the arts, but her inclination towards beauty and ease tended to be irresponsible and lazy. She showed positivity, determination, strength of will and masterfulness, but with some hardness and selfishness, i.e. a nature apt to be self-centred and difficult to influence. Her earnestness, self-confidence, pride, passion, desire to rule (megalomania?), management ability and dramatic instinct were stimulated.

Jill tended towards materialistic thought, had some revolutionary inclinations, in which her feeling of independence was strong, and her desire for revenge, when thwarted, was keen. She was ready to get rid of the old, and to begin the new. Her manner appeared to be cool, cautious and more limited than she was really. She showed some reserve, some lack of enterprise and a tendency to be timid through a feeling of personal inadequacy. But duty, conscience and orderliness were of importance. There may have been keen appreciation, sterling qualities, musical talent, and excellent business ability, but on the more coarse side, there may have been tendencies to become too exacting and a carping critic.

More negatively, Jill tended to be self-insistent and also disruptive, awkward, brusque, precipitate, avaricious, harsh and perhaps even brutal.

<u>Mentality:</u> Jill's personality was quick-witted and mentally able, seeking knowledge wherever it may be found. She was subjective, of quick speech and showed general, intellectual ability. This brought into activity all her mental expressions. Both her mentality and self-expression would have been critical and detailed. Literature and science would have been equally attractive. Her mind was practical and sensible, in which forethought and patience would have been good. Her internal nature was awakened, and hence so were intuition, discrimination and practical business ability, but, at the same time, there was a tendency to become overly critical, and although clever, there would have been temptations to be both selfish and overly acquisitive. However, her mind and mental outlook were improved as far as charm of speech and pleasantness of manner were concerned. She became clever at using the right words at the right

time, to get the effects she wanted. The tendency was that she had a capacity for devising a variety of ways to express herself. She thought "young" and was generally optimistic about life. Attracted to younger people, she found it easier to express 'radiating' qualities to them, rather than naturally introverted tendencies. She was attracted to reading romantic novels, as well as to stories about how people reached greatness, but had difficulty putting the knowledge gained into practice. There may have been an inclination to concentrate on utilitarian things; and forever wanting the next thing on the list. Communication would have taken place in affairs to do with the possessions of others, and to do with the emotions aroused by them.

Jill was overly self-conscious and saw much of her outer World as threatening to her own personal ego. This was the reason why she tried to create situations, of which she could prove herself to be the master. As a result, she was often too aggressive with others, hardly giving them the time/chance to think. In this way, she was sure that her ideas would not have been rejected. She had been building her self-identity, and spent an enormous amount of time/energy defending any ground that she had gained previously. In her life, she needed, "to learn, to see and to be" in the 'here and now', so that she did not over-react to situations that she, herself, had created.

Jill's keen mind led to an expansive, contented and pleasant existence, in which she was thoughtful, philosophical, conventional and jovial. Her mind was capable of much development. This self-expansion took place in a noble, dignified, loyal, high-minded and good-hearted way. But there may have been a certain amount of mental inflation, leading to conceit. There would have tended to be width of mind, here, rather than grasp of detail. On the other hand, and constructive in a narrow, one-track way, orderliness could have become rigid discipline and dreary planning. Hence, there was also an inclination towards mental limitation, but her mind would not have wandered, but would have organised and controlled in practical, cautious and methodical ways. However, mental loneliness could have resulted, perhaps because of fear and apprehension, leading to a lack of poise that forced brusque speech and writing.

Although conducive to sharp, acute and clever mental action through perceptive, revolutionary thought, Jill's communicativeness became too brusque and independent so that it lost good contact with others. Her addiction to the unusual and unconventional could have become so strongly and awkwardly expressed that she risked becoming odd, eccentric and tiresome.

Jill could have appeared to be on the strict, cold side, showing little tolerance for disorder. Also, she held strong views about what was right and wrong in terms of how others should live their lives. Yet Jill herself, changed her approach to life, according to the ways the winds of chance happened to be blowing at any particular time. Hence, she was more interested in how she got by, rather than by having her life stand for any particular principle. Thus, she was less honourable, than she was adaptable, to whatever life threw her way.

Jill shied away from entangling relationships, feeling much more comfortable when there was a slight distance between herself and those around her. While not being particularly warm, regarding personal relationships, she did have the abilities of a highly skilled, impartial thinker. Her happiness and joy came from her confidence in solving problems that involved details that others were unable to handle.

Jill had a highly fertile imagination that contained great kindness. Her sensitivity and impressionability made a mind that could take various patterns just like wax takes on an imprint. Sensitivity opened her psyche through her unconscious and much may have been given out following her reception of ideas and influences. She was curious and fond of everything mystical, occult and progressive. However, her intangibility could have resulted in vagueness and muddles. She may have had many ideas, but poor fulfilment; she may have become deceitful, or the object of treachery.

Jill could have concentrated deeply. She had invention, faith in her own ideas, ambition, spiritual energy, a compelling need to achieve fully creative self-expression and she could read character. However, suspicion, over-carefulness and/or being foolhardy, could have proved a hindrance to her success. She was fond of arguments, just for the love of arguments, rather than for any desire to get at the truth. However, her mind could have become energised to the point of over-strain, leading to bad temper, irritability and breakdown. Incisiveness then tended to become satirical and carping. Although talkative, times of quiet and withdrawal were also needed.

Earlier, Jill had tried to leap ahead of herself but could not make a reality of all that she had wanted to do. Instead, this made her nervous. Later, she reflected on all that had been completed, studying its flaws and matching it against the ideal in her mind. Also, earlier, she underwent experiences that taught her a particular method of thinking of how to relate all the intricacies within herself, to her World. She learned to see a major gap between how her World worked in reality, with how it could have worked in her ideals. She saw that machinery of all kinds could have been closer to her ideals, than was the machinery of human relationships. Thus, in all her dealings with people, she tried to make everything fit into these computer-like ideals that she had established years earlier. Experiencing some difficulties in focusing her mental energies, she had worked on how to make her mental productivity creative. Curiosity led her to leap ahead into the multitude of ideas that she would have liked to have created. Yet it was much easier for her to think about creating, or of telling others, about what she would have liked to create, than actually to have carried out her creative projects completely. Often, she thought that she should have been doing more than she was, and this kept her mind racing further and further into the future, but she kept receiving glimpses of how little she had accomplished in her past. She had to have learned how to overcome these frustrating mental pictures that kept impeding her in all that she thought that she could have become.

Mental curiosity had pushed her into future experiences. She became keenly interested in all that she had not yet perceived. She expressed outwardly that which she was already sure of, while testing that which she had not yet experienced. She became overly worried about her actions. Sometimes, she caused over-reaction in herself, as her restlessness caused her anxiety during this introspective period. Being curious had not been enough. She had to have worked at finding the answers to her numerous questions about herself, and about the people around her. She had to have learned who she was, through how she had related with other people, and that the intense desires that she had seen in others, were really her own. Also, she had to have found the best ways to fulfil her obligations to them, and to herself.

She had tried to project herself into the future that she had desired currently. When she had not made things happen instantly, she had used a great deal of thought projection, bringing others into her desires, until, ultimately, she had actually believed that she could have made the future happen faster than she sensed that it would have happened, had she not taken a hand in it. Because of her impatience, she appeared to go through much seemingly needless activity and behaviour, trying to create all that would have taken place naturally, of its own accord. She was the isolated warrior of earlier desires, re-manifesting currently, wanting others to join her, and yet not truly allowing anyone into her own psychic spaces. Thus, she lived much of her life alone. All told, she needed to become able to understand how to organise, and how to create, the present, from all that she had become conscious of, earlier.

Lifestyle: Examination of Jill's Epoch chart shows that she had an eccentric balance in that a free, one third span of her experience was set-off against an occupied two-thirds part, containing a related, but limited span of experience. Her power lay in the 2 : 1 disproportion of these two parts. She felt a sense of need, or strong sense of lack, or of a task to be achieved, or of a problem to be solved, in the social and intellectual World around her. Thus, she had a self-driving individuality, an executive eccentricity that was neither queerness, nor unbalance, but rather was power. She showed a dynamic, and exceptionally practical capacity, which was neither a broad universality, nor a special obsession with some particularly narrowed aspect of experience. Her self was found to be moved more by external factors in her environment, than by aspects of her own character. The point of application for the power of her self, is shown by her "leading planet", i.e. Uranus (conjoint Mars) in Gemini in the 1st House, and this is the planet (+ Mars) that is vital for her Epoch chart's analysis. Her desire for a fulfilling life is in harmony with the emotional satisfaction that she derives by being helpful. Her personality is out-of-the-ordinary, clever, original, seeking new and interesting ways, even if letting go of the old. There was a tendency to express this in science (or in aviation). Possible troubles could include eccentricity, difficulties for others to live with and a readiness to alter her life at too short notice. Change was to be expected in financial ways, and money, itself, was earned in unusual ways. Change also worked with flashing genius and quick inventiveness, within which a quick-change mentality sought advancement in any swift and unconventional way. Speech could have been off-hand, abrupt and without enough thought for others.

Additionally, the course of Jill's life would have been held between narrow bands of opportunity (see the 'bundle' shape of her Birth chart), in which her energy would have been apt to sway first to one way and then to another. She tended to be inhibited, but was capable of making much out of little, or for building small beginnings into great, and often with unanticipated final results. A total World may have been moulded out of some highly centralised force of self-concentration. She may have taken a little, central point within her, and have made a vital impact upon the entire World around her.

Indulging in personal pleasures might have been limited by lack of funds. However, once she had established herself in her career, she could have afforded to enjoy herself more freely. Her behaviour seemed to have been based on a belief in the survival of the fittest and so she took enormous chances that she wouldn't have encountered someone, who would have resisted her more strongly than she had bargained for.

There was a desire for the unusual and unconventional in her home, accompanied by independent behaviour. She could have been explosive, likely to have ended conditions, and so forced new beginnings, but with good results, after a crisis that had been painful. Thus, changeful happenings, even though violent, could have been turned to good account.

Relationships

<u>Others:</u> Jill had gentle charm, she shared ideas and she enjoyed having people admire her seemingly inspired actions. She was ready to give a helping hand to another to make life go happily. She reached out to people, eager to get to know them. She understood their needs and was sensitive to their failings. Usually, she saw through people who distorted the truth, or whose ethical standards proved questionable. But she permitted them to do what they wanted, as long as they didn't try to interfere with her. Normally, people trusted in her talent and in her professional competence, and they sensed that they could tell her their problems and that she would do what she could to help them to find solutions.

Jill admired people with strong personalities, and she had a fondness for children. But she had a lot of growing-up to do herself. Probably, she had been overly indulged as a child and she hadn't outgrown it. She made whatever concessions were necessary to create greater harmony in her daily affairs. When she disagreed with others, she gave them the benefit of the doubt, and sometimes even took the blame for their errors. Sometimes, when her opinion was challenged, she should have taken a firm stand. She gave the impression that she felt that she was unimportant, so that people tended to take advantage of her. In the company of contemporaries, or of those older, she became inhibited. Also, her relations with women (and with her mother) were not easy. She was confronted with the conflict of being the actor at the centre of her life, or of being the spectator of it, through observing the reactions of others.

<u>Friends:</u> Friendship and hospitality were marked features. There was a love of pleasure and of social life that helped to bring popularity. But an inclination to have been too easy-going, could have led to difficulties, unless it had been kept under control firmly. Much effort was made to obtain companionship, but perhaps with little success. She was inclined to quarrel with intimates. However, if she had cut the lines of communication with the people who could have enriched her life, then she would have become lonely. She may not have made many friends, but those who were close to her, would have been discriminately hand-picked.

<u>Family:</u> Jill's strong family ties were an asset (and there would have been pleasant and advantageous relationships with siblings). She was vitally interested in, popular with and much concerned about, relatives, such as uncles, aunts and cousins, as well as with neighbours.

Perhaps there had been a cleavage in her life relating to parents, or to early childhood, causing disharmony in her nature, but that could have urged her to accomplishment, later. However, she continued to have a good relationship with her parents, who gave her the self-confidence to make her own way, without having to depend on their support. Also, they taught her to apply herself diligently to achieve family security, and she was grateful to them for encouraging her to accept responsibility. Probably, her parents gave her every opportunity to develop according to her own creative needs. Her early conditioning had stimulated her to make the most of any situation, for which, again, she should have been grateful to her parents. She was impressed by the domestic harmony she had enjoyed while growing up, and she hoped to raise her own family in a similarly fine environment.

Jill would have extended herself for her partner and children, because they gave her so much joy. This may have provided the stimulus she needed to capitalise on her creativity. If she had truly cared about the people she loved, then she would have tried to live up to her potential. In fact, she enjoyed working for her family and children, and wanted them to have all possible comforts. But she hadn't to have forgotten the people who had helped her in the past, especially her parents. It's not likely that she would have forgotten, for she felt a close tie with them. Their contentment gave her great happiness, but she had to have been careful, not to have short-changed herself, as a result.

Jill was generally permissive, which her children may have resented. Although they may have admired her exciting lifestyle, they may not have wanted it for themselves. Possibly, there would have been a tendency for her to project her personal childhood inadequacies onto her own children.

Lover: Usually, Jill was attractive and good-looking. She would have been prettily dressed, even when not well-off. She had a happy, charming and lovable nature. 'In love with love', she was happiest with a congenial "other", either for work, or play. She had receptive sensitivity, harmony, rhythm and beauty all combined, resulting in sweetness of character and behaviour. There was an inclination to all forms of artistic expression, including dancing, things of the sea and a psychic sensitivity needing rapport for expression. Her self may have been deluded as to the realities of life, through too much living in the clouds, lovely though these may have been. Partnerships may not have been what they seemed. Conditions of love were often kept hidden. Her ideals and 'hunches' would have come easily, since her imagination was strong. Generally, she was permissive in her attitudes to sex, and she didn't get upset when individuals decided on a moral code that differed from that of society. However, there was weakness in becoming too easily attracted.

Yet her affection was difficult to express. A sense of lack intensified her shyness and prevented easy response to what could have brought happiness. There was sorrow and loss through affection and any partnership brought responsibility. Life tended to become solitary. On the other hand, there was unusualness in Jill's expression of love, or in artistic accomplishment, or in any kind of partnership, which tended to become delightful, intriguing and fascinating. There would have been an easy slipping away from one attraction and the quick forming of another. Partings may have been likely for good reasons, and with pleasant replacements, or reunions. However, she could also have been explosive, likely to end conditions and force new beginnings, but with good results after a crisis that had been painful. Thus, her affections and partnerships were subject to disclosures, upheavals and new starts.

Jill's feelings and emotional responses could have been galvanic and tense. She had a strong desire nature and wouldn't have accepted "no" for an answer. Her ability to love and enjoy sexual life, and all things of beauty, was strong and robust, but less delicate. However, her strong physical desires may well have been chilled by people who were coarse and vulgar. She needed to appreciate that ~~that~~ the intense desires she saw in others, were really her own. She may have become inclined to shy away from the opposite sex, as childhood problems were re-projected onto men, both in the present and their future. Sexually, she may have experienced a coldness, which sometimes led her to judge others, particularly in terms of their motives. Avoiding deep involvements, she tended more to superficiality, than to expressing life on a deep level. She would have sabotaged relationships that she felt she could not have dominated. She may have become highly insecure, particularly about her sexuality, which, in most instances, seemed to have become fixated in her youth.

Jill wanted a lover who would have sustained her in her defeats, as well as have shared in her losses. She felt that to win the one she loved, she had to have shown her ability to develop according to her own creative needs. It might have been better, if she had postponed making close ties, or making a permanent relationship, with others, until she had built independence in her career, without losing her identity.

Jill will have attracted, as a mate, someone who had certain deficiencies that she could have compensated for. As long as she was assured that her partner was grateful for her unselfish devotion, she was happy. But she had to be wary of accepting a submissive rôle with him.

Career

Early: Jill's destiny lay in her own hands, but more so, in those of others and depended on circumstances. There was an ability to adapt to circumstances – good, or bad – that would have persisted throughout her life. Her fate would have been influenced by external, and concrete, matter-of-fact, experiences. But there was a lucky journey through life. She will have had plenty of good opportunities combined with a feeling that 'good luck' was to have been expected. Possibly there will have been good fortune concerning money, legacy, property, or honours and dignities, but also, just possibly, loss in any of these directions. She could have changed her occupation, or have followed two at once. She may have gained public success, and become a person of some note, along these lines, but often, there may have been loss of opportunity in her life, arising from irresolution. Misfortune may have led to misery. She must have guarded against this, if only to safeguard her health.

Jill's early conditioning led her to believe that her role in life was to serve others. Her desire to exploit her creativity may have been frustrated in the beginning, but eventually, she would have found the freedom to assert herself. She would have shown that she could control others, organise, plot, plan, scheme, exert tact and diplomacy, and exhibit qualities useful in a master, or leader, whether in business, or in politics. She had compassion for people's problems, and she asserted herself in ways that served their needs. However, in her desire to help people with problems, she also attracted those who make no effort at all to help themselves. Yet her success came from her ability to understand people. Her upbringing showed her how to provide effectively the services that people needed. Also, this medium of self-expression gave her the opportunity to gain a high degree of skill. With greater confidence, her earnings would have increased, and she would have established her professional credibility. She may not have wanted a position of high visibility, but it would have been satisfying to know that she was respected by those in authority for the excellence she showed in carrying out her tasks. She communicated effectively to people that she could handle their needs, and they were impressed when she lived up to her promises. She had always known that the public would buy her services, when she had had the time to develop her ideas, and to make them work. She adapted to job assignments well and learnt new skills easily. She wanted people to consider her to be responsible, trustworthy and she took every opportunity to improve her skills when special training became available. She became fully aware of her creativity, and quite satisfied that, with any luck, she would have fulfilled her goals. She was fully satisfied with her frame of reference, and she knew that to succeed, she had to depend on her own creativity. Overall, she was happy in work as long as it was neither ugly, nor dirty. She was good at getting others to work harmoniously, either as co-workers, or as employees. She longed for all life's comforts and luxuries, and she would have exploited every available resource to get them. But with a little ingenuity, she could have chosen a career that would have given her a substantial return for her efforts.

Originally, it was difficult for her to stand on her own, because she lacked the necessary self-confidence. She needed to be appreciated by those she served (including her partner) who may have taken her for granted. Although she had some feelings of insecurity, her need to express herself in a worthwhile endeavour assured her of eventual success. With even a moderate amount of effort, she could have adequately satisfied her needs and even have accumulated a substantial financial reserve. Even though she had educational advantages, she needed to analyse herself to determine what motivated her best. Often, serving the public involves sacrifice, but what better way to show her credentials and win approval for her efforts? Her ability to plan would have netted her optimum results from even the most meagre assets. She was able to apply herself to improve her skills, and hard work was no deterrent. She knew that she would have had to apply herself diligently to achieve security for herself and her family. Her energy became expressed in hard work and she expected the same from others. Success would have followed from self-development, because she knew that her ideas had the potential to provide long-term yields. She became unafraid to knock on doors because she knew that, in time, her persistence would have been rewarded. But mainly she needed to know that she had made the only decision possible, namely to alert others to her talents and skills. Now, she knew how to communicate her ideas to those who had the resources to promote them. Thus, she would have had to make some personal sacrifices to attract the patronage she wanted for her services. On the way, she had had to accept full responsibility for exploiting her creativity as the foundation for her achievements/actions. Her sense of caution and reserve would have helped her to reduce the possibility of any financial losses. She had applied herself in developing her skills, knowing that this would have improved her image with others, especially with those to whom she was attracted romantically.

As a rebel at heart, Jill insisted on being able to develop in her own way. Any kind of limitation seemed intolerable to her. She thought 'free', and so she was. But her irresponsibility may have irritated those who accept their responsibilities, and her disregard for rules made her seem somewhat unstable. She knew she could not have been free, unless she had developed her creativity. Her future could have been in her own hands, to shape as she wished. With her many ideas, she could have achieved the security and independence that she needed.

Jill's early conditioning may have restricted, or have inhibited, her from becoming more independent. And yet these frustrations may have provided her with an added stimulus that she needed to force her to rely on her own resources. She underestimated her abilities, and so failed to capitalise on them. She had an obligation to herself to take advantage of her creativity, but her fear of risks made it difficult for her to exploit it fully. It wasn't always easy for her to put her ideas to work, because sometimes she doubted that they would have succeeded. Her only alternative would have been to promote them at every opportunity. More often than not, her suggestions would have been accepted. Eventually, she would have stood on her own, but first she had to mature and accept the fact that she had to have earned her independence.

Jill's natural reticence came from suspecting that others might have tried to exploit her talents. This would have diminished when she had realised that, in fact, they sought her services to fulfil their needs. When she had accepted the responsibility for working with and for others, she would have been well-rewarded for her efforts. Also, she would have gained the respect that she needed so desperately. Being uninformed was her greatest liability and would have kept her from accomplishing as much as she could have. She must have been willing to apply her talents, but had to ask herself if she was ready to become the best in her field. She had to have learned to listen to others, if only to have realised that she was as talented, and as capable, as they were. She needed to dramatize her creativity, and to have communicated with people outside her family, to have become assured of her gifts. Knowing that she needed to become secure financially, she needed to take advantage of her imaginative and intuitive ideas to achieve independence. But, importantly, she had also to learn to postpone taking any action until she was sure that her plans were valid. Lack of money could have taken the wind out of her sails, until she had learned to conserve her resources.

Vocation: Jill was fit for receiving a good education, and for following some scientific, or professional career, in which intellect was more important than practical, business ability. She should have chosen a career that allowed her to use her creativity in helping people to manage their material resources. But her ability to serve the public may have been restricted by family obligations. Working with young people would have given her the satisfaction of knowing that she had helped them to prepare for the future, so that they could achieve greater fulfilment. There is success in educational matters, writing and communication. Although she could have succeeded in the communications field, her prospects were even better as an investment counsellor. Because she had a talent for dramatizing her ideas, she might have considered writing as a suitable medium for self-expression, in which ease and balance are shown. Medicine, physical therapy, psychological counselling, vocational guidance, ecological enterprise, nutrition and family planning were some of the many fields available to her. She would have done well as a clerk, reporter, editor, agent, or traveller. She would have been fortunate in travel, liking rapid locomotion and having vital experiences. The unknown and the occult would have excited and appealed to her, as did anything that might have contained hidden danger. This was the reason why she wanted a career that incorporated some of the skills required in dealing with secrets.

Middle: In general, Jill was concerned about the fact that people in powerful, government positions could apply financial leverage that altered the destinies of many people. Yet in her personal dealings, she applied similar pressures to win compliance with her own desires.

Jill looked for ways to show her concern for people, especially those who had problems. She communicated freely to people that she was willing to help them. However, she hoped that she was not being naïve when she offered to help others, assuming that she would have been repaid later for her efforts, when she would least have expected it. She was grateful for any opportunity to show how much she cared about people. But despite this, she complained often that she didn't have enough time to take care of her own needs, and she resented the fact that others expected her to do everything. Satisfyingly, however, it was good to know that her actions had helped to improve others general well-being, and when they appreciated her efforts, she became inspired to continue. As soon as she got the feedback that convinced her of her abilities, she would then have made her most significant contribution to society, and to herself. She could have enjoyed financial rewards, while, at the same time, have helped those who had required her services.

Not content just to be proficient in her skills, Jill looked for new ways to apply her talents. She put a lot of effort into her work, because she expected increased benefits from her accomplishments. Her resourcefulness in capitalising on her basic skills, allowed her to earn a comfortable income. And she didn't hesitate to take a chance when there were material benefits to be gained. But a lack of concreteness might not have helped in her work, which may have become unsatisfactory through muddles made, and through two-facedness of work people.

However, Jill's combination of initiative and will-power, in unusual ways, could have produced unusual results. Her ideas were carried out into actuality by unusual power of leadership in scientific and advanced ways. There was a tendency that a galvanic force pointed to results of an outstanding nature, possibly in science. As a result she would have been brought into an eminent position, which, nevertheless, may not have been retained. Constructiveness could have forced to a patient working-out of what had been begun, but not with ease. Her results had to have been battled for. Narrowness engendered could have produced selfishness and egocentricity. Hardness was endured and sternness given. She would have tended to become compulsive and magnetic, so that her leadership was either obeyed, or violently broken.

Generally, Jill showed enthusiasm for the arts, dancing, psychic sensitivity, or for any form of idealism. There was also interest in connections with the sea, in mysticism and in hidden things, which were all pursued with energy and with a desire to experiment in new ways.

<u>Middle (charity)</u>: Her sensible mind was inclined to approach charity at home positively. Her work-a-day, passionate response to carefully considered charity at home came easily. Hence, her creative, but critical and detailed philanthropy, would have become strengthened and vitalised.

<u>Late:</u> There were no interpretations found for inclusion in this section.

Appearance and Health

<u>Appearance:</u> Jill was above average height, slight/ slender, yet inclining to plumpness, while still remaining well-proportioned. There would have been a tendency to a square shape of body, later. There was physical strength, endurance and some tendency towards a muscular physique. She would have had a longish face, tending to a square shape, later and with a sanguine complexion. Also, she would have had a longish nose, chin and strong neck, with dark hair (possibly curling) and quick-sighted hazel/dark eyes inclining to be round and

prominent. Her forehead, lips, nose, cheeks and mouth all tended to be full. Although arms, hands and fingers inclined to be long they also had a certain plumpness. She would have had an erect, active walk with a tendency to stoop somewhat, later.

Health: Jill's health generally, physically and mentally was strong, favoured and good. However, her health varied according to her moods and circumstances. When she was positive and optimistic about life in general, she would have accomplished a great deal. On the other hand, when her spirits were low and she was miserable, she suffered from many kinds of discomforts, because of nervous tension, which could have played havoc with her digestive system. She had a responsive and harmoniously working nervous system resulting in general benefit. However, it was exposed to all that touched it, becoming energised to the point of over-strain. There would have been a likelihood of disruption and bad temper. Also, trying to leap ahead of herself unrealistically, made her nervous. Although times of quiet and withdrawal were needed, escapism was possible with an inclination to avoid the concrete by day-dreaming, or by the effects of either drugs, or alcohol.

For completeness: Jill's chest and lungs were perhaps her most vulnerable parts. Hence asthma, bronchitis, consumption and nervous disorders, were possible. Also, there may have been a tendency towards incurable and rare diseases that would have affected both her nerves and psychic aura. Hidden, toxic substances could have spoiled her attempts to maintain good health, such as, for example, fish-poisoning and gas escapes.

Her throat could have been sensitive to diphtheria, soreness and abscesses. There may have been a liability to suffer from chills, colds, falls, poor circulation and obstruction. Potential chronic disorders would include rheumatism and wasting diseases. Alternatively, there may have been feverish and inflammatory complaints, possibly burns and scalds, as well as the risk of physical overstrain that depleted her energy. On the other hand, she may well have been protected, and/or preserved from accident, while travelling.